Resource Sharing Today

Resource Sharing Today

A Practical Guide to Interlibrary Loan, Consortial Circulation, and Global Cooperation

Corinne Nyquist

ROWMAN & LITTLEFIELD
Lanham • Boulder • New York • Toronto • Plymouth, UK

Published by Rowman & Littlefield
4501 Forbes Boulevard, Suite 200, Lanham, Maryland 20706
www.rowman.com

10 Thornbury Road, Plymouth PL6 7PP, United Kingdom

British Library Cataloguing in Publication Information Available

Library of Congress Cataloging-in-Publication Data

Nyquist, Corinne.
  Resource sharing today : a practical guide to interlibrary loan, consortial circulation, and global cooperation / Corinne Nyquist.
    pages cm
  Includes bibliographical references and index.
  ISBN 978-0-8108-9316-0 (hardback) — ISBN 978-0-8108-8803-6 (paperback) — ISBN 978-0-8108-8804-3 (ebook) 1. Library cooperation. 2. Library cooperation—United States. 3. Interlibrary loans. 4. Interlibrary loans—United States. 5. Document delivery. 6. Document delivery—United States. 7. Cooperative collection development (Libraries) 8. Cooperative collection development (Libraries)—United States. I. Title.
  Z672.N97 2014
  021.6'4—dc23

                                                                        2014008521

♾™ The paper used in this publication meets the minimum requirements of American National Standard for Information Sciences—Permanence of Paper for Printed Library Materials, ANSI/NISO Z39.48-1992.

Printed in the United States of America

Contents

Acknowledgments   vii

Introduction   ix

Part I: Building an Efficient Resource Delivery System

1   Teaching One Another ILL since the Library Schools Don't Do It   3

2   MARC: Library of Congress Did It and Changed It, and It Affects ILL   15

3   OCLC: How to Get Them to Listen to Us   29

4   Innovation Can Come From Us: ILLiad Is One Example   41

5   Rethinking Library Resource Sharing: The Future of Interlibrary Loans   55

Part II: Adding Personalized, High-Quality Service

6   Don't Just Say "No" When Faced with Rules and Policies   73

7   Showing Users What They Missed in the Library: ILL as Reference   85

8   Buy or Borrow? Getting What the Patron Needs   97

9   Conundrums: Confusing and Difficult Problem or Question   109

10   Going Global: It's Easier Than You Think   125

11   On-the-Spot Interlibrary Loan   135

12   Enhancing Discovery: Taking Responsibility at the Local Level   147

Appendixes

A   Code of Ethics of the American Library Association   157

B   Interlibrary Loan Code for the United States   159

C   Interlibrary Loan Code for the United States Explanatory Supplement   163

D   ALA and ARL Response to the Section 108 Study Group Regarding
    Interlibrary Loan and Other Copies for Users   173

E   Interlibrary Loans: ALA Library Fact Sheet Number 8   183

F   Five Things Every New Resource-Sharing Librarian Should Know   187

G   About IFLA   193

H   IFLA Guidelines for Best Practice in Interlibrary Loan and
    Document Delivery   195

I   Libraries Very Interested in Sharing (LVIS) Fact Sheet, Illinois
    State Library   199

Index   201

About the Author   213

Acknowledgments

This project would never have been completed if Charles Harmon, my wonderful editor, had not guided me through the process of creating and submitting a book outline. Then he encouraged me to write, commented on what I sent, scolded me when I had writer's block, and extended my deadline when I had an accident. My son, Jon, introduced me to DropBox and answered my technical questions. My daughter, Lynn, along with her daughter, Jenna, provided a book cover proposal. And, of course, my husband, Tom, provided moral support throughout the many months devoted to this book.

Everyone needs a good colleague and friend like Judy Fischetti, who read every word I wrote and recommended needed changes, which only another ILL librarian could do. Collette Mak wrote a great introduction, revealing that she has done ILL as long as I. Beth Posner looked into her crystal ball and predicted alternative ILL futures as she is part of the new resource sharing movement. And Judy Kuhn filled in when I lost my other contributor. Thanks also to library colleagues Elizabeth Strickland, Madeline Veitch, Nancy Nielson, as well as to two friends who knew what I was getting into: Ronald Knapp, and Jack Zand. Also, thanks to an anonymous reviewer for excellent suggestions and supportive statements.

At OCLC, I want to thank Tony Melvin for answering questions and referring me to Linda Gable, who provided RDA changes and computer code. And my investigation of OCLC's Global Council brought answers from George Needham and Pam Bailey.

Introduction

Why a practical guide? Because it's desperately needed. When I started in interlibrary loan (ILL), Mansell was only up to the Ms, there was no WorldCat, and we communicated through multipart paper forms. Increasingly, librarians and library staff no longer know what Mansell or TWX mean, and for that I am grateful. Mansell was the publisher of a gigantic national book catalog, and TWX was a Telex messaging system. Those tools worked but were cumbersome and slow, and ILL was a specialized service appropriate only for serious scholars with lengthy time frames. In the days of paper verification, the operation was headed by a degreed librarian dedicated to the function. With the addition of even modest levels of technology, for instance, Online Computer Library Center's (OCLC) Interlibrary Loan Subsystem, as it was then called, ILL became accessible to all library users and is now considered a core service.

While no academic library questions the necessity of ILL, many have no idea where to put it or how to staff it. Increasingly, interlibrary loan is relegated to a back room and combined with another, somewhat related function, for example, acquisitions. In terms of efficiency for the library, there's clearly synergy to be gained, but it comes at the price of community and, potentially, customer service.

As ILL and document delivery become backroom operations, the library may well see benefits through cross-training, allowing staff to better cover vacations and staff vacancies, but it will find it more difficult to develop the skills necessary to negotiate a facsimile of a manuscript or locate a government document from before the breakup of the Soviet Union. When the practitioners are removed from both their clients and their counterparts at other institutions, it is far too easy to see the work as a series of unrelated transactions instead of being part of a global community that functions on trust and generosity.

Without that underlying community, resource sharing would not be possible; we trust one another to respect one another's policies and be faithful stewards of the materials we borrow. Libraries that fail to respect that trust soon find themselves on "do not loan" lists. As I have told many a library user, until the book arrives, we're working for you; as soon as that book arrives, we're working for the library that lent it to us.

Clerical support staff seldom become members of the American Library Association (ALA), let alone the Reference and User Services Association's Sharing and Transforming Access to Resources Section (RUSA STARS), and they rarely travel to state, regional, or national conferences. With the dissolution of U.S. regional networks, even attending training becomes problematic. Another victim of the backroom consolidation is the understanding that resource sharing is a relationship business, that the relationship with the patron and the lending library are equally important.

In my own writings and presentations, I've stated that ILL and document delivery are production operations that must appear as boutique services to customers. The only way that libraries can offer the high-volume production aspects, as well as the high-touch personal service, is through industrializing as many of the functions as possible through such services as the OCLC's Direct Request, Relais' Discovery-to-Delivery, or ILLiad's Trusted Sender. By offering self-service and using the technology to its greatest potential, libraries are able to offer the personalized services required by researchers with truly difficult needs that may require weeks or sometimes months to fulfill. The ability to serve both the generic and the highly specialized is the hallmark of service excellence in support of research.

ILL is also a mission-critical service that graduate students, faculty, and unattached scholars depend on to conduct their research. At my institution, Notre Dame, ILL serves more than 3,500 individuals in more than 100 academic departments and centers; those 3,500 individuals include 75 percent of our faculty and 61 percent of our graduate students.

So what are ILL, document delivery, and resource sharing? These are umbrella terms that cover a number of functions, all of which can be described as getting and sending content. Traditional ILL is just that, a transaction that occurs between two libraries. Document delivery can mean purchasing content from a commercial supplier or delivering content from the local collection to a local user. Remote circulation differs from ILL in that while the content is coming from another library, the transaction is between the lending library and the end user. Resource sharing is broader yet and covers all these topics and more. It includes a community of practice that literally spans the globe.

This book, as well as others that have come out in recent years (*Interlibrary Loan Practices Handbook*, 3rd edition, *Twenty-First Century Access Services*, and the forthcoming IFLA *Handbook for Document Delivery, Interlending, and Resource Sharing*) seeks to address the need for helping staff and supervisors learn best practices, resources, and obligations, and begin to address the gap between expedient service and excellent service.

Collette Mak
Head of Access Services
Notre Dame University

I

BUILDING AN EFFICIENT RESOURCE DELIVERY SYSTEM

1

Teaching One Another ILL since the Library Schools Won't Do It

I thought I'd be a librarian, until I met some crazy ones.

—Edward Gorey, *Boston Globe*, 17 December 1998

Before writing about whether you should go to library school, particularly when you work in interlibrary loan (ILL) and believe that you won't learn much more about it than you already know, let us ask, Why should anyone go to school at all? My library is named after Sojourner Truth, who lived her first thirty years here in Ulster County. We recently dedicated a statue to her. She never attended school, and she never learned to read or write. Yet, she dictated a book about her life, created the words to several songs that she sang at gatherings, and became a nationally famous orator. One of her famous quotes is, "I can't read books, but I can read the people." She asked children to read the Bible to her, knowing they would just say what was on the page, and she listened to many speakers before she could make a point even better than they could do it. To learn more about her, go to http://www.newpaltz .edu/sojourner_truth.

THE PROVERBIAL PIECE OF PAPER

Why must anyone get any schooling at all? Reading, writing, and arithmetic are needed, because you are going to grow up and need to get a job and support yourself. You might like some of the subjects you were taught and look forward to learning more. In 1900, only 6.4 percent of American teenagers graduated from high school, and only one in 400 attended college. Yet, many went on to "every career, from shop-keeper, mechanic, and farmer, big entrepreneur, author, politician, and including engineer, architect, and even lawyer." Apprenticeships, mentoring, business training programs, and using libraries helped many make their way ahead. Paul Goodman, who served on the New York City School Board, writes that it was a "misconception that being in school was the only appropriate way of being educated." He "roamed the public libraries" growing up, and as a novelist, playwright, poet, and social critic. Goodman believed that the "creative, whether in the arts, sciences, or professions, do not especially thrive by formal school." Yet, he attended City College in New York City and received his BA at the age of twenty-two. He continued formal school at the University of Chicago and received his PhD there at forty-two (Goodman, 1963, 13).

While the first American library school was established by Melville Dewey in 1887, at Columbia University, most library training was on the job. The University of Chicago offered the first master's degree in library science, as well as the first doctoral degree in the field. In the 1950s, additional schools opened, and the American Library Association (ALA) began its accreditation program. The need for a library degree has been questioned many times, most recently by the former editor of *Library Journal*, Michael Kelly.

Although he had worked for twenty-five years as a reporter and never thought about attending journalism school, Kelly writes that he did well in the newsroom; however, he calls it a "white collar job with a blue collar rhythm." He went on to library school, got his MSLIS, and has even been a visiting library school instructor at Pratt Institute in Brooklyn. In his editorial, he says that his master's degree in library science is "nice to have," but he "questions its value." He complains about the situation where people "start working in a library to get a foot in the door and gain experience only to confront an expensive and time-consuming certification blocking advancement, or spend time and money to obtain the credentials only to find it difficult to get in the door owing to a lack of experience or overqualification." Twice he states, "And did I mention that the pay is absurdly low?" He concludes by asking, "Can we have a rational discussion about this?" (Kelley, 2013, 8). There were 165 comments continuing the discussion online.

ANALYSIS OF LIBRARY SCHOOL CURRICULA

There are currently fifty-eight library schools in the United States accredited by the ALA. An e-mail survey asking if they taught ILL in a course or part of a course brought twenty-four responses within a few days that listed at least one course that included ILL.

Administration and Management
Bibliographic Organization and Resource Development
Collection Development or Collection Management (listed by almost everyone)
Computer Applications and ILL Exercises

Copyright in Libraries (part of other courses)
Information Sources and Services
Introduction to Managerial and Administrative Services with ILL and Document
  Delivery
Libraries Cooperation and Networking (listed by several)
Library Skills and Practices (usually a workshop)
Online Information Retrieval
Reference and Information Research (listed by several)
WorldCat Assignment

One school had an actual ILL course at one point. Three listed hands-on workshops that were useful to ILL. One had a continuing education course that covered ILL. Nine others sent a link to their full course list or suggested that kind of review, which brought the responses to thirty-three. E-mails were sent to the admissions staff. Those who were referred to the program director or a specific instructor got the most useful responses.

An interesting e-mail came from Andrew Wertheimer (2013), chair of the Library and Information Science Program at the University of Hawaii. He was an ILL librarian "many moons ago" and therefore does cover ILL/consortia/resource sharing briefly in his collection management course. He also provides one of the earliest online responses to the *Library Journal* editorial, saying that it is "far from a new argument." He then draws attention to another *Library Journal* article entitled "Why People Really Hate Library Schools" (1985), by the late Samuel Rothstein, who was a professor at the University of British Columbia School of Librarianship. Rothstein's article is an analysis of our personalities and how we respond to "rapid change and financial exigencies."

Andrew Wertheimer's online comments responding to Michael Kelly about library school and its curriculum represents another interesting viewpoint.

> Basically, the challenge for LIS [library and information science] schools is to find a balance between theoretical and applied, and also allow students to prepare for emerging careers in the field, while also still respecting what is needed today. It is always a challenge for educators to balance the needs and skills of students who enter our programs. . . . Fine tuning professional education is a complex process involving many stakeholders. All schools routinely survey our students, alumni, and their employers. These always provide fascinating results. We usually find that current students complain about some hard classes that seem either too demanding or too theoretical. Within something like five years later, they often ask me why we didn't require more of the same content they once complained about. As I said, it is a hard balance.

Wertheimer notes that during his sabbatical in Japan, where the library degree is an undergraduate minor or certificate, those positions have about 1,000 applicants, as it is so easy to meet the requirements.

PROFESSIONAL, PARAPROFESSIONAL, OR CLERICAL

In the 1990s, a discussion on the ILL-L listserv showed that many disagreed about the requirements needed for ILL supervisors. Structures have changed, and controversy continues about which library tasks are professional and which are not. It is accepted that clerks or paraprofessional staff supervise service at the circulation desk. They hold responsible positions in cataloging, serials, acquisitions, and ILL. The controversy centers on the need for librarians in ILL. Virginia Boucher asserts that ILL had complexities. She describes the many roles played by the ILL librarian: manager, bibliographic reference practitioner, legal advisor, automation counselor, network consultant, teacher, defender of rights, and public relations expert (Boucher, 1989).

So what are the things that anyone holding a responsible position in ILL should know and should have been taught in library school? The following is a summary of two dozen responses to this e-mailed question:

- rules—I knew they had to exist but had no idea where or what they were.
- policies—ILL and collection development policies differ yet serve the same people.
- copyright—There are so many situations and questions that are hard to answer.
- codes—Understanding these gives us the "big picture" of ILL.
- holdings—Information in the serials catalog record and holdings should be improved.
- theory—Theory behind the importance of ILL should be taught.
- automation—It is important to know how systems interact with the Online Computer Library Center (OCLC) and one another.

Responders also revealed what kinds of training they have received and what kind is best:

- OCLC webinars are good, but small, in-person workshops are best.
- Recorded training has the advantage of webinars but is best used when you have time.
- The ILL listserv provides tips and practical training.
- Conference networking works well.
- It is useful to have someone demonstrate how to do it first and then monitor the steps the second time through.
- Hands-on classes were a great start (Solinet/Nylink, etc.).
- Webinars now are better.
- Online training is better than nothing, but the presence of a human being in a room to answer questions is best.

ILL IN THE WORKPLACE

One of the problems with online training programs is that the jobs in the ILL workplace vary greatly. Look at ads for librarians posted on the ILL-L listserv, in professional journals, and even in newsletters and you will see that there is no standard ILL position. The duties for librarians, paraprofessionals, clerks, or even students vary from library to library. Attend a regional online training session and you will see people bringing up their e-mail or Facebook page when the topic covers something not part of their job. The ILL policies of libraries also vary greatly depending upon who you serve, what you will get for them, and when you will pay.

ILL is a department often under stress trying to meet the requests received each day. It is said that both MLS and non-MLS people are "meticulous, painstaking, and indefatigable in their pursuit of elusive and obscure document requests" in an environment where fast decisions [must] be made throughout the day and a heavy workload managed" (Hawley, 1995, 93). Reference and circulation face this too, but they have shifts and time away from the service desk. We do not. On the other hand, we have many grateful patrons who praise us in person and on library surveys.

HELP IS AVAILABLE

ILL staff should be aware of the ALA Reference and User Services Association (RUSA), which has a section called STARS, a lovely acronym for Sharing and Transforming Access to Resources. I assume we were put in RUSA because we started in reference and have not found another home. On their website, start by looking at "5 Things Every New Resource-Sharing Librarian Should Know" (http://www.ala.org/rusa/sections/stars/5-things-every-new-resource-sharing-librarian-should-know). The STARS website page covers the following:

1. guidelines and laws
2. technology
3. customer service
4. assessment
5. education and networking

The following annotated resources list was prepared by Judy Kuhns, Assistant Librarian, Technical Services, Macdonald DeWitt Library, Ulster County Community College, Stone Ridge, New York.

PRINT AND ELECTRONIC RESOURCES

Against the Grain: Linking Publishers, Vendors, and Librarians
Based at the Citadel, College of Charleston, South Carolina
ISSN 1043-2094
    Print only, this is a unique collection of reports about libraries, publishers, book jobbers, and subscription agents. Blog: http://www.against-the-grain.com/atg-blog network/

IFLA Journal
Sage
ISSN 0340-0352 eISSN 1745-2651
    Each issue covers news of current International Federation of Library Associations and Institutions (IFLA) activities and information profession issues. http://www.ifla .org/publications/ifla-journal

Interlending and Document Supply
Emerald Group
ISSN 0264-1615
    Long published in the United Kingdom, issues include articles from countries worldwide. Installments will keep you informed of IFLA and OCLC international efforts and activities. http://www.emeraldinsight.com/products/journals/journals .htm?id=ilds

Journal of Interlibrary Loan, Document Delivery, and Electronic Reserves
Taylor and Frances
ISSN 1072-303X
    Peer-reviewed, this periodical provides a mix of practice and theory. As a North American journal, it expanded to electronic reserve to be more useful to all libraries. http://www.tandfonline.com/toc/wild20/current

INTERNET RESOURCES

RUSA STARS Professional Tools
Resources listed on this website were developed by individuals in the reference and user services profession. The tips and resources are particularly useful for those new to resource sharing and ILL. http://www.ala.org/rusa/sections/stars/resources

ShareILL
This tool is a gateway to electronic and print resources pertaining to all aspects of ILL, document delivery, and resource sharing. Designed to be comprehensive

and international in scope, ShareILL features links to resources that will help practitioners locate materials for their clientele, manage the ILL process, and keep up with developments in the profession. http://www.shareill.org/index .php?title=Main_Page

RESOURCE MANAGEMENT SOFTWARE SUPPORT

DOCLINE
National Library of Medicine
Customer Service
8600 Rockville Pike
Bethesda, MD 20894
E-mail: custserv@nlm.nih.gov
Telephone: 1-888-FINDNLM (346-3656)

OCLC WorldShare ILL
OCLC Customer Support (U.S.)
6565 Kilgour Place
Dublin, OH 43017
E-mail: support@oclc.org
Telephone: +1-614-793-8682 (direct)
800-848-5800

OCLC Customer Support (Canada)
E-mail: canada@oclc.org
Telephone: +1-888-658-6583
+1-800-848-5800
Fax: +1-450-618-8029

ILLiad
Atlas Systems
244 Clearfield Avenue, Suite 407
Virginia Beach, VA 23462
E-mail: service@atlas-sys.com
Telephone: 800-567-7401, ext. 1

The New CLIO System
CLIO is a family business based in New Hampshire, with staff in Texas, California, and Michigan, that focuses on small medical and public libraries.
E-mail: support@cliosoftware.com
Telephone: 817-726-3475

LISTSERVS

CLIO-L
This listserv acts as an international forum for users of Clio products and software, including Clio, ClioDoc, ClioWeb, and ClioAdvanced developed by Clio Software. List address: CLIO-L@LISTSERV.UCONN.EDU

ILL-L
Hosted by OCLC, this listserv is for all types of libraries and is especially useful for problem requests and hard-to-find items, as it goes out to a large audience. Their archives are available from December 2003 to the present. List address: ill-l@webjunction.org. Subscription address: http://listserv.oclc.org/scripts/wa.exe?REPORT&z=3

ILLiad-L
ILLiad-L is a listserv for users of ILLiad, and for others interested in automating ILL. Subscription address: http://www.ill.vt.edu/illiad-l.htm

LIS-ILL
This is a discussion of ILL and document delivery, based in the United Kingdom. List address: lis-ill@jiscmail.ac.uk

OCLC Sharing-L
This broadcast-only list periodically announces the latest news from OCLC's ILL and resource-sharing line of services. Subscription address: https://www3.oclc.org/app/listserv/sharingl/

For more discussion lists and blogs, go to http://www.shareill.org/index.php?title=Discussion_lists_and_blogs.

LVIS
Libraries Very Interested in Sharing (LVIS) was established in 1993, and represents the first global OCLC no-charge resource-sharing group agreement. It began as the goal of the Illinois State Library and the Missouri Library Network Corporation (MLNC) to promote free sharing throughout the Midwestern United States. During its first year, membership grew to more than two hundred libraries of all types in Missouri and Illinois. Today, members worldwide number more than 2,700. See appendix I for more information, a list of members, and instructions for joining by completing a LVIS Participation Agreement Form. Subscription address: http://www.cyberdriveillinois.com/departments/library/libraries/OCLC/lvis.html

WHAT ELSE TO LEARN ABOUT ILL

The e-mail survey mentioned earlier asked for instruction about rules, policies, copyright, codes, holdings, and automation. The eleven chapters that follow, along with the appendixes, answer these and more questions than were asked; however, I cannot supply the proverbial piece of paper. This book provides the background that will prepare you to attend regional and national workshops and enter into the discussions. If you hear acronyms sprinkled throughout the discussion, just ask questions. Or you can turn to the ALA Library-Related Acronyms online list. It includes ALA units and publications known by acronyms, plus those for other library and related organizations, as well as abbreviations commonly used in library literature. Go to www.ala.org/tools/library-related-acronyms/.

There are links to the OCLC products/services glossary and a multilingual glossary in two parts: 1) language table with terms in six languages and 2) definitions with explanations for all the terms. Finally, there is a link to *ODLIS: Online Dictionary for Library and Information Science*, created by Joan M. Reitz, a librarian at Western Connecticut State University. The dictionary is also available in print. (See the link for *ODLIS* at http://www.ala.org/tools/library-related-acronyms.)

Most interesting was the suggestion calling for a theory supporting the importance behind ILL. Library science programs dwell on the factors affecting the performance of libraries. Thus, library schools teach classification, collection development, indexing and retrieval, reference interviews, information technology, library history, and such specializations as archives or skills needed in public, academic, hospital, special, and school libraries. Since we are service organizations, we periodically apply surveys to discover the satisfaction level of our patrons. ILL always ranks high. This may be because of our philosophy, which is, "Get them what they want," but I believe it is because we have mastered the art of cooperation. That could be presented as theory of the importance behind ILL.

ILL THEORY

There is a theory of cooperation developed as part of ecology, the science of the relationships between organisms and their environment. Why cooperation exists is a question raised by anthropologists, biologists, economists, psychologists, sociologists, and environmental scientists. So why can it not be applied to library science? If it is, we in ILL win the prize. The problem is often told as a parable of the "tragedy of the commons" (Hardin, 1968).

> Here, a community of herdsmen graze their cattle on a common pasture. At the level of the community, there will be an optimal level of exploitation of the pasture [that] balances both profits, in terms of fed animals that can be sold at market, and costs, in terms of sustainability of this shared resource. However, while the costs of overexploitation are shared among all individuals who graze their animals on the commons, the benefits of

grazing additional livestock accrue directly to the individual herdsmen. This leads to each individual deriving a net benefit from grazing more and more animals on the commons, until the pasture is destroyed from overgrazing—to everyone's detriment. Here the problem is what stops—or could stop—the self-interested behavior of the individual from damaging the interests of the group.

Social behavior that costs one and benefits another is altruism. Behavior that benefits both is mutual benefit. These two helping behaviors define cooperation. Cooperation can be enforced if there is a mechanism for rewarding cooperation or punishing those displaying only self-interested behavior. These exist in the ILL community. Those who regularly show cooperation will receive preferential treatment from those they have aided in the past. Those who do not show cooperation can be blocked.

Another way to express ILL cooperation is "reciprocal cooperation," which refers to those who are cooperative "either directly (help those who help you) or indirectly (help those who help others)." This type of cooperation applies almost entirely to humans, although a few examples exist amongst animals. While this analysis results from reading a biological paper, I would agree with Gardner and colleagues (2009) that, "we need better integration between theory and empirical work." Gardner and associates also state that, "one could be forgiven for thinking that human, primate, and social insect literatures on cooperation concerned completely different topics, rather than attempts to develop and test the same body of theory" (7).

Libraries view ILL as special service that is limited to what would be similar to a commons. Cooperation theory does work for ILL, but when we get too much demand, libraries call it expensive (even though it is not), or an imposition upon the local users (only when checked out to ILL), or too staff intensive (so make it all electronic processes and materials). Cooperation or coordination is promoted for every aspect of libraries but works the best in ILL. So we have become too successful. The herders are the people doing research who want so much as they access the online databases, the expanded WorldCat, Google Docs, and the Internet. Administrators did not expect this, so the commons allotted to us has become overused.

In addition, our overall costs ($17.50 to borrow and $9.27 to lend) are seen as very expensive, while other library costs—acquisitions, cataloging, book storage, or librarians answering reference questions or teaching patrons how to find more information—are calculated but not talked about as much. Must we force our patrons to evacuate the commons? Are we accusing them of self-centered behavior? Are there other, better solutions? Read on to learn more about ILL and its wonders and dilemmas.

WHAT ELSE YOU NEED TO LEARN

In the past, networking was a "system made of libraries for the purpose of providing access to shared resources" (Gilmer, 1994, 40). Now we think of it as computerized systems that provide a communications mechanism of some kind. Networks are used by libraries in various ways—cataloging, reference services, collection development, and especially resource sharing. The mechanism to facilitate lending and borrowing began in the United States as the Library of Congress began to print and distribute catalog cards beginning in 1901. Later, transmitting this information required the development and acceptance nationally, and later internationally, of a machine-readable format for bibliographic data. How that began and continues today is detailed in chapter 2.

ADDITIONAL THOUGHTS

The work in any kind of library is fascinating. We hear about special projects from our patrons and try to make the information they need more accessible. Hope Leman, who calls herself a "research raven," is a librarian at Samaritan Health Services in Oregon (www.researchraven.com/hope-leman.aspx). She created Leman's Lexicon as an "aid for those trying to gain a grasp of some of the terminology in the increasingly interconnected worlds of the life and information sciences." The following poem, written by Leman, expresses achievement, but also the efforts and worries we feel as librarians.

> I fritter all my time away
> Spending much of every day
> Diligently working on
> My very silly lexicon
> For what could possibly be more fun
> Than working hard from sun to sun
> With words and terminology
> That get defined by little me
> And if I am ever corrected
> By scientists much respected
> I will acknowledge my mistake
> And offense and umbrage will not take
> But will promise that I'll try
> To do much better by and by
> And will thank them for their efforts to
> Ensure I don't misinform the rest of you

REFERENCES

ALA Reference and User Services Association (2013). "5 Things Every New Resource Sharing Librarian Should Know." Available online at http://www.ala.org/rusa/sections/stars/5-things-every-new-resource-sharing-librarian-should-know (accessed December 13, 2013).

Boucher, Virginia (1989). "The Interlibrary Loan Librarian." *Interlending and Document Supply* 17, no. 1: 11–15.

Gardner, Andy, Ashleigh S. Griffin, and Stuart A. West (2009). "Theory of Cooperation." In *Encyclopedia of Life Sciences.* Chichester, UK: John Wiley & Sons.

Gilmer, Lois (1994). *Interlibrary Loan: Theory and Management.* Englewood, CO: Libraries Unlimited.

Goodman, Paul (1963). "Why Go to School?" *New Republic.* 149, no. 14: 13–14.

Hardin, G. (1968). "The Tragedy of the Commons." *Science* 162, no. 3,859: 1,243–48.

Hawley, Lorin M. (1995). "Why You Do Not Need an MLS to Work in ILL." *Journal of Interlibrary Loan, Document Supply, and Information Supply* 6, no. 1: 89–94.

Kelley, Michael (2013). "Can We Talk about the MLS?" *Library Journal*, April 29. Available online at http://lj.libraryjournal.com/2013/04/opinion/editorial/can-we-talk-about-the -mls/ (accessed October 11, 2013).

Rothstein, Samuel (1985). "Why People Really Hate Library Schools." *Library Journal* 110, no. 6: 41–48.

Wertheimer, Andrew (2013). E-mail response to Michael Kelly's posted editorial, 29 April. Available online at http://lj.libraryjournal.com/2013/04/opinion/editorial/can-we-talk -about-the-mls/ (accessed October 11, 2013).

HANDBOOKS

Hilyer, Lee Andrew (2006). *Interlibrary Loan and Document Delivery: Best Practices for Operating and Managing Interlibrary Loan Services in All Libraries.* Binghamton, NY: Hayworth Press.

Knox, Emily (2010). *Document Delivery and Interlibrary Loan on a Shoestring.* New York: Neal-Schuman.

Weible, Cherié L., and Karen L. Janke, eds. (2011). *Interlibrary Loan Practices Handbook.* Chicago: American Library Association.

2

MARC

Library of Congress Did It and Changed It, and It Affects ILL

A reader may know the work he requires but cannot be expected to know all the peculiarities of different editions, and this information he has a right to know from the catalogues.

—Sir Anthony Panizzi, 1797–1879

Do you wonder why you should know about MARC records and if they affect interlibrary loan (ILL)? Judy Fischetti, a librarian who trains staff in academic, public, medical, school, and specialized libraries to submit ILL requests, believes "an overview is needed . . . not for everyone working in ILL . . . but for supervisors and librarians." As the member services librarian at the Southeastern New York Library Resources Council (SENYLRC), Fischetti serves libraries in eight counties of the Mid-Hudson Valley in New York.

Yes, an ILL librarian [and staff member submitting requests] should care about MARC records. After all, ILL is all about the details. Details of edition, author of a preface or forward, editor, date of publication, title of volume in a multivolume work, abridged edition versus unabridged, and electronic format versus print format are some of the details that an ILL person needs to consider when requesting an item.

An accurate MARC record helps the ILL person to correctly identify the precise item needed. I worked with many authors when I worked at the Woodstock Library. There were many times an exact item was needed. Musicians had very specific needs when requesting sheet music. Sometimes it doesn't matter. The public patron requesting a copy of a novel may not care if it is a paperback or a hard cover edition, reprint or other. (Fischetti, 2013)

Chapter 2

THE MARC PROJECT

In 1965, the Library of Congress (LC) held a conference to report on a study of converting cataloging data into machine-readable format prepared through a contract to Inforonics Ltd. At the second conference in 1966, all parties agreed to "stop hypothesizing and . . . take action." During the next two years, 35,000 LC records were converted, and sixty-two magnetic tapes containing MAchine-Readable Cataloging (MARC) were sent to sixteen participating libraries for review. Changes were made in the codes to represent the place of publication, language, and publisher, and alterations were also made to the procedures for collection, preparation, and processing of MARC data (Avram, 1968).

The MARC project began when the LC hired Henriette Avram as systems analyst to develop the binary configuration and formats necessary to interpret the long list of characters entered into a computer as a bibliographic record for an automated catalog. She had the aid of five librarians, three computer systems analysts, five programmers, one data technician, three editors, and two input typists.

Avram continued to refine MARC until she retired in 1992. At that time, she was responsible for the LC's networking and automation, while supervising a staff of 1,700. The MARC standard was adopted by the LC in 1970. It became an international standard in 1973, and within a decade it had been adopted by most large libraries (Blumenstein, 2006). According to Avram,

> In my opinion, libraries and librarians are needed more than ever, and the literature is noting this more often. In the development of MARC, it was clear to me that we needed two talents, i.e., computer expertise and library expertise. Neither talent could have succeeded alone. We need this more than ever today. Librarians must become computer literate so that they can understand the relationship between technology applied and the discipline of their profession. (Pattie, 1998, 77)

The computer needs a place for bibliographic information (author, title, call number, etc.), which is called a field, and it needs fields of different lengths because, unlike a telephone number, the space needed for this information varies in length. A three-digit number called a "tag" identifies each kind of field. Most fields have subfields. A book's physical description in field 300 is subdivided as:

300   ## $a 590 p. : $b illus. ; $c 24 cm.

MARC records can be used with the LC, Dewey Decimal, or some other classification scheme. The most popular book of English fiction, *Pride and Prejudice*, celebrated its 200th birthday in 2013. Following this paragraph is a listing of its original MARC format using Anglo-American Cataloging Rules (AACR). All MARC fields use a three-digit tag, followed by indicators and subfields, made up of numbers, letters, and symbols that are needed by the computer to interpret what we enter. The MARC 245 field has a "1" to indicate that the title should be displayed and a "0" for the number of letters to be ignored for filing. Subfields have their role in the 245-field role, with the delimiter "|a" indicating the title and "|c" stating responsibility for the work. Another common subfield delimiter representation is "$" instead of "|" since various cataloging software packages use different characters to represent subfield delimiters.

MARC	AACR
020	|a 0396085369 [ISBN] [International Standard Book Number]
035	|a (OCLC) 12405045
100 1	|a Austen, Jane, |d 1775–1817.
245 1 0	|a Pride and prejudice/ |c. Jane Austen Illus. by Charles E. Brock.
260 0	|a New York: |b Dodd Mead, |c 1985.
300	|a 269 p., [13] leaves of plates: |b illus.; |c 22 cm.
490 0	|a Great illustrated classics. [Series statement]
700 1 0	|a Brock, C. E. |q (Charles Edmund), |d 1870–1938. [Added entry]

MARC soon became the standard in the United States and other countries, but variations existed in UKMARC and CANMARC. Canada and the United States worked to combine and revise changes until the twenty-first version of MARC was published in 1998. MARC was also adopted by the British Library in 2001. The result allowed for more content in the notes fields, and access points in the subject added entries fields. In the following example, 520 is a summary notes field. And 650 has new subject headings, which are topical; 651, which is geographic; and 655, a LC indexing term. MARC 21 uses the revised Anglo-American Cataloging Rules, Second Edition, called AACR2. What follows is that most popular book again in MARC 21:

MARC 21	AACR2
020	|a 9780955881862 [ISBN]
035	|a (OCLC) 319501589
100 1	|a Austen, Jane, |d 1775–1817.
245 1 0	|a Pride and prejudice/ |c Jane Austen.
260	|a London: |b White's Books, |c 2009.
300	|a 376 p. ; |c 24 cm.
520	|a "For some readers Pride and Prejudice is a delightful comic novel, for others it is a Study of social and personal values—no other English novel is as popular. The binding illustration is by Kazuko Nomoto" —Publisher's description.
650 0	|a Young women |z England |v Fiction.
650 0	|a Courtship |z England |v Fiction.
651 0	|a England |x Social life and customs |y 19th century |v Fiction.
655 0	|a Love stories.

Another MARC Change

MARC 21 provides media formats for AACR2. The 020 subfield after the ISBN shows that this is an e-book that can be read on a mobile device. The 856 fields provide electronic information and method of access. The record also provides a website to learn more about access through the Mobipocket Reader platform.

MARC 21	AACR2
020	|a 9781775411857 (electronic bk. : Mobipocket Reader)
035	|a (OCLC) 586185609
100 1	|a Austen, Jane, |d 1775–1817.
245 1 0	|a Pride and prejudice/ |h [electronic source]/ |c Jane Austen.
260	|a [Waiheke Island] : |b Floating Press, |c c2008.
300	|a 1 online resource (626 p.)
500	|a "First published in 1813"—P.2.
520	|a In early nineteenth-century England, a spirited young woman copes with the suit of a snobbish gentleman, as well as the romantic entanglements of her four sisters.
650 0	|a Social classes |v Fiction.
650 0	|a Young women |v Fiction.
650 0	|a Courtship |v Fiction.
650 0	|a Sisters |v Fiction.
651 0	|a England |x Social life and customs |y 19th century |v Fiction.
650 0	|a Domestic fiction.
655 4	|a Electronic books.
655 7	|a Love stories |2 gsafd [*Guidelines on Subject Access to Individual Works of Fiction, Drama, Etc.*, 2nd edition, 2000.]
856 4	|3 Image |u http://images.contentreserve.com/imageThpe-100/1785-1/{D6472FA5-3ADE-41116-B15F-0A0FD90F1C2}Img100.jpg.
856 4	|u http://qqq.xonrwnrewawecw.xom/TitleInfo.AP?is={D6472FA5-3ADE-4116-B15F-0A0FD90F 1FC2}&Format=50 |z Click for information on Adobe Digital Editions version.
856 4	|u http://www.contentreserve.com/TitleInfo.asp?ID={D6472FA5-3ADE-4116-B15F-0A0FD90F-1FC2}&Format=900 |z Click for information on Mobipocket Reader version.
938	|a EBSCOhost |b EBSC |n 314142.

Following the communication code is one of the three previous records of *Pride and Prejudice* shown in computer code. See if you can guess which one it is. That is what the computer sees and reads in one continuous stream without the line breaks that are needed to make it visible to the human eye. But the organized display of data that is transferred between systems would not be possible without MARC's machine-readable cataloging format. This computer view of a MARC record was supplied by Linda Gabel at the Online Computer Library Center's (OCLC) WorldCat Quality Management unit.

01593cam a2200397la
450000100130000000300060001300506010007000704000730009402000
150016702000180018203500200020003700700022004300120029005000
210030204900090032310000300033224500740036226000340043630000
520047049000310052252001250055365100610067865000350073965000
330077465000310080765000540083865000560089270000530094883000-
3201001938006901033938004001102938003901142994001401181--OCoLC-20
130401034545.0-850820s1985 nyuaf 000 1 eng d- a 84072208 - aNLNbengcNLN-
dlAEdOHldOCLdBAKERdBTCTAdXY4dYDXCPdOCLCGdOCLCQ- a0396085369-
a9780396085362- a(OCoLC)12405045- bDodd, Mead & Company, Inc., 79
Madison Ave., New York, N.Y. 10016- ae-uk-en- 4aPR4034b.P7 1985- aOCLC-1
aAusten, Jane,d1775-1817.-10aPride and prejudice /cJane Austen ; illustrated by
Charles E. Brock.- aNew York :bDodd Mead,c1985.- a269 p., [13] leaves of plates
:bill. ;c22 cm.-1 aGreat illustrated classics- aA spirited young woman copes with
the suit of a snobbish gentleman as well as the romantic entanglements of her
sisters.- 0aEnglandxSocial life and customsy19th centuryvFiction.- 0aYoung women-
zEnglandvFiction.- 0aCourtshipzEnglandvFiction.- 0aSisterszEnglandvFiction.-
1aBenet, Elizabeth (Fictitious character)vFiction.- 1aDarcy, Fitzwilliam (Fictitious
character)vFiction.-1 aBrock, C. E.q(Charles Edmund),d1870-1938.4ill- 0aGreat
illustrated classics.- aBaker & TaylorbBKTYc3.98d3.58i0396085369n0001699205-
sactive-aBaker and TaylorbBTCPnbl 99948809- aYBP Library ServicesbYANK-
n354567-aC0bOCLCQ-01233cam a2200361Ki

MARC is a standardized way to format bibliographic information so that when
entered into a computer, it creates an understandable record for the item. For all
data elements that appear in MARC 21 records, developed in 1999 and last updated
September 2013, see the "MARC 21 Format for Bibliographic Data Field List" at
http://www.loc.gov/marc/bibliographic/ecbdlist.html.

Serials Midlife Crisis

The term *midlife crisis* was coined by Elliott Jaques, an organizational psycholo-
gist. According to Kay G. Johnson (2006), the "constantly changing nature of serials
[can be] compared to a 'psychological midlife crisis'" (35). Therefore, bringing our
problems to our serials colleagues, who make constant changes in MARC records,
may not solve all ILL problems with journals. If ILL librarians and staff members
read this, they will know where to turn for commiseration.

Serials librarianship is in a constant midlife crisis because of the continual changing
nature of the serials information chain. The traditional complexities of serials combined
with the rapid advancement of technology create an explosion with fallout. . . . The
explosion of serial publications and emergence of alternative forms of journal access and
delivery are transitions that have no apparent end. (Johnson, 2006, 35)

What we want to know is why journals keep changing their names and which libraries have made holdings changes. The new names, referred to as "rebranding," confuse databases that attribute new articles to old journal names or vice versa. Journal names are cited incorrectly by authors and by patrons entering citations manually into ILL requests. "What's in a (Journal) Name?" was asked by Phil Davis, an independent researcher and publishing consultant specialist, in his blog entitled "The Scholarly Kitchen." He cites a change by the American Medical Association (AMA) for nine journals beginning with the prefix "Archives of" to "JAMA."

Thus, *Archives of Internal Medicine* became *JAMA Internal Medicine* in 2013. In answer to his query, the AMA responded that "archives" led readers to believe that they did not publish "important and current research." Aware of Davis's research showing that a "journal name change depresses the journal's impact factor, as citations in the next two years are split between the old and the new title names," the response was that, "they would be in a stronger position in the near future." Responders to Davis's blog named many other examples for which they saw no good reason. And, David Flaxbert, a librarian at the University of Texas at Austin made the following comment (Davis, 2012):

> This is a good point usually overlooked by market-obsessed publishers. I'd like to add that more than just subscriptions can get messed up. Libraries must spend significant time updating their catalogs and link resolver databases so that access to the new titles (and old) [is] not interrupted. These aren't trivial tasks and require relatively high-level staff to work on [it]. Indexing services also have to make changes. And of course reader confusion about such changes persists for years.

Before we blame it all on the publishers, let us learn that librarians can cause the same problems for their colleagues in serials and ILL. The following section includes discussion of a serial with more title changes than our *Journal of Interlibrary Loan*.

What's in a Name Change?

On March 13, 2012, the American Library Association (ALA) sent out a news brief about a journal name change by the AASL division, known as the American Association of School Librarians. Its online, refereed journal, *School Library Media Research*, had officially changed its name to *School Library Research (SLR)*. The journal's coeditor, Jean Donham, said that the new title gave them the "opportunity to reimage and expand the journal's reach, while still providing high-quality, original research from scholars in [their] field." Then we learned that *SLR* is the successor to *School Library Media Research* and *School Library Quarterly Online*. School librarian creativity and serial librarian detail has given the AASL division eighty-two entries in WorldCat, for ten title changes (Habley, 2012). Note that an ISSN (International Serial Standard Number) is assigned to each title change (xxxx–xxxx) but not to different formats.

> *Newsletter,* vol. 1, no. 1–v. 1, no. 4, Sept. 1951–June 1952.   Print
> *ISSN 0899-580X* OCLC 17389453 *33 holdings*
> Followed by
> *School Libraries,* Quarterly, v. 2–21; Oct. 1952–summer 1972.   Print
> ISSN 0036-6609 OCLC 1765127   377 holdings, 9 records with 1–14 holdings
> *School Libraries,* Quarterly, v. 2–21; Oct. 1952–summer 1972.
> Electronic resource
> ISSN 0036-6609 OCLC 760252279   1 holding, plus 9 with 1–2 holdings
> [Google books record entered 2012]
> Followed by
> *School Media Quarterly,* Vol. 10, no. 1, Fall 1972–Summer 1981   Print
> ISSN 0361-1647 OCLC 1773523 507 holdings, plus 8 with 1–40 holdings
> Followed by
> *School Library Media Quarterly,* vol. 10, no. 1, 1981–vol. 24, no.4, 1997   Print
> ISSN 0278-4823 OCLC 7831305 673 holdings, plus 8 with 1–45 holdings
> Followed by
> Split into two: Knowledge quest [print] and School library media quarterly online
> *Knowledge Quest,* Bimonthly, Began with vol. 26, no. 1, Nov/Dec. 1997   Print
> ISSN 1094-9046 OCLC 37395440 507 holdings, plus 8 with 1–17 holdings
> *Knowledge Quest,* Bimonthly, Began with vol. 26, no.1, Nov/Dec. 1997 Internet
> ISSN 2163-5234 OCLC 60618523 341 holdings, plus 7 with 1–45 holdings
> *School Library Media Quarterly Online,* vol. 10, no. 1, 1981–vol. 25, no. 4, 1997
> ISSN 1098-738X OCLC 38490845 337 holdings OCLC 614960611 42 holdings
> Plus 2 with 0 holdings and 1 with 1 holding Internet
> Followed by
> *School Library Media Research,* Annual began with vol. 2, 1999–. Internet
> access ISSN 1523-4320 OCLC 40665167 469 holdings OCLC 644225739 58
> holdings
> Followed by
> *School Library Research,* Annual, vol. 15, 2012-Internet access
> ISSN 2165-1019 OCLC 768422879 18 holdings, plus 1 with1 holding.

Use the "780" and "785" MARC fields in OCLC records to verify these kinds of changes. Also check in after two years for the further results of this rebranding. Librarians made the title change promptly; commercial databases continue to use the former title, so it may take longer to attain their goal of growth and respect. Showing the relationship among these many journal changes will require more changes to the descriptive cataloging and computer representations.

Various Media Formats

With media, the carrier is important, particularly if the video is produced overseas. North American productions simply differentiate between videotapes and DVDs. Sometimes records add NTSC (National Television System Committee). This is the analog system used in North America and parts of South America. PAL (Phase Alternating Line) is used in most of Europe and elsewhere, but SECAM (Sequential Color with Memory), used by France and Russia, is also used in regions once connected with them. Check the "300" and "538" fields, as follows, and then discover if the patron has access to the correct player.

MARC 21	AACR2
035	(OCLC) 62501329
245 0 0	Extranjeras |b FoRibes, Federico.reign women [Title main entry]
260	Pamplona, Spain: |b Lamia Producciones audiovisuals; |a [Bilbao, Spain]; |c c2003.
300	1 videodisc (75 min.): |b sd., col.; |e 1 study guide (46 p.:col. Ill.: 24 cm.)
538	DVD, PAL, Regions 2–9; Dolby Digital. System details]
546	In Spanish; optional subtitles in English or French.
508	Cinematographer, Federico Ribes; editor, Tiago Herbert. [Creation/ production credits]
500	Videodisc release of the documentary motion picture produced in 2002.
520	Shows the experiences of immigrant women from China, Bangladesh, South America, Africa, the Middle East and Eastern Europe in Europe. [Summary]
650 0	Women immigrants |z Spain |x Social conditions. [Topical subjects]
650 0	Assimilation (Sociology).
650 0	Culture conflict |z Spain.
655 7	Documentary films. [Genre, Form]
700 1	Taberna, Helena. |4 aus [author] |4 drt [director] |4 res. [researcher] [Personal name added entry]
700 1	Pomar, Charo M.|4 res.
700 1	Ribes, Federico.
700 1	Illarramendi, Angel. |4 cmp [composer]
710 2	Afrika Lisanga. |4 cmp |4 prf. [composer, performer] [Corporate added entry]
710 2	Lamia Producciones Audiovisuales.|4 dst. |4 pro.

A VERY SHORT HISTORY OF CATALOGING

Whether we talk about clay tablets, animal parchment scrolls, paper books, or plastic compact discs, a large collection needs organization. Efforts to organize a library collection by describing each item and noting its place of access is usually traced back to Anthony Panizzi, an Italian trained in law who became in charge of the books at the British Library, but it has evolved. The following is a brief history of cataloging:

1841   Panizzi's 91 rules for the first and subsequent British Library printed author catalogue are published.

1876   Charles Ammi Cutter, a Bostonian, creates a classified card catalog with an author index. The catalog is best known for call numbers where letters and numbers put books in order.

1953   Seymour Lubetsky, of Belarus, as LC cataloger, issues *Cataloging Rules and Principles*, which is the basis for relationships of editions and formats.

1961   The twelve principles known as the Paris Principles for international author/title headings are promoted by the International Federation of Library Associations and Institutions (IFLA).

1967   Discussions lead to the AACR Anglo-American cataloging rules for British and North American versions.

1971   International Standard Bibliographic Description (ISBD) for order and punctuation, and then covering map, serials, and electronic sources by the IFLA, appear, influencing MARC changes.

1978   Revisions in 1988, 1998, and 2002 bring about a single version called AACR2.

1989   S. R. Ranganathan of India publishes his *Classified Catalogue Code*, in which he puts the user at the center of the library and reminds us that the catalog only has value when needed information is found.

2004   AACR3, still a draft, calls for a new approach and standard for digital and analog records.

2005   RDA (Resource, Description, and Access) is the new standard established by AACR2.

JUMPING INTO RDA

RDA (Resource, Description, and Access) is being developed by the English-speaking library associations at the same time that IFLA is working to revise the Paris Principles into FRBR, which stands for Functional Requirements for Bibliographic Records. RDA is now using FRBR terminology to name bibliographic entities (work, expression, manifestation, and item). They will also incorporate FRBR tasks (Find, Indentify, Select, and Obtain) as the method of defining data elements. To some it seems as if we have been using the same cataloging rules for more than forty years, and to others the many changes taking place are implementing Lubetsky's concepts of works distinguished from editions, translations, and versions for a new future (Welsh and Batley, 2012).

Meanwhile, the MARBI (Machine-Readable Bibliographic Implementation Committee), which is responsible for MARC, has introduced changes that make the implementation of RDA possible for libraries using the MARC 21 format. Many libraries are already using them, while others ignore them. So before we discuss when or if "MARC must die," as is suggested in much of the current literature, and before BIBFRAME is presented, with its goal to go fully into the online world with links to people, events, publishers, etc., let us review RDA.

SEARCHING FOR RDA IN MARC 21

According to the OCLC, there are more than 150,000 records in WorldCat that are cataloged according to RDA. There are currently 238 records using RDA in my library. To do a search limited to just RDA records, merely add "dx:rda" to your search statement. You may have to use the expert search screen to accept the addition. To simplify the major differences between AACR2 and RDA, you will see the following types of changes. The $ symbol is used here instead of "|."

- Elimination of media format following the 245 (title) $h in the following new 33x fields: 336 (content type), 337 (media type), and 338 (carrier type) in RDA. This places books on an equal footing with other formats.
- Removal of abbreviations in favor of spelled out words. In the 300 (physical description field), change "29 p. : $b illus." to "29 pages : $b illustrations." Latin abbreviations in the 260 (imprint) field are $a [S.l. : $b s.n.], $c [ca. 1820]. Sine loco (without a place) becomes [Place of publication not identified], sine nomine (without a name) becomes [Publisher not identified], and circa (about) becomes [1820?].
- Use of the "take what you see" approach. So under AACR2, the publisher Rowman & Littlefield would be transcribed like that even if it appeared as Rowman Littlefield. Now it is what appears. The same goes for capitalization. RDA gives the cataloger the right to transcribe what is seen on the title page even if it will be presented as follows: 245 1 4 THE COMPLETE HISTORY OF EVERYTHING.
- Use of "Department" instead of "Dept." in headings for government and corporate bodies. Headings for books of the Bible will omit "N.T." and "O.T." unless it is necessary to distinguish, in which case "New Testament" and "Old Testament" are used. More efforts to differentiate people with the same name will be constructed.
- Encouragement of explicit relationship information. Record the relationship between a heading and the role played in the work, and the relationship of the work to other works.
- Elimination of the "rule of three" (related to the "transcribe what you see" point). In the past, if there were more than three authors, the cataloger would only record the first one and indicate the rest by [et al.]. Now all names can be recorded and traced. This also means that there will be fewer title main entries.
- Increased granularity in describing publication information. While the 260 field is still valid, catalogers can now specify more clearly the difference between publication and production or distribution by using the 264 fields. (Welsh and Batley, 2012)

RESOURCE DESCRIPTION AND ACCESS LINKS

To visit the RDA Toolkit site, go to http://www.rdatoolkit.org. This site includes information on subscriptions, an RDA Toolkit blog, development and release information, and much more. Notice that here a different format has its own ISBN (International Standard Book Number).

The following are RDA records, first as presented to patrons, and second as presented to catalogers. Note that the additional 3xx fields do not appear in the online catalog presentation. There are thousands of RDA records now in WorldCat. Patrons often send e-book records when they want print, and we are better informed if they tell us this in the request note field. They seldom check for media formats as well.

Online Catalog RDA Record in AACR2 Presentation

Title:	Bach gold.
Authors:	Bach, Johann Sebastian, 1685–1750, composer.
	Bradley, Kate.
Publication:	CD edition.
Year:	2012
Series:	Easy piano collection.
Standard No:	ISBN: 9781780382852; Publisher: CH78672; Chester Music; OM49687; Omnibus Media.
Descriptor:	Piano music, Arranged.
	Piano music – Simplified editions.
Notes:	27 pieces for piano, either arrangements or simplified editions/ CD contains demonstration tracks. / CD published by Omnibus Media. / Includes biographical note by Kate Bradley/ Score only originally published: London, Chester Music, c2007.

RDA Record in MARC 21 Communication Presentation

MARC 21	RDA
020	9781780382852
100 1	Bach, Johann Sebastian |d 1685–1750, |e composer
245 1 0	Bach Gold
264 1	London : |b Chester Music, |c [2012]
300	1 score (64 pages) : |c 31 cm |e 1 CD
336	notated music |2 rdacontent
336	performed music |2 rdacontent
337	audio |2 rdamedia
338	audio disc |2 rdacarrier
490 1	Easy piano collection.

500	27 pieces for piano, either arrangements or simplified editions.
500	CD contains demonstration tracks.
500	CD published by Omnibus Media.
500	Includes biographical note by Kate Bradley.
500	Score only originally published by London, Chester Music, c2007 (publisher's note).
650 0	Piano music, Arranged.
650 0	Piano music |v Simplified editions.
700 1	Bradley, Kate.

THE FUTURE OF CATALOGING

The Internet and Wikipedia appear to be creating new directions for cataloging. The LC is developing a bibliographic framework (BIBFRAME) initiative. Kevin Ford, who works in the LC's Network Development and MARC Standards Office (NDMSO) presented updates at ALA Midwinter 2013 and 2014 for their initiative launched in May 2011. It emphasizes "the network" and makes linking and "interconnectedness commonplace." It is a "high-level model" for the library community that has been presented for discussion and evaluation, but it is also a model that will look far beyond the library community.

We are reminded that LC efforts led to machine-readable cataloging in the 1960s so that the work of one cataloger could be shared with many others using technology

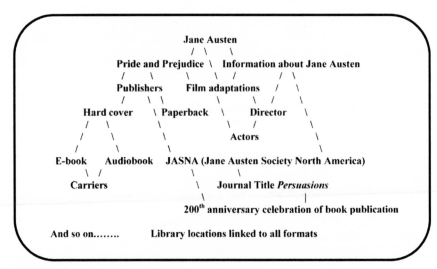

Figure 2.1.   BIBFRAME Model for Linked Relationships

to create "economies of scale" (Ford, 2012). Similar notes and discussion from Ford's presentation can be found online.

The new model is not just a replacement for MARC; it is the future for our bibliographic description of library materials "as part of the Web and the networked world we live in." The objectives are:

1. Differentiate clearly between conceptual content and its physical manifestation(s). (Referring to the works and its many instances.)
2. Focus on unambiguously identifying information entities. (Includes all those involved.)
3. Leverage and expose relationships between and among entities.

Explaining the information presented in bibliographic records through linkages will make it more understandable. Relationships are fundamental and will suggest to users other items they may be interested in based upon their previous searches. BIBFRAME will be using the RDA vocabulary, and changes will soon be available at http://www.loc.gov/bibframe/.

CONCLUSION

Accurate MARC records are important to ILL. When an ILL staff member requests the wrong item or has requested the correct item but the lending library sent the wrong item, the patron is upset because the item must be requested again. The delay affects the work of the faculty member, student, physician, musician, or professional writer who required the material by the definite "need by" dates indicated on the request. How these automated bibliographic records became part of a global online library catalog is explained in chapter 3, along with its development into a large nonprofit vendor that manages many of our library operations and has enhanced the importance of ILL.

REFERENCES

Avram, Henriette D. (1968). "MARC: The First Two Years." *Library Resources and Technical Services* 12, no. 3: 245–50.
Blumenstein, Lynn (2006). "Avram, MARC Pioneer, Dies at 86." *Library Journal* 131, no. 10: 18, 20.
Davis, Phil (2012). "What's in a (Journal) Name?" *The Scholarly Kitchen*, December 18. Available online at http://scholarlykitchen.sspnet.org/2012/12/18/whats-in-a-journal-name/ (accessed March 12, 2013).
Fischetti, Judy (2013). E-mail to author, May 2.
Ford, Kevin (2012). "Changing Futures: Exploring the Future of Cataloging and Metadata in Libraries." *Cataloging Futures*, December 7. Available online at http://www.cataloging

futures.com/catalogingfutures/2012/12/ (accessed March 28, 2013). This presentation is available in two formata: Video and Slides.

Gabel, Linda (2013). "RDA Records." E-mail to author, March 6.

Habley, Jennifer (2012). "AASL's Research Journal Announces Name Change and Debuts New Logo." *American Libraries*, March 13. Available online at http://www.ala.org/news/press-releases/2012/03/aasl%E2%80%99s-research-journal-announces-name-change-and-debuts-new-logo (accessed June 14, 2013).

Johnson, Kay G. (2006). "Serials: The Constant Midlife Crisis." *Serials Review* 32, no. 1: 35–39.

"MARC 21 Format for Bibliographic Data Field List." *Library of Congress*, 1999. Available online with lastest updates at http://www.loc.gov/marc/bibliographic/ecbdlist.html (accessed November 19, 2013).

Miller, Eric (2013). "BIBFRAME and the World Wide Web." LC Bibliographic Framework Initiative Update Forum, Seattle Washington, ALA Midwinter, January 27. Available online at http://www.loc.gov/bibframe/pdf/ALAmw2013-bibframe-lcupdate-20130127_Miller.pdf (accessed November 18, 2013).

Pattie, Ling-yuh W. (Miko) (1998). "Henriette Davidson Avram, the Great Legacy." *Cataloging and Classification Quarterly* 25, no 2/3: 67–81.

Welsh, Anne, and Sue Batley (2012). *Practical Cataloging: AACR2, RDA, and MARC 21*. Chicago: Neal-Schuman.

3

OCLC

How to Get Them to Listen to Us

Go to the people at the top. Do not moan and groan with like-minded souls. Do not write letters or place a few phone calls and then sit back and wait. Stand before the people you fear and speak your mind—even if your voice shakes. When you least expect it, someone may actually listen to what you have to say. Well-aimed slingshots can topple giants.

> —Maggie Kuhn, social activist instructions in her book
> *The Life and Times of Maggie Kuhn* (1991)

In 2005, Leslie R. Morris, editor of the *Journal of Interlibrary Loan, Document Delivery, and Electronic Reserve*, spoke up for interlibrary loan (ILL) staff in his editorial, saying, "OCLC seems to have lost its way" (1). Leslie is no longer with us, so now we are on our own. The four issues he raised after listening to us complain to our listservs were:

- The decline in productivity of the new Web-based systems
- A lack of testing before new software is released
- The loss of library mission
- Inadequate user support

User support has improved. Technicians staffing the support desk work to answer our questions, but most of them have no real-life library experience, unlike the days when the Online Computer Library Center (OCLC) was being developed. That is one of the OCLC's biggest challenges. Tony Melvin, product manager for WorldCat Resource Sharing, now monitors our listservs, which keeps him in the loop with ILL issues. He is knowledgeable and, we suspect, high enough in the chain that his voice

is heard. As we transition to WorldShare Resource Sharing we are again in indefi-
nite Beta. Before returning to these concerns, the following is a brief history of the
OCLC, the monolith that both impresses and annoys us.

HOW IT ALL BEGAN

The OCLC, first known as the Ohio College Library Center, was organized in July
1967, as a nonprofit corporation in Ohio to serve its fifty-three academic libraries.
They ranged from small liberal arts and community college libraries to large research
universities and specialized colleges. Prior to 1967, a special committee from the
Ohio College Association expressed interest in developing a revised union list of
serials, cooperative acquisitions, and a storage center. They hired a consultant, who
recommended a "bibliographic center to facilitate interlibrary lending."

Bids to develop this bibliographic center were requested, but the special committee also brought in two more consultants. They were Ralph Parker, University of
Missouri library director, and Frederick G. Kilgour, Yale University associate director
for research and development. These consultants recommended nonacceptance of
the bids received; then they offered a very different plan. They said that the "best approach would be to create a centralized, computer-based, machine-readable file that
could be used for many functions," including the union catalog desired by the first
special committee. This report was accepted and the corporation formed, and after
a search for leadership, Kilgour was chosen as the director, a position he assumed in
September 1967. In fewer than three years, the computer-based operation was ready
for off-line catalog card production (Hopkins, 1973, 309).

Judith Hopkins, a catalog librarian who worked for the OCLC in those early
years, explained that members sent in an IBM card with the Library of Congress
(LC) card number assigned to the book for catalog cards to be ordered. At the
OCLC, this information was keypunched and run against the MARC II database. If
the record was found, MARC catalog cards, with variation only in call number format, were produced, batched, and mailed to customers. Call number variation was
very important to librarians at that time. In August 1971, the OCLC went online.
It started with one library, and soon all members could not only modify a MARC
record, but input a record for an item not in the LC, which then became available to
all members. Cards were mailed from the OCLC to the library within five to seven
days. By January 1973, the OCLC database contained 635,000 records, of which
245,000 were input by user libraries (Hopkins, 1973).

THE REGIONAL ADVANTAGE

Between 1972 and 1977, twenty American networks joined the OCLC by invitation
or just organized to join the project. Some of these organizations, like NELINET,

already existed, but they were willing to support the OCLC. Others, like SUNY/ OCLC, which later became NYLINK, had formed just to be service centers, but they also provided technical support and training. When you search the OCLC policies directory, some of the following names still appear:

- Cooperative College Library Center (CCLC)
- New England Library Information Network (NELINET)
- Pittsburgh Regional Library Center (PRLC)
- Five Associated University Libraries (FAUL)
- Federal Library Committee (FEDLINK)
- Interuniversity Council of the North Texas Area (AMIGOS)
- Pennsylvania Network Area (PALINET)
- Missouri Library Network Corporation (MLNC)
- Illinois Research and Reference Center (ILLINET)
- Southeastern Library Network (SOLINET)
- State University of New York (SUNY, NYLINK)
- Bibliographic Center for Research (BCR)
- Consortium of Universities of the Washington Metropolitan Area (CAPCON)
- Indiana Cooperative Library Services Authority (INCOLSA)
- Michigan Library Consortium (MLC)
- Wisconsin Library Consortium (WiLS)
- OCLC Western Service Center (PACNET, OCLC Pacific)
- Minnesota Interlibrary Teletype Exchange (MINITEX)
- Nebraska Library Commission (NEBASE)
- Midwestern Regional Library Network (MRLN)

NEW NAME, NEW STRUCTURE

OCLC Inc. became the new corporate name in 1978, and the abbreviation came to stand for Online Computer Learning Center. A new governance structure was formed of regional networks or service centers where no network existed, along with an expanded Board of Trustees. Ohio libraries formed OHIONET (Schieber, 2009). The OCLC developed relationships with these regional service providers in an effort to reach out to libraries in all fifty states, "because the Ohio membership would not approve operation outside of Ohio . . . except in Pittsburgh" (Alford, 2009, 572).

For thirty years, the networks served as members by electing representatives to serve on the OCLC Users Council. Regional networks provided technical support and face-to-face technical workshops, as well as promoted OCLC services, but they added a few of their own projects. Starting in 2005, the OCLC reduced compensations provided to these "former sales partners," resulting in mergers of some and the dissolution of others. The OCLC was now focusing on global expansion and direct delivery of its own products and services (Bailey-Hainer, 2009). The OCLC continues to receive input from its various user/member groups, but the necessary communication provided by the regional networks was lost.

VISION AND ACTION

Kilgour was an academic librarian and historian of science and technology for thirty years before he was hired by the Ohio College Association in 1967, to create the world's first computerized network. He introduced a shared cataloging system in Ohio in 1971, and, in 1979, he launched the online ILL system. There were only four ways to search for a record at that time: 1) title (4,2,2,1); 2) author title (4,4); 3) OCLC accession number; and 4) LC card number (Schieber, 2009).

While most librarians consider the shared cataloging database and the provision for online resource sharing to be his main contribution, this was not his view. At the May 13, 1972, annual meeting of the Association of Research Libraries, Kilgour outlined his three goals for library cooperation:

1. The establishment of new objectives for a group of cooperating libraries. He believed that too often a library joined a cooperative "to further its own goals."
2. The sharing of resources without cost to the institution providing the resources. His example was not ILL but original cataloging that cost a library nothing to share.
3. "Pooling of human and financial resources to achieve a system unattainable by individual libraries." This achieves a computer system like no library could afford.

With this system, he believed that librarians were offered the opportunity through computerization to "treat an individual person . . . as a unique event" and "supply information to a person when and where that person needs that information" (Kilgour, 1973, 138).

Interviewed a few years before his death in 2006, Kilgour stated that his vision was to "build a comprehensive database that would *promote learning* on a global level." That database is WorldCat, built by librarians from throughout the world during a span of forty-four years. In 2008, for the first time, it contained more non-English records than English-language ones (Alford, 2009). The WorldCat database currently contains more than 30 million records and more than 2 billion holdings.

LEADERSHIP MATTERS

The OCLC has had four presidents since its formation. Frederick G. Kilgour served from 1967 until 1980, but he remained on the Board of Trustees until 1995. He also served on the faculty of the School of Information and Library Science at the

University of North Carolina at Chapel Hill from 1990 until he retired at the age of ninety-two, in 2004. Author of many scholarly papers, he was also the founder and first editor of the journal *Information Technology and Libraries*.

Kilgour was succeeded by Rowland C. W. Brown, a lawyer with a business leadership background. Brown served the OCLC from 1980 until 1989. He opened the first office outside the United States, in Birmingham, England. The number of member libraries increased from 2,300 in North America to 9,400 in twenty-seven countries. WorldCat records grew from 5 million to 18 million.

Dr. K. Wayne Smith was an economics professor, a business consultant, and publisher of the *World Book Encyclopedia* before becoming president and chief executive officer of the OCLC in 1989. During his tenure, library membership increased to 30,000 libraries in sixty-four countries, and WorldCat grew to 38 million records. The OCLC created the first online end-user reference service known as FirstSearch and did innovative work in electronic journals.

Jay Jordan has served the OCLC the longest, beginning in 1998. Although he tried to retire at the age of sixty-eight in 2012, he continued until June 2013. Jordan came to the OCLC after twenty-four years in management, including as president of Information Handling Services, a publisher of databases internationally. He actively increased OCLC library membership to 72,000 libraries, which contributed 290 million bibliographic records. After investing in a new computer infrastructure that could handle non-Roman scripts, it was easy for users to search by entering either Dostoyevsky or Dostoïevski for the same books.

A gateway for WorldCat to access digitized special collections and art treasures holdings in libraries, museums, and elsewhere was opened using CONTENTdm, digital management software developed at the University of Washington. To promote public libraries as a place "where everyone is welcome," where "almost anything can be explored," and where you can "debunk" any misinformation, he launched the website "Geek the Library." A joint project with the LC, Deutsche Nationalbibliothek, and Bibliothèque nationale de France, along with many other national libraries, resulted in a Virtual International Authority File (VIAF) that combined their name authority files into a single service. See http://geekthelibrary.org/geek -the-library/, http://www.oclc.org/research/activities/viaf.html, and http://www .oclc.org/about/leadership/presidents.en.html.

CHALLENGE AND CONTROVERSY

The OCLC was incorporated as a nonprofit, but it often displayed aggressive for-profit corporate behavior. It has an advantage due to its tax-exempt status and two sources of steady income—membership dues and service fees—as well as grants like those from the Council for Library Resources (CLR) and the Gates Foundation. Objections came from both the library and the business community, as seen in the following clashes and the ways in which they were resolved.

1972   Richard Abel, "father of the computer-assisted library approval plan," makes an early effort to provide a computer-based cataloging system with LC records plus those produced by his firm for scholarly, current, backlist, and grey literature. Abel's plan to automate the catalog of the California public university system was the only proposal that met requirements. Concern by their cataloging staffs that this would put them out of work led instead to acceptance of catalog-card purchasing from the newly started OCLC. This forward-thinking business lost many libraries to the OCLC and then went bankrupt; however, the OCLC had the same impact on catalogers (Abel, 2011–12).

1979   The OCLC also has nonprofit competitors, all of whom eventually agree to merge; however, the Research Libraries Information Network (RLIN), created by the Research Libraries Group (RLG) in 1974, will not go quietly. Columbia, Harvard, and Yale, along with the New York Public Library, formed this consortium of university libraries, although a small library with a unique collection like the Fashion Institute of Technology could join. The OCLC and RLIN "cross swords" publicly as each tries to promote its advantages. The RLIN focuses on reference support by being the first to add subject searching to their online catalog, which also retained the "record version of every member library." They would remain a restricted group and were about to go online for ILL. The OCLC emphasizes its new nationwide ILL system, LC authority files, and planned circulation system. The RLIN provides members with "elite" status ("OCLC and RLIN Backers Cross Swords at Mid Atlantic," 1979, 2,389).

2003   The OCLC sues Library Hotel, in New York City, for unauthorized use of the Dewey Decimal System (DDC) trademark while decorating, room numbering, and placing books in rooms. The OCLC acquires Forest Press and rights to DDC in 1988, to update it for worldwide use and develop it online. Librarians are upset that the OCLC sought more money than the hotel had earned during the three years it had existed. The hotel survives after it agrees to acknowledge the DDC trademark and donate to a children's reading charity (McElfresh, 2009).

2006   The RLG's 150 member libraries are integrated into the OCLC, with many of their leaders being absorbed into the OCLC Programs and Research Division, but the RLIN was dissolved (Oder, 2006). The RLG catalog is integrated into WorldCat, including the SCIPIO database of Hand Press Books and Art Sales Catalogs, and ArchiveGrid for loan of archival materials. SHARES, their resource-sharing partnership with special access for former RLG members, continues (Wilson et al., 2009).

2008   The OCLC works to gain complete control of bibliographic records in WorldCat, even limiting use by members, to protect "against unreasonable use." Librarians, who see this as taking ownership of their work, protest through their professional associations. Member libraries had not been consulted, or even notified, of the planned policy change. This leads to the creation of an OCLC Review Board. Their survey, with 1,620 responses (50 percent academic and

21 percent public libraries), showed that librarians, unlike the OCLC, "do not see the problem, and where they do, how the proposed policy will address this problem" (McElfresh, 2009). The new OCLC policy is withdrawn and later replaced with a policy responsive to member concerns (Richardson, 2012).

2010   SkyRiver and Innovative Interfaces sue the OCLC in California federal court, "alleging anticompetitive business practices" that have eliminated choice involving cataloging, bibliographic data services, interlibrary lending, and integrated library systems. One example cited is Michigan State University ending its use of the OCLC's cataloging system but retaining OCLC membership. A fee for batch loading records cataloged by SkyRiver is expected, but the OCLC's high quote eliminates any savings, and a large fee is also added for ILL services. Innovative continues to lose clients for online public access catalogs (OPACs) and discovery platforms as the OCLC develops an integrated library system (ILS), beginning with WorldCat Local in 2008. The OCLC becomes the "back end" for every ILS needing access to bibliographic records for copy cataloging and ILL (Richardson, 2012). Innovative absorbs SkyRiver, drops the suit, and is then "excited" to "engage with OCLC." The OCLC is pleased and looks "forward to possible future engagement with Innovative where it benefits libraries" (Schwartz and Warburton, 2013).

PROFIT OR NONPROFIT

WorldCat is the largest catalog in the world, the flagship of the OCLC, containing more than 300 million bibliographic records from 72,000 libraries throughout the world. As a nonprofit, the OCLC has a public purpose as follows (go to http://www .oclc.org/en-US/worldcat/catalog.html):

> We are a worldwide library cooperative, owned, governed, and sustained by members since 1967. Our public purpose is a statement of commitment to each other that we will work together to improve access to the information held in libraries around the globe and find ways to reduce costs for libraries through collaboration.

During the same time that the OCLC was developing exciting new services itself, it was also absorbing numerous innovative nonprofit and commercial corporations. See the following chronology for a listing of many of the acquisitions (go to http:// www.oclc.org/en-US/about/sustainability/mergers.html):

1982   Purchases Claremont Total Library System from Claremont Colleges
1983   Purchases National Library of Medicine Lister Hill Center's Integrated Library System and acquires Avatar to assist in development and launch of LS/2000 library automation system
1987   Acquires Data Phase's software and launches as LS/2 but sells to Ameritech in 1990

1991   Acquires University of Toronto Library Automated System (UTLAS) from Thomas Canada Ltd.

1993   Acquires Information Dimensions from Battelle and sells to Gore Technologies in 1997

1997   Acquires Blackwell North America's authority control service

1999   Acquires Washington Library Network (WLN) and enters joint ownership with PICA

2000   Buys Public Affairs Information Service (PAIS) but sells in 2004. The OCLC becomes sole distributor of ILLiad software, developed by Virginia Tech and ATLAS Systems.

2002   Enters partnership with Olive Software; enters partnership with DeMeMa Inc. for CONTENTdm; and acquires netLibrary and then sells it in 2010 to EBSCO

2005   OCLC PICA acquires Sisis Information Systems and Fretwell-Downing Informatics Group. OCLC buys the remaining shares of OCLC PICA, created in the Netherlands in 2007.

2006   Research Libraries Group, with its 150 member libraries, including its RLIN database, combines with the OCLC. The OCLC acquires the assets of Openly Informatics, with a database of 1.2 million records, with links to electronic resources and Digital Media Management known as DiMeMa.

2008   Acquires EXProxy from Useful Utilities and AmLib library management system from Australia

2009   Acquires OAIster, a union catalog of more than 25 million records representing open-access resources gathered by the University of Michigan from more than 1,100 contributors

2011   Acquires assets of German library system provider Bond GmbH & Co. KG (Richardson, 2012)

In 2013, it appeared that collaboration, rather than takeover, of competing enterprises would be the new direction for the OCLC. The OCLC is offering Proquest's discovery service, Summon, and its ebrary through WorldCat Local's interface. In return, Proquest will have direct access to WorldCat and OCLC resource sharing. Another exchange is discovery of popular Gale databases with full text and archives in WorldCat Local for mutual subscribers ("New Partnerships," 2013).

A GLOBAL ORGANIZATION

The first organization was made up of presidents and library directors of the fifty-four colleges in Ohio that created the OCLC. In 1978, a report from Arthur D. Little Associates suggested that changes take place to involve the membership, which came from forty-five states. The Board of Trustees was expanded and a User's Council formed to include representatives from regional networks and OCLC service centers in the states without networks (Alford, 2009).

In 2009, Larry Alford, who served for six years as chair of the OCLC Board of Trustees, described the fourth stage of OCLC governance that he saw evolving. Decisions are made by the Board of Trustees, with input from the Global Council, which is made up of representatives holding leadership positions in libraries, museums, and archives, as well as related areas in business, publishing, and information technology. They are chosen by the regional councils that now represent continents. Meetings are held to consider what kinds of services, charges, and training will be available. "These representatives will advise the OCLC on its strategic directions and represent thousands of librarians and millions of library users both to OCLC management and its board" (Alford, 2009, 570).

OCLC Regional Councils

There are four regional councils representing Europe, the Middle East and Africa, Asia Pacific, and the Americas. They have the following responsibilities:

- Elect delegates to the Global Council—one from Canada, one from Latin America/the Caribbean, and three from the United States
- Hold at least one in-person annual meeting and other meetings as necessary
- Expedite the flow of information amongst regional members and to OCLC management, the Board of Trustees, and the Global Council

OCLC Global Council

The Global Council meets in person at least once each year in an Annual Global Council Meeting and may hold other meetings in person or electronically. Delegates are elected for three-year terms by members of their respective regional councils, but they must be elected from various types and sizes of institutions to offer different perspectives. These representatives of member libraries are called ambassadors. Global Council exercises its responsibilities in four ways:

- Electing six members to the OCLC Board of Trustees
- Ratifying amendments to the OCLC Code of Regulations and Articles of Incorporation
- Discussing interests of mutual concern and making recommendations to OCLC management and members of the OCLC Board of Trustees
- Ensuring regular and open communication between the membership and OCLC

OCLC Board of Trustees

In addition to six members elected by the Global Council, the board consists of the president of the OCLC and nine trustees elected by the board itself, five of whom come from fields outside librarianship. Members own the cooperative, and librarians guide and shape its services, policies, and direction through a sixteen-member Board of Trustees—more than half of whom are librarians, but usually library directors. This governance structure ensures regular and open dialogue between member libraries and the OCLC management.

Americas Regional Council

The website for the Americas Regional Council (ARC) lists current delegates to that regional council. The ARC holds at least one annual meeting in the United States at ALA Midwinter or ALA Annual. The meetings are open in person or virtually to all library staff regardless of ALA membership. An ARC Communications Committee was set up in 2010, to "provide meaningful opportunities for librarians to discuss issues that matter to them and to contribute ideas to the further development of the OCLC." To learn what they do and communicate with them, go to http://www.oclc.org/councils/americas.en.html.

Whatever the method of communication used since this governance structure began in 2010, the OCLC has yet to develop a way for this structure to reach out to librarians and library users. A first innovative step has been the organization of topical meetings at the opening of ALA Midwinter. The 2014 program is set to include an OCLC Americas report by Skip Pritchard, a luncheon, a panel lead by Pritchard on MOOCs (Massive Open Online Courses) and libraries, and a reception. Anyone interested can attend in person or virtually. The Americas ambassadors organized this very interesting panel.

WE LOVE PROGRESS BUT NOT ALL THE CHANGES

In 2013, ILL librarians faced with a transition to WorldCat Resource Sharing, away from using the FirstSearch platform, were again overwhelmed with problems as they transitioned into the cloud for WorldShare. The OCLC claims that it is "working together with members of the library community to build a platform for exchange, innovation, and collaboration to help libraries operate at Webscale" (see http://www.oclc.org/en-US/worldshare-platform.html).

The OCLC provided many WorldShare free tutorials in an attempt to introduce this change. The ILL listservs were filled with questions. Tony Melvin, who monitors the ILL listservs for the OCLC, asked that these concerns go directly by telephone to the OCLC technical staff. To handle the heavy call volume, the OCLC spent a weekend upgrading ILL customer service.

Those who are hesitant to call can send e-mails to "OCLC Customer Support" at support@oclc.org. If you are not on the ILL-L listserv, for WorldShare tutorials, go to http://oclc.org/support/training/portfolios/resource-sharing/worldshare-ill.en.html.

OCLC upgrades telephone prompts for more personalized and streamlined support.

Beginning June 21, 2013, OCLC users who call OCLC Support (in North America) –including technical support, training, library services, billing, and order processing—will select from a new set of prompts. Easier and faster for users to navigate, the new streamlined options will feature the following capabilities:

Select a Spanish language option.
Dial a known extension to contact a specific support representative.
The system will tell you how many members are ahead of you in queue.
Bypass the queue and enter your direct phone number so that you may be contacted as soon as a support staff member becomes available.

We look forward to assisting you and hearing what you think. Give us a call

Direct phone: 1-614-793-8682
Toll free phone: 1-800-848-5800   Use it. See that your staff uses it.

Figure 3.1.   OCLC Customer Support Upgrade Instructions

OCLC'S NEW LEADER

On July 1, 2013, David "Skip" Pritchard became the president and chief executive officer of the OCLC, succeeding Jay Jordan, who retired after fifteen years as the OCLC's leader. Pritchard has a strong business background, having recently been head of the Ingram Content Group, the world's largest distributor of books, music, and media to retailers, libraries, and schools in the United States and abroad. Before that he held executive positions at ProQuest and LexisNexis. He has a B.S. from Towson University, near Baltimore, Maryland, and a J.D. from the University of Baltimore School of Law. Unfortunately, he has had no prior experience with nonprofits or librarianship, "[b]ut he wants to do a lot of listening and let members decide what they want" ("Newsmaker: Skip Pritchard," 2013).

One form of listening that the OCLC does well is to recognize innovation within libraries. They are one of the sponsors of the Rethinking Resource Sharing awards listed in the next chapter. It is always a good idea to attend ALA meetings, regional meetings, and other gatherings where the OCLC will have a presence and make a presentation, give a suggestion, or state a concern. The OCLC says that they have no plans revive the ILL Advisory Committee due to the cost of covering the expenses; however, if we urge our directors to vote for ILL representatives to the ARC, we can have more involvement in guiding our future and learn more about the paths that our recommendations will take through the OCLC policy-making groups.

REFERENCES

Abel, Richard (2011–12). "Papa Abel Remembers—The Tale of a Band of Booksellers, Fasicle 17: The Theatre of Bibliographic Control." *Against the Grain* 23, no. 6: 67–69.

Alford, Larry P. (2009). "Governing a Global Cooperative." *Journal of Library Administration* 49, no. 6: 567–74.

Bailey-Hainer, Brenda (2009). "The OCLC Network of Regional Service Providers: The Last Ten Years." *Journal of Library Administration* 49, no. 6: 621–29.

Hopkins, Judith (1973). "The Ohio College Library Center." *Library Resources and Technical Services* 17, no. 3: 308–19.

Kilgour, Frederick G. (1973). "Computer-Based Systems: A New Dimension to Library Co-operation." *College and Research Libraries* 34, no. 2: 137–43.

Kramer, Marilyn McMann (2005). "An Interview With Judith Hopkins." *Cataloging and Classification Quarterly* 41, no. 1: 5–22.

McElfresh, Laura Kane (2009). "Good Things Come in Small Libraries: Much Ado about the New OCLC WorldCat Policy." *Technicalities* 29, no. 2: 3–6.

Morris, Leslie R. (2005). "Library Staff and OCLC: Making OCLC Do What You Want Them to Do." *Journal of Interlibrary Loan, Document Delivery, and Electronic Reserve* 15, no. 3: 1–5.

"New Partnerships: ProQuest, Gale, FamilySearch, and DOGObooks" (2013). *NextSpace* no. 21: 20.

"Newsmaker: Skip Pritchard." (2013). *American Libraries* 44, nos. 9/10: 16–17.

"OCLC and RLIN Backers Cross Swords at Mid Atlantic" (1979). *Library Journal* 104, no. 20: 2,389–91.

Oder, Norman (2006). "RLG to Become Part of OCLC." *Library Journal* 131, no. 10: 16–17.

Richardson, Ellen (2012). "Ain't No (Sky) River Wide Enough to Keep Me from Getting to You: SkyRiver, Innovative, OCLC, and the Fight for Control over the Bibliographic Data, Cataloging Services, ILL, and ILS Markets." *Legal Reference Services Quarterly* 31, no. 1: 37–64.

Schieber, Phil (2009). "Biographical Sketch of Frederick G. Kilgour Librarian, Educator, Entrepreneur, 1914–2006." *Journal of Library Administration* 49, no. 6: 561–65.

Schwartz, Meridith, and Bob Warburton (2013). "III Drops OCLC Suit, Will Absorb SkyRiver." *Library Journal* 138, no. 6: 12.

Wilson, Lizabeth, James Neal, James Michalko, and Jay Jordan (2009). "RLG and OCLC: Combined for the Future." *Journal of Library Administration* 49, no. 6: 585–89.

4

Innovation Can Come from Us

ILLiad Is One Example

We look before and after. We pine for what is not.

—Percy Bysshe Shelley, "Ode to a Skylark"

The idea of sharing books between libraries goes back more than a thousand years, and some individuals in certain instances made it work by traveling to the place where the book could be found. But the idea of sending the book to another library for use faced many barriers. To create a loaning system required catalogs for discovery, rules to support cooperation, procedures and equipment to make it work, and ways to send the books. It now seems easy after almost a century of American Library Association (ALA) codified rules, standardized request forms, interlibrary loan (ILL) procedures, and the U.S. postal service. What is complicated now is changing technology, grander patron expectations, and time-sensitive workflows. But we once had dreamers, and we still have them. Some take action but leave it to others to do the developing and testing. Let us start with our early dreamers and doers.

ILL COOPERATION DEVELOPS

Cooperation is the catchword, motto, slogan, or mantra of ILL. Cooperation was nurtured by our professional associations but initiated by the innovative librarians who were the founders of the ILL movement as we know it.

On September 4, 1876, Samuel S. Green, librarian of the Worchester Public Library in Massachusetts, wrote a letter published in the new *Library Journal* stating,

> It would add greatly to the usefulness of our reference libraries if an agreement should be made to lend books to each other for short periods of time. . . . I should think

libraries would be willing to make themselves responsible for the value of borrowed books . . . should the books disappear in transit. . . . Libraries, it is true, all have exceptionally valuable books that they would not be willing to lend.

In September 1892, another letter appeared in the *Library Journal* from Bunford Samuel, librarian of the Ridgway Library in Philadelphia, beginning as follows:

> But why should not libraries enter into an agreement in virtue of which books may be furnished by any institution . . . under its own rules as to loaning books. . . . The institution making request guarantees safe return of book and at the same time protects itself by agreement with the individual on whose behalf book is borrowed.

On July 7, 1898, the ALA Cooperation Committee was read a paper from Green, not a member, that began with this reminder:

> Twenty-one or twenty-two years ago I sent a communication to the first number of the *Library Journal* to awaken an interest in interlibrary loans. Today, after having, as a librarian, borrowed books from other libraries and lent books to other libraries for twenty years, and having done so extensively to other libraries, I am again to present the subject to librarians. . . . I am of the opinion that the system of interloaning should be more widely extended, and that small libraries should lend to one another, as well as the smaller libraries borrowing from larger ones.

The committee had received other reports of libraries that were loaning their collections. One was the Boston Public Library, which had a special request form shared with libraries in New England in the 1890s. Another was the National Medical Library in Washington, DC, which shipped books to anyone who deposited $50. In the West, the University of California was offering to make reciprocal agreements with any library in the United States (Stuart-Stubbs, 1975, 649–52).

Ernest C. Richardson, Princeton University librarian, chaired the ALA's College and Reference Section in 1899, so he put himself on that program to present a paper entitled "Cooperation in Lending among College and Reference Libraries." In his paper, he calls for a national library and regional libraries, similar to what exists today for medical information. He also states that research in this country at that time faced the following three barriers:

1. Many titles were not in any of this country's libraries.
2. Titles held were not easily located.
3. Travel to libraries was expensive. (Richardson, 1899, reprinted 1982, 51)

CATALOGS OF DISCOVERY

Richardson recommended the development of union catalogs, library cooperative purchase specialization, and the "adoption of some practical scheme whereby, without hardship to the larger libraries, the great expense of travelling to books may be eliminated, so far as American libraries are concerned, by sending books from one library to another." Actually, Richardson wanted a national lending library like the British Library and would have liked a national, government-supported, country-wide collection plan akin to what Germany has today, but the librarian of Congress, Herbert Putnam, declined the national role, stating a policy to "aid the unusual need with the unusual book" (Stuart-Stubbs, 1975: 653–54).

National union catalogs developed in Europe in the late nineteenth century. Germany was first with the *Deutscher Gesamtkatalog*, and then came the *Bibliothèque nationale de France* and the *British Museum Catalogue*. Our *National Union Catalog*, which includes Canada, was issued serially beginning in the 1950s by the Library of Congress (LC) through 1979, primarily to aid catalogers with their printed copies of catalog cards (Gilmer, 1994, 8).

POLICIES, PROCEDURES, AND PARCEL POST

It was the U.S. Postal Service (USPS), through parcel post delivery, beginning on January 1, 1913, that encouraged the national lending of books. Previously, private delivery companies were used and referred to as expressage. USPS package service was primarily created to support the economy that involved the majority of the population living in rural areas and promote the mail order business. The Smithsonian maintains an online exhibit called "Parcel Post: Delivery of Dreams."

Finally, in 1917, an official ALA Interlibrary Loan Code, written by librarians for librarians, established the framework for ILL policies and procedures. The code has been modified numerous times, the latest revision coming in 2008, a copy of which appears in appendix B. Early requests were mailed as a request letter or sent with a form enclosed created by each library or its consortia. Each code revision added or specified different information and additional recommended procedures.

A four-part, multiple-carbon ILL loan request form for use among the eight campuses of the University of California was created in 1950. The next year, the Association of College and Research Libraries (ACRL) recommended to the ALA that all libraries use this form. Once copiers were invented and available, a standard photocopy request form was developed by the ALA Resources and Technical Services Committee in 1963. This was the next boost to ILL procedures (Gilmer, 1994, 32–33).

Committees work well when they have many best practices from which to choose. ALA committees take months or even a year or two to develop new policies and procedures. They are at the top of the library organizational pyramid, and the improvements they make trickle down to benefit the entire library world. Individuals can dream new ideas, or they can think of different or better ways of doing things. Such figures as Green, Samuel, and Richardson are innovators we can learn from. We have many of their examples in the library world.

AUTOMATION NEEDS OVERWHELMED ILL

MAchine-Readable Cataloging (MARC) records were first produced at the LC for automated catalog card production. This was followed by an online cataloging system created by the Online Computer Library Center (OCLC) for MARC records, plus shared original cataloging contributed by the OCLC's many members. By 1975, the OCLC realized that communication for ILL would be beneficial because online catalog records provided locations, and, in 1977, the catalog was functional. There were other bibliographic utilities using MARC records, and this use resulted in what can be called an explosion as libraries were automated.

A community college in Morris, New Jersey, reported that it processed 351 ILL requests in 1980, but, in 1985, the same staff numbers were overwhelmed by more than three thousand requests. Most libraries can report similar statistics. ILL is labor intensive. Records must be kept on patrons, loans, overdue fees, charges, and statistics. The volume workflow of materials between libraries, to patrons, and even within the library must be understood. Management involves organization, training, costs, reporting, and statistics. Automation increased requests but did not provide the required changes in workflow, record keeping, or management (Gilmer, 1994, 105, 108).

ILLIAD FROM VIRGINIA TECH

ILL was a "back-office operation" at Virginia Tech, just as it was in libraries throughout the country, but there it changed rapidly. Harry Kriz, a librarian for special projects and head of ILL, became aware that in fiscal year 1996–1997, ILL ordered 20,716 items, an 8 percent increase from the year before. During the same period, Collections Development and Acquisitions ordered 20,540 items, a decrease of 11 percent from the previous year.

Kriz believed that this difference would increase, and he was aware that while almost all ILL items would be used, studies showed that many library purchases sat unused on the shelves. He also saw ILL as an important library function in need of substantial improvements in automation. He worked with his ILL technician, M. Jason Glover, to automate the entire borrowing process. They named it ILLiad, an acronym for InterLibrary Loan Internet Accessible Database.

ILLiad was modeled using a flowchart that started with 490 steps and decisions, but even now it continues to grow. Even so, Kriz and Glover considered this the easiest part of making ILLiad. The hardest part was choosing the "software environment." They developed a Web-based user form that replicated those already widely used. They chose the Microsoft SQL Server as the relational database because it worked well with the Windows NT server used with the ILL department's personal computers. They were to meet the borrowing goals set by Kevin Ford, which were as follows (Kriz, Glover, and Ford, 1998):

- Customer identification through registration to ensure successful delivery of materials, eliminate repetitive input of customer information, and prevent unauthorized use
- Customer-initiated requests submitted through online forms
- Customer interaction to allow altering a request after submission, renewing a request, and tracking the progress of a request
- Tracking and reporting of requests at every stage
- Elimination of all paper records and manual record keeping
- Statistical reports that could be shared with customers

ILLiad performs actions that staff need no longer do (e.g., overdue notices), or it alerts them to an action they need to perform (e.g., search OCLC for lenders.) Another step could be automated and added to ILLiad (e.g., verifying that a photocopy meets fair-use guidelines) (Kriz, Glover, and Ford, 34).

ILLIAD FROM ATLAS

By 2000, Glover had gone from a Virginia Tech library employee to an Atlas Systems vice president, at the company that then developed the lending component of ILLiad. Kriz developed the 50-10 rule as he continued to review ILL service, meaning that 50 percent of the items requested were requested by 10 percent of their customers. Although many did not use the service often, he learned that this did not correlate with studies of those who chose electronic delivery. Electronic delivery imposes printing responsibilities upon the customer that include configuring your computer to view and print the PDF files, as well as supplying the printer, paper, and ink costs (Kriz, 2000).

One professor who requested 250 articles did not want to spend time learning how to do electronic delivery and so preferred paper delivery. Even though Virginia Tech ranks as one of the campuses with the "most wired professors," Kriz passed on the following useful advice: "Correctly choosing what services to impose on our customers and what services to offer as value-added options is fundamental to maintaining the credibility of libraries during these times of very rapid change" (Kriz, 2000, 32).

ONLINE BEFORE THE INTERNET

The Internet as we know it today only dates back to 1991. Prior to 1991, you needed to feel comfortable using a command line interface in which you typed commands instead of choosing them from a menu or selecting an icon. An example follows:

```
Display disk directory [C:]
     C: \ >DIR /
        Directory of C: \
[DOS]  [MOUSE]  [PROGRAMS]  [TEMP]  [TOOLS]  [WINDOWS]
```

If you wanted to search an online bibliography, you contacted a librarian who did it for you. But one of the earliest examples of user-oriented online bibliographic retrieval originated in a library in Syracuse, New York.

Biomedical Literature Database

SUNY Upstate Medical Center library director Irwin Pizer oversaw the development of the Biomedical Communications Network, the first online information retrieval service for biomedical literature in libraries, and it operated from 1968 to 1977, with thirty-two member libraries at its peak. Terminals were found in Minnesota, Illinois, Indiana, Ohio, Massachusetts, and Maryland, as well as in New York. There was close cooperation with the National Library of Medicine (NLM), which shared its catalog records and journal article citations. State support was received, along with that from IBM.

From the start, users could input their own terminology without assistance, although some training was required. Dr. Alexander Cain, as medical bibliographer, mapped vernacular medical language to the medical subject headings developed by the NLM that were called MeSH. An example could be the common term *shoulder blade*, linked to the medical term *scapula*. Indexing of books, chapter by chapter, was combined with cooperative cataloging and a union list of serials.

The union list was to aid ILL, and availability of books was to be checked against circulation records, but no system tied these elements together. Requests from nonmedical libraries to join and add additional nonmedical databases led instead to discussions for a commercial online service when state funding was lost. This led to the formation of BRS (Bibliographic Retrieval Services), which began service after signing agreements with most of the network members (Lipscomb, 2001).

Bibliographic Retrieval Services (BRS)

BRS started commercial operations with twenty databases, including the first commercial availability of MEDLINE, using IBM Storage and Information Retrieval System (STAIRS) software. In 1980, BRS was sold to Indian Head, a subsidiary of the Dutch company Thyssen-Bornemisza. In 1989, Robert Maxwell acquired BRS Search Services and BRS Search Software as part of his Maxwell Online group. At that time, BRS was serving medical and academic libraries with more than 150 databases. Maxwell died, and, in 1994, his subsidiaries were sold separately, with BRS Search Software being sold to Dataware Technologies and BRS Search Services being purchased by CD Plus Technologies.

Kurt Mueller, owner of BRS Search Software, was interviewed in 1995 for *Searcher* magazine about this special search software, which could handle unstructured information, much like the Internet today. He signed a worldwide deal with Thomson to use the software. Components added to BRS Search in 1995 were natural language, enhanced relevance ranking, semantic networking, and thesaurus functionality modules in eleven foreign languages. In his interview, Mueller tells of this strategy to "provide server software for the Internet," since he is listening to Gopher, Mosaic, and Z39.50 clients. He concluded by saying that, "One nice thing about BRS/Search compared to its competitors, because its heritage lies in the online services world, [is] it has very sophisticated security administration and accounting features. That's important to Internet providers (IPs)" (Quint, 1995, 42–44).

GREAT SERVICE FOR PHYSICIANS, MEDICAL LIBRARIES, AND YOU

DOCLINE is an automated ILL system formed by the National Library of Medicine (NLM) in 1985. The system became widely available in 1987. It searches a biomedical serials database called SERHOLD, which includes the NLM's journal holdings and the journal holdings of every library that participates in DOCLINE. Entering your complete holdings is a requirement for medical libraries, but not for academic membership. What is unique is that there are ten holdings cells that each library must create for itself, numbered 1 through 10. The lowest numbers are the libraries with which your library has a reciprocal agreement or the system in which your library is a member. The lower-numbered cells do not charge one another. The higher-numbered cells are the designated regional medical libraries (RMLs) and other libraries that do charge. DOCLINE first searches cell 1 for the needed issue, and if not matched, it searches cell 2, then 3, and so forth. The NLM fills cell 10 as the library of last resort (Young, 2011).

Entering requests into DOCLINE is easy, but it wasn't always that way, so the inventive James Daly, at Beth Israel Hospital in Boston, created QuickDOC to manage the ILL data for the Web version of DOCLINE, which started in 2000. Early routing rules were carefully developed so that libraries would not go directly to libraries in the highest cells. FreeShare membership is open to any DOCLINE library, except borrow-only libraries, and it does not require an agreement form. FreeShare libraries should be entered into one of the cells, usually a lower one. For regional contacts, search http://nnlm.gov/rdd/freeshare/. It should not be confused with FreeForAll (FFA), another collaborative effort to provide health professionals in developing nations with journal articles, and it will be placed in a separate cell (Young, 2011).

DOCLINE was built on the work of OCTANET, an idea developed in St. Louis, when, in 1982, local hospital libraries applied to this pioneering system at Washington University's School of Medicine (WUSM) to provide automatic routing of ILL requests within their region and to NLM. In 1985, NLM created DOCLINE nationwide and adopted the OCTONET routing design, which allowed libraries to take advantage of the reciprocal routing groups that already existed. Automated management of serial records using PHILSOM (Periodical Holdings in the Library of the School of Medicine), developed by Dr. Estelle Brodman, librarian and professor of medical history at WSUM, led to the recognition of the value of updating serial holdings and detailed serial holdings. OCTONET took advantage of online access to serial records, allowing ILL to search for a specific volume and issue, a capability now in DOCLINE that is not found in any other online ILL system. OCTONET also took advantage of the technology that became e-mail and was useful for ILL referrals. We should appreciate the clearness of Dr. Brodman's vision and her belief that not only the largest libraries can contribute to progress, and also that problems and mistakes, as well as successes, should be provided in publications (Peay and Schoening, 2008).

RETHINKING RESOURCE SHARING
(RRS) INNOVATION AWARDS, 2008 TO 2013

Beginning in 2005, librarians, product vendors, and library technology specialists got together in ad hoc groups in several venues to explore needed change in resource sharing. In 2007, they produced "A Manifesto for Rethinking Resource Sharing" (discussed in the next chapter), by Beth Posner, current chair of the Steering Committee. The group is advocating for a "complete rethink in the context of the global internet revolution in the way libraries share resources." Funding for the initiative award is provided by numerous businesses, consortia, nonprofits, and professional organizations. Awards of $1,000 each are given to projects that make changes and innovate in ways that improve ILL service to their users.

North Carolina NC LIVE Media Collection

In 2008, NC LIVE was one of two winners of the first RRS Innovation Awards. They were the first virtual library cooperative in the United States to offer statewide access to more than 500 hours of licensed PBS videos to their 198 member libraries, paid for by grants from the State Library of North Carolina. Since January 2008, more than 93 percent of member libraries accounted for more than 24,000 individual viewings. They believed that streaming video would improve viewer access and eliminate the need to circulate physical copies.

Included in the collection are the Emmy Award-winning television series *American Experience* and *Frontline*, as well as such popular programs as *The Civil War*, *Baseball*, and *Jazz*, by Ken Burns. Many items and other projects have been added in the following years. Any resident can access the video link at a local member library using the following link: http://media.nclive.org/video_home.phtml.

Information Delivery Services (IDS) Project

The IDS Project also received a 2008 RRS Innovation Award. SUNY Geneseo, one of twelve arts and sciences public colleges in New York, responded to reductions in state funding and inflationary price increases by calling together the library directors of similar units, including this author's, to develop a cooperative approach to resource sharing beginning in 2004. They began by adding ILLiad software to the OCLC ILL system at each library. Then the Geneseo Milne Library set turnaround benchmarks, followed by developing a unique Transaction Performance Analysis Module (TPAM) to analyze and evaluate data from each project library. The "user-centric definition" of an ILL transaction and its improvement appears in table 4.1.

An annual contract committed each library to performance standards, common workflow and delivery practices, sharing of data, and participation by staff in an annual conference. In addition, a special tool called the "Article License Information Availability Service (ALIAS)," created by Mark Sullivan, a Milne Library staff member trained as lawyer and now a credentialed librarian, provided relevant ILL licensing information. Holdings data for project libraries was taken monthly from Open URL resolvers. The licensing data was updated by a team of three librarians. Results showed that 35 percent of journal requests could be filled by the collective electronic journal holdings (see http://idsproject.org/about/description.aspx).

Kentucky Libraries Unbound

Three RRS Innovation Awards received recognition in Dublin, Ohio, at OCLC headquarters on May 13–14, 2009. One award honored Boone County Public Library, named for Daniel Boone, in Burlington, Kentucky, for making local history materials available throughout the state in downloadable formats, including e-books, audio books, music, and online video. Being present, it was fascinating to learn how Jennifer Gregory, virtual services librarian, and Bridget Striker, local history librarian, chose almost every kind of Boone County history item or format, from Civil War history to flute music, to add to their downloadable collection. Next they invited other libraries to join in, resulting first in contributions from three Kentucky counties and later from twenty-seven more libraries in the regions of the commonwealth (see http://www.bcpl.org/lhg).

RapidILL

When RapidILL was receiving the 2009 RRS Innovation Award in Dublin, pictures were shown of the July 28, 1997, flood of the main library building at Colorado State University, which led to the formation of this concept. Approximately

Table 4.1. The "User-Centric Definition" of an ILL Transaction and Its Improvement

Outcome Measures	Spring 2004	Fall 2007
Loans filled within 72 hours	32 percent	58 percent
Articles filled within 48 hours	52 percent	88 percent
Total filled requests	3,794	23,513

half a million books and bound periodicals were destroyed by a cloudburst of several hours. It was the ILL staff at Morgan Library that designed this resource-sharing system for ILL staff. The system promises twenty-four-hour turnaround of articles and book chapters.

Each library joins a pod of similar libraries, but libraries receive copies from the Center for Research Libraries (CRL), Canada Institute for Scientific and Technical Information (CISTI), and Linda Hall Library at reduced rates. An automated system matches a request against a database of more than 3 million open-access articles, and when a match is made, the article is sent to the requesting library in three to five minutes. There is no pulling material from shelves; no scanning, updating, or reshelving; and no staff intervention. The percent of article requests filled is 96, and average fill time is less than thirteen hours (see http://rapid2.library.colostate.edu/Default.aspx).

Orlando Memory Project

Winner of a 2009 RRS Innovation Award, also presented in Dublin, the Orlando Memory Project is a digital archive of images, documents, as well as audio and video resources, but this project focuses on the "people's history" of Central Florida from 1880 to 1930. With this archive, it is primarily the users that select and contribute the content of photos, comments, letters, diaries, maps, and postcards that show how the region has changed throughout time.

In addition, beginning in 2002, there were three contributing institutions that cooperated using grant funding for organized online access to their collections to provide educational materials for teachers to use to enthuse their students, especially those in fourth grade, about local history. The three are the University of Central Florida Library, the Orange County Regional History Center, and the Orange County Library System.

In 2004, grant funding added items from the Olin Library at Rollins College and the Museum of Seminole County History, and 2008 funding involved the Bethune-Cookman University and the DuPont-Ball Library at Stetson University (see http://www.cfmemory.org//Share/About/).

DataCite (Data That Might Come from a Database but Might Not)

In 2010, a RRS Innovation Award was given to a not-for-profit organization formed in London, in 2009, to help researchers locate, identify, and, particularly, learn to cite datasets, data that is temporarily stored but needs to be processed to be understood. The dataset registration form, which provides the research community with a simple and effective way to cite datasets and also create links to the datasets themselves, can be found at http://crosscite.org/citeproc/. It calls for creator, publication year, title, version, publisher, resource, type, and identifier. In library language we call this metadata.

COKAMO

COKAMO won a 2010 RRS Innovation Award for its ILL interstate delivery efforts. In 1913, the USPS created parcel post to ship loans cheaper than expressage. Almost a century later, we are trying to create courier services that are cheaper than the USPS. COKAMO uses Greyhound buses with extra storage space to deliver loans between Missouri, Colorado, and parts of Kansas and Wyoming. Transportation of tubs to and from buses, as well as to and from libraries, involves a courier delivery service called Mid-America Library Alliance (MALA) (see http://mid-americalibraryalliance.org/). COKAMO claims that costs are a fraction of postal rates and turnaround time is faster (see http://www.collaborativelibrarianship.org/index.php/jocl/article/viewFile/114/75).

Samaritan Health Services "Access for All" Projects

Hope Leman, a research information technologist and librarian, accepted the 2011 Innovation Award during the Interlending and Document Supply Conference held in Chicago in September 2011. Access for All consists of two Web-based services, ScanGrants.com and ResearchRaven.com, which are available to the five thousand employees, medical residents, and students affiliated with the community health system in the Willamette Valley of Oregon.

ScanGrants is a public service that lists hundreds of grants and other funding for support of health research programs and scholarships. ResearchRaven focuses on the information search needs of all those involved in health, medicine, and basic science, as well as public and community health. It lists conferences, calls for papers, publications, job openings, and funding opportunities (see http://www.samhealth.org/aboutus/newsevents/news/Pages/innovativepracticesrecognized.aspx).

UBorrow

The 2012 RRS Innovation Award was given during the ALA Annual Conference in Anaheim, California. The recipient was the Committee on Institutional Cooperation (CIC) consortial project called UBorrow. This service offers access that is more rapid than traditional ILL to more than 90 million books from the collections of thirteen university libraries in the Midwest due to their proximity, and also the Center for Research Libraries.

The unmediated request then uses Relais D2D to search the CIC library catalogs through Z39.50 to learn which libraries have available copies, while the OCLC and ILLiad manage the processing of the requests. Books arrive on campus within a week, can be checked out for twelve weeks, and can be renewed for four more weeks. Atlas and Relais have worked together on developing this innovative approach to consortial borrowing that retains the borrowing library responsibility detailed in the ALA Code (see http://www.cic.net/projects/library/reciprocal-borrowing/uborrow).

IDS Wins Again

Mark Sullivan, now executive director of the IDS, accepted the 2013 RRS Innovation Award during ALA Annual in Chicago, on June 29, during the ILL Discussion Group. The IDS Project has grown from twelve state colleges to seventy-three public and private academic libraries, plus the New York State Library and the New York Public Library.

The project has a strong community that meets at a yearly conference, but also regionally as User Groups twice a year. The three User Groups provide a platform to share expertise through presentations on borrowing, lending, and best practices. It is a workshop setting with hands-on activities and a Workflow Toolkit binder that helps participants gain experience with new features. Present are ILL librarians, along with their staff and library technicians, who meet with those from other campuses in the region and also gain the benefit of mentors, who are also available to visit their campus. For a mentor contribution to the Workflow Toolkit online, go to http://toolkit.idsproject.org.

CONCLUSION

Let us begin with a discussion of ILL before the existence of the OCLC and MARC, but we will not call it the dark ages. We did well with typewriters, multipart forms, and first-class and package postage. Verification came from the *National Union Catalog of Pre-1956 Imprints*, and update files were paper. Turnaround time was weeks. Things got a little better with OCLC verification and OCLC ILL. Turnaround time was a week or two. Then the number of requests exploded. ILL went from a privilege to a necessity, then to a right.

ILL has been greatly affected by technology, but our success has not been met with increased staff, only more technology. Before we look at the next chapter, which predicts the future of ILL, let's contemplate the future of technology as imagined by a visionary, Norbert Wiener. He was known as a mathematician connected with engineering who provided basic ideas for all kinds of inventions, from radar to communications networks, to computers, to artificial limbs.

Years after he died, a manuscript was found in his papers. It was published in 1994, as *Invention: The Care and Feeding of Ideas*, by MIT Press, connected to the institution where he was a professor. In the introduction, Steve Heims says that the message from Wiener is that,

> truly original ideas cannot be produced on an assembly line, and that their consequences are often felt only at distant times and places. The intellectual and technological environment has to be right before the idea can blossom. The best course for society is to encourage the best minds to pursue the most interesting topics, and to reward them for the insights they produce. (Wiener, 1993)

REFERENCES

Gilmer, Lois (1994). *Interlibrary Loan: Theory and Management.* Englewood, CO: Libraries Unlimited.

"Innovation Awards Past Winners" (2013). *Rethinking Resource Sharing Initiative.* Available online at http://rethinkingresourcesharing.org/innovation-awards/winners/ (accessed October 29, 2013).

Kriz, Harry M. (2000). "Electronic Interlibrary Loan Delivery with Ariel and ILLiad." *Journal of Interlibrary Loan, Document Delivery, and Information Supply* 10, no. 4: 25–34.

Kriz, Harry M., M. Jason Glover, and Kevin C. Ford (1998). "ILLiad: Customer-Focused Interlibrary Loan Automation." *Journal of Interlibrary Loan, Document Delivery, and Information Supply* 8, no. 4: 31–47.

Lipscomb, Carolyn E. (2001). "SUNY Biomedical Communication Network: Irwin Pizer." *Bulletin of the Medical Library Association* 89, no. 2: 231–34.

"Parcel Post: Delivery of Dreams" (2013). *Smithsonian Libraries.* Available online at http://www.sil.si.edu/ondisplay/parcelpost/cf/view.cfm (accessed October 1, 2013).

Peay, Wayne J., and Paul Schoening (2008). "Estelle Brodman and the First Generation of Library Automation." *Journal of the Medical Library Association* 96, no. 3: 262–67.

Quint, Barbara (1995). "Whatever Happened to BRS Software?" *Searcher* 3, no. 1: 42–44.

Richardson, Ernest C. (1982). "Cooperation in Lending among College and Reference Libraries." *Collection Management* 4, no. 3: 49–60.

Stuart-Stubbs, Basil (1975). "An Historical Look at Resource Sharing." *Library Trends* 23, no. 4: 649–64.

Wiener, Norbert (1993). *Invention: The Care and Feeding of Ideas.* Cambridge, MA: MIT Press.

Young, Diane (2011). "Not Just Another Interlibrary Loan Librarian." *Journal of Hospital Librarianship* 11, no. 1: 78–86.

5

Rethinking Library Resource Sharing

The Future of Interlibrary Loans

Beth Posner

> *Plus ça change, plus c'est la même chose.* The more it changes, the more it's the same thing.
>
> —Jean-Baptiste Alphonse Karr,
> French critic, journalist, and novelist, 1808–1890

CONSIDER TWO FUTURES

How can interlibrary loan (ILL) librarians rethink current practices as they anticipate, prepare for, and shape the future of ILL services? ILL services face dilemmas as they consider the future. On one hand, libraries collect less print material as more information is created. The demand for global information increases as the discovery becomes easier than ever. Thus, need for ILL is likely to increase, putting more and more pressure on understaffed and underfunded departments. At the same time, with more information freely available online or through library-licensed, full-text databases, and as publishers impose embargoes and fight for copyright and license restrictions, demand for ILL services is likely to decrease.

ILL departments still have a great deal to contribute by connecting people and information; however, a variety of challenges exist. As the future unfolds, developments in libraries, technology, and education will drive changes in what ILL services encompass, some of which will go far beyond what is recognizable today as traditional ILL.

There are challenges that face any field when rethinking current practices with an eye toward preparing for, and trying to positively shape, the future. First, the future develops out of the interplay of innumerable interactions within our inextricably interrelated world. There is chance involved, as well as the kindness of friends and strangers. So, despite our insatiable curiosity, it is inherently unknowable. Nonetheless, there is continuity in the past, present, and future, as well as causes and effects that make it possible to formulate informed and likely predictions. For librarians to continue to provide relevant and high-quality information services, today and in the future, it is essential that they try to make these connections.

POSITIVE, NEGATIVE, AND VALUE-NEUTRAL CHANGE

Equally problematic for forecasters is the real but partial truth of the old adage, "The more things change, the more things stay the same." Librarians generally remain confident that, in the future, as in the past, they will continue to facilitate access to information. Librarians who value the goal of connecting people and information see this service as relevant in a world with a scarcity of time and a surplus of information, as it was in a world with a scarcity of information. Many believe that like television, film, and radio, digital information will coexist with print, rather than supplant it. Yet, it is wise to acknowledge the Buddhist nature of reality as one of constant change. Librarians cannot afford to be complacent. Continual and rapid technological change is a given in the library and information world. It is what makes the processing of transaction after transaction interesting and challenging for ILL specialists.

In future, there will be positive and negative developments, as well as rewards and challenges. So, while approaching the past with thankfulness and the present with appreciation, it is more productive to look at the future with hope. Librarians and those they serve, including society as a whole, would all benefit from efforts to peek around the corner. By staying engaged with trends and developments in the larger world, surprises will be limited. This will support rational choices made in the best interest of information users and society, no matter what particular technology exists or what information is needed.

Librarians need to understand what is coming to make compelling arguments for needed resources amidst competing services to receive the level and type of support necessary to provide quality services. For libraries to remain helpful and relevant, library services, policies, and procedures must evolve alongside other developments in the information world, which, today, means the world of digital information.

KNOW THE PAST TO UNDERSTAND THE FUTURE

Librarians can do this by studying how the past shaped the present, analyzing current trends, framing the larger information landscape in which they operate, and identifying relevant questions. Of course, librarians do not want to risk not meeting the information needs of the current generation of library users, either by being overly focused on the future or stuck in the past. One need not disregard history to be forward-looking. Many of the decisions made today will affect future patrons, just as past decisions shaped libraries today. This is more than a matter of the butterfly effect, wherein the smallest action can have multiple, larger effects. Individual librarians, and the profession as a whole, can work to create positive change. Twenty years ago, Association of Research Libraries (ARL) librarians called for librarians to work with vendors to automate more of the ILL process (Jackson, 1995).

Today, automation greatly helps ILL librarians to decrease costs and increase volume. Ten years ago, Mary Jackson identified ten trends in ILL. They are as follows:

1. rising user expectations
2. mediated ILL services
3. user initiated services
4. increased access to electronic resources
5. copyright and licensing
6. implementation of portals
7. enhancements to online catalogs
8. blurring of collections and access activities
9. technical standards
10. globalization (Jackson, 2004, 88–92)

These trends continue to define and affect ILL services. As far back as 1939, Sydney Mitchell recognized that it is the "present-day trends in interlibrary loans [that] will have become so emphasized as to constitute the practice of the future" (75).

To some, libraries and librarians have a reputation for being traditional, old-fashioned, or even reactionary. Yet, their policies, procedures, priorities, and services have all continually and meaningfully evolved throughout time. ILL specialists, in particular, are practical and eager to embrace any technology that will be useful—from union catalogs a century ago, to OpenURL today—for the delivery of print, and now digital, information. Again, in the past few decades, there has also been a technological revolution in online discovery and automation, although even more remains to be done in both areas. By learning how change has been successfully implemented in the past, librarians can confidently navigate the future.

They can also see how ILL services have developed out of chosen limitations, or a chosen focus, in vision and mission, as well as unchosen resource limits. ILL has long been a core service in many libraries. This is the case for net borrowers who need access to information for their patrons, and it is no less true for net lenders, with large, rich collections that enable them to demonstrate their value and even recoup costs by charging fees. There have been millions of successful ILL transactions, and ILL specialists are justifiably proud of a successful tradition of service. It must also be acknowledged that ILL remains labor intensive and, in far too many libraries, prohibitively slow, expensive, and bound by rules. Physical delivery time, in particular, remains problematic, as do costs, understaffing, copyright, and license restrictions.

Librarians should not be blinded by traditional ways of doing things. Technology enables new possibilities for information access, be the information free or available to buy, borrow, or rent (Radnor and Shrauger, 2012). Technology has helped greatly by automating much of the processing of ILL transactions, enabling efficiencies, decreasing turnaround time, and supporting new services. Articles can be ordered, processed, and delivered in just minutes, and more than 9 million ILL requests are processed annually by the Online Computer Library Center (OCLC) alone. So, although it is safe to predict that, in the near future, the traditional ILL work of lending and borrowing of print, and now also electronic, information will continue to be safe, it is best not to strictly define "near."

MOVEMENTS WE SHOULD JOIN

To effectively rethink current best practices, librarians also need to adopt relevant advances in such related fields as information technology, marketing, and user needs assessment. Any change requires energy, training, and time, so it can be challenging to plan for the future, while also keeping up with the daily processing of lending and borrowing transactions. Fortunately, individual ILL specialists do not have to do this alone. There are professional library organizations, for example, the committees of the American Library Association (RUSA, or Reference and User Services Association) and International Federation of Library Associations and Institutions. ALA has a STARS section (Sharing and Transforming Access to Resource Sharing), and IFLA has the Interlending and Document Supply (ILDS) section and the Rethinking Resource Sharing Initiative (RRSI). These sections provide forums and workshops for training and discussion.

The mission of RRSI is to "rethink resource sharing for the twenty-first century." In 2005, they declared their goals to "foster an updated framework of cooperation and collaboration, be a catalyst movement for systematic change, become an influential 'think tank,' define and promote best practices, inspire a change in attitude in providing services, and encourage libraries to open up to find new ways to serve not just their patrons, but all potential users" (Posner and Simpson, 2011, 144). The RRSI manifesto consists of seven principles that can guide libraries toward the future of information sharing, and they are being endorsed by libraries throughout the world:

1. Restrictions shall only be imposed as necessary by individual institutions with the goal that the lowest possible barriers to fulfillment are presented to the user.
2. Library users shall be given appropriate options for delivery format, method of delivery, and fulfillment type, including loan, copy, digital copy, and purchase.
3. Global access to sharable resources shall be encouraged through formal and informal networking agreements with the goal toward the lowest barrier to fulfillment.
4. Sharable resources shall include those held in cultural institutions of all sorts: libraries, archives, museums, and the expertise of those employed in such places.

5. Reference services are a vital component to resource sharing and delivery and shall be made readily accessible from any initial "can't supply this" response. No material that is findable should be totally unattainable.
6. Libraries should offer service at a fair price rather than refuse, but should strive to achieve services that are not more expensive than commercial services, e.g., bookshops.
7. Library registration should be as easy as signing up for commercial, Web-based services. Everyone can be a library user. (Rethinking Resource Sharing Initiative)

In rethinking library resource sharing for the twenty-first century, Tom Bruno describes the combination of digitization, declining budgets, and the rise of Google as a competing information provider and a "perfect storm." Nonetheless, he remains confident that ILL services and specialists will "continue in the spirit of innovation, collaboration, and experimentation" (Bruno, 2013, 58). This acknowledgement of the spirit of ILL and its practitioners is what ultimately underscores the success of ILL services in the past and present, and promises great things from ILL in the future.

INCREASING, DECREASING, AND CHANGING NEEDS

By identifying issues that are crucial to the future of libraries and ILL services, librarians can effectively focus their own learning and development. To predict, prepare for, and shape the future, they need to ask questions about the larger landscape of information, technology, and education in which they operate. Even if these cannot be completely answered, it is dangerously simplistic to ignore them. Such issues, albeit ones beyond the scope of this chapter, include the following:

- How will educational goals change in the future? (Heick, 2013)
- What will access to free information do to publishing and society? (Lanier, 2013)
- Will people need to join virtual libraries to have access to information because local libraries will disappear?
- Will local libraries remain to help content creators and replace bookstores as places people can browse new books?
- Will bookstores or online booksellers replace libraries?
- Can librarians create ways to share access to datasets?
- Can they manage institutional repositories?
- Can they serve participants in massive open online courses (MOOCs)?
- How will the OCLC develop in the future?

Perhaps the most important question for the future of ILL and libraries is whether libraries will continue to build and maintain collections to share or whether they will focus on temporary access as needed for local patrons. This is not for ILL librarians alone to decide, but they should bring their perspective and understanding to the discussion and decisions. Other important issues impacting the quickly approaching future of ILL—the increasing, decreasing, and changing need for ILL services—are ones that we can consider here. The most immediate is, How will ILL services develop, given the increase of commercial information providers, open-access (OA) publishing, regional print depositories, plus restrictive copyright laws and license terms, as digital information licensing increases and print holdings in libraries decrease?

CONNECTING PEOPLE TO EVERYTHING

The explosion of online information, as well as online discovery of print and online information, and the globalization of information are making ILL work more valuable than ever. Discovery through free search engines and commercial or library databases is easier than ever, so people are requesting more locally unavailable information from domestic, as well as international, sources. Despite the potential of such digital archives as Google Books, HathiTrust, Internet Archives, or the Digital Public Library of America (DPLA), not everything is online. Nor is everything that is online free. Not everyone wants to use digital information or has good e-readers or online access; therefore, the core of library resource sharing—that is, connecting people to locally unavailable information in print, digital, or any format from libraries throughout the world—is a need that still exists. ILL services remain well poised to help people access this universe of information. Thus, to meet user demand in the future, even more libraries can and should develop and market high-quality ILL services, now and in the future.

In addition to ease of discovery, there is also more print and digital information being created than ever before, and ILL specialists are still needed to provide access to new and existing information, whether it is posted online or published in print, or both; however, their work, and often the information, comes at a cost, and as librarians pay more for access to more digital information, there is less in their budgets for print. This can lead to more ILL requests for print material and the need for all libraries, especially those with smaller collections, to turn to larger research libraries, consortial partners, reciprocal agreements, and/or regional print depositories.

OUR UNDERLYING COMMUNITY

Fortunately, librarians, especially ILL librarians, have always collaborated. Today, they are working together more closely than ever before. More libraries throughout the world are joining the OCLC. The next step is to encourage them to become suppliers and use their automated payment system to make information sharing more efficient. Successful consortial groups in the United States include the Information Delivery Services Project (New York); the Committee on Institutional Cooperation (Midwest); Borrow Direct (Ivy League schools plus MIT); Orbis Cascade (Oregon, Washington, Idaho); the MLA Resource Sharing (Massachusetts); Illinois Heartland; and ASERL in the Southeastern United States, which claims to be the largest. These partnerships can enable cooperative collection agreements, the development of innovative technology, and the sharing of knowledge through group training. Regional print depositories and membership organizations the likes of the Center for Research Libraries (CRL) or such shared remote storage facilities as RECAP (storage for Columbia, New York Public Library, and Princeton) generally lend to member libraries for no fee and to others for a reasonable fee.

ILL services can facilitate access to these holdings, just as they do now with individual libraries. Large research library collections that are maintained in the future could also recoup costs by charging other libraries lending fees. One evolution in ILL philosophy is that rather than insisting that ILL should be free, its value is increasingly recognized and librarians understand that reasonable fees are necessary to keep the system going. Assuming that they have a budget to do so, they would rather pay other libraries processing fees to support sharing, as well the preservation of information, than pay exorbitant publisher prices.

COMMERCIAL ALTERNATIVES

Even as ILL demand is growing in some libraries for the aforementioned reasons, the traditional lending and borrowing of print and digital information amongst other libraries is seeing decreased demand. Commercial information providers that offer unmediated information access directly to information users, the licensing of full-text databases, and the growth of OA publishing are positive developments that can increase information access; however, their growth also points to the need for libraries and ILL service to refocus their strategies, changing what they do, while not abandoning traditional lending and borrowing entirely.

There are sobering and chilling recent examples of libraries cutting back on information sharing. For instance, the National Library of Canada has stopped providing international loans, and some Illinois libraries have left the System Wide Automatic Network (SWAN), a large resource-sharing network, because of costs (CBC News, 2012; Mannion, 2013). Yet, it is important to recognize that many people do successfully connect to information without the assistance of libraries. Commercial alternatives come with their own pros, for instance, convenience and low cost, and cons, for example, costs, sometimes high ones, and the lack of preservation or privacy concerns for purely educational interests.

Google has made the discovery of information easier than ever, but commercial library databases are still difficult to search. Online information providers and other vendors, for example, Amazon, Google, and ReadCube, offer fast, inexpensive access to information. Librarians can learn a great deal from them about what information users want; however, these companies work for profit, while libraries share costs and work for information access for people with and without resources, whether or not it is commercially profitable or politically expedient.

Full-text library databases currently help people access information directly, without librarian assistance. Libraries license access to a great deal of information that people can connect to from anywhere through their library portal. Library users often have to be taught to search these sources, and ILL staff members regularly do this as they receive requests for information that their library already owns or subscribes to. Some even provide direct links to the online information, enabling ILL to facilitate access to more information, locally available or not.

OPEN-ACCESS PUBLICATIONS

Because information costs are rising, because technology enables easier online publishing, and because of calls for government-funded research to be made available to the public, OA publishers of scholarly and academic information, creative commons licensing, institutional repositories, and other repositories (e.g., www.academia .edu or www.researchgate.net) are likely to lead to a decline of traditional lending and borrowing amongst libraries. Even academic libraries have limited budgets to purchase materials, while their faculty members are the ones providing the content. Scholars that contribute to OA care more about being read than being part of the commercial publishing world. ILL departments are not needed to access such information, yet they can help people with its discovery by checking OA sources before turning to other libraries.

When OA sources are found, librarians can notify library users and demonstrate the value of this sort of publishing. When not found and not available in libraries, they can also directly contact authors and start this same discussion, while asking if they can share their work with a library patron who needs it for study or research. OA does not include popular and commercial publishing, so ILL requests for such materials will continue to be made. Nonetheless, academic librarians are likely to see, and want to see, more scholarly information available freely online.

INFORMATION ACCESS BEYOND ILL

Responding to the changes with ILL, Cyril Oberlander writes that,

> Interlibrary loan is well positioned to handle requests that are increasingly global in scale, customized in services, and resolving the tensions of should we buy it or borrow it in an age of economic woes, increased emphasis on e-book packages, right-sizing print collections, and purchase on demand. We are moving from optimizing interlibrary loan workflow and systems to increasingly transforming libraries. (Oberlander, 2012)

In the future, as in the past, the traditional work of ILL departments will continue to evolve. ILL today cannot satisfy all information needs, often because of costs or policies, but also because some print material is too rare, fragile, or costly to ship or copy. And copyright laws or license terms can prohibit copying or digitization. Thus, librarians must always be thinking of new ways to provide access to information.

Traditional ILL only works if some library, somewhere, owns or has permission to share licensed content. Print is still preferable to many people because of ease of reading or a need to see the physical manifestation of an object. Print is also sometimes the only option because of copyright and license restrictions on information sharing. Yet, most libraries are collecting less print because of limited budgets and a need for more space and other services. In the United States, fair use and other library exceptions to copyright law, as well as the right of first sale, allow libraries to share print information.

When licensing digital material, librarians may agree to terms that restrict the use of e-resources to local patrons only, or that include embargoes of recent e-serial issues. This means that unless the information is available in print form in some library, made OA through some institutional repository, or shared by the author directly, it may be unavailable through ILL and accessible only by purchasing it directly from publishers or booksellers at a significant cost and through a process completely outside existing library ILL procedures.

RIGHTS OR TERMS OF ACCESS

Regardless of what happens to library print collections, the concomitant rise of digital information means that libraries need to provide access to digital information as well. This is made challenging by publishers that do not want to sell libraries digital books at all, or who will do so only under restrictive costs or terms. This limits the ability of ILL services to facilitate access to e-books, although there has been success in negotiating license terms that allow the sharing of e-journal articles. ILL specialists, now and in the future, need to continue and increase their involvement in ensuring that license language for digital content permits ILL.

The copyright guidelines and laws that currently guarantee the right of libraries to share print material are also being rethought as new digital copyright laws are being crafted. Such laws differ from country to country, something that greatly complicates and limits global ILL. In the United States, such exceptions as fair use of information for education remain essential to the future of library resource sharing. There is also a need for advocacy in the area of digital rights management (DRM), through which publishers make sharing, and even using, information technically restrictive. Librarians respect author and publisher rights to compensation for their work, but, at the same time, they also see the limits to scholarly communication, education, and progress that this creates; therefore, they are in a good position to advocate and educate their constituents and all stakeholders about these issues. This is a new role for ILL librarians, but one that fits with the belief in information access and is crucial to the future of libraries and society as a whole.

Copyright limits mean that libraries can only request a certain number of recent articles from any journal title, and publishers often charge high fees beyond this limit. New services like the Copyright Clearance Center's (CCC) "Get It Now" and ReadCube are attempting to decrease such costs through agreements with publishers. Librarians or library users can order material from the CCC directly, and ReadCube is designed for patrons to use without librarian mediation. This is less than ideal from the library perspective, however, because although prices are reasonable and a price limit can be set, ILL staff members can often get the same information quickly, and for no cost, from another library.

Even as publishers are restricting the sharing of e-books, new models of information access are possible. Rick Anderson (2012) points to the difference between sharing print and copying digital information and believes that ILL should not do what it has always done in this new environment. He argues that libraries exist to facilitate access to information, not purchase and preserve it or provide traditional ILL services. Instead of libraries facilitating information access through a first-sale emulation model, where a library buys a copy of an e-book and only one user, local or distant, uses it, publishers could offer short-term leases of e-books. According to Anderson,

> For interlibrary loan, the future is much less clear; today it's becoming increasingly possible to provide access both effectively and affordably without entering into the legally and semantically difficult realm of "sharing." And I think we need to accept and actively acknowledge that this is a good thing—not a betrayal of our core values.

CORE VALUES: ACCESS, PRESERVATION, AND SHARING

Many librarians continue to see both preservation and sharing as core values, and ILL as a core service, because this is how libraries are able to provide information access today and ensure that information will remain available tomorrow. Whether libraries focus on access and preservation, or both, will be the fundamental question of twenty-first-century librarianship. Meanwhile, when no library owns or licenses certain information, librarians still need to help people access it. This includes recent books and journal articles that are only published online or are available through libraries but come with embargoes. In response, ILL specialists are increasingly working closely with commercial document suppliers, publishers, booksellers, and authors, in addition to library partners.

Some libraries are willing to pay high per-article prices because subscription prices are even higher. Others, needing to adopt completely new workflows and permissions, are being reluctant or are unable to purchase information for individual patron use, although they could still let people know where else they could access the information, even if it comes only at a cost. More libraries would be interested and able to facilitate such access if per-article fees were as low as ILL fees, and if publishers would work with the OCLC to facilitate payment through such automated features as their IFM system.

As librarians rethink how they can help people connect with information through their policies and procedures, they are also rethinking their services. Historically, libraries were created and maintained to ensure preservation. Recently, their focus has been on teaching people how to find information. And, increasingly, librarians are providing even locally available information to people, as they need it through what are often called document delivery services. This is in response to busy patrons who need more time to read and create new knowledge, and the success of such commercial online information providers as Google and Amazon. More and more libraries will scan local material that local users request, rather than just pointing them to the stacks. Libraries serving distance learners are also providing home delivery of ILLs, as well as local material. Such new services are only possible if ILL departments are adequately staffed, but when they are, without a doubt, this serves the real needs of busy citizens, scholars, and students, while demonstrating the continued value of library collections and services.

HAVE NO FEAR OF THE FUTURE

Another way to look at the future of libraries and ILL is that, perhaps, all library work will simply become integrated into ILL. It is, after all, about access to information (Bruno, 2013). Or, then again, it is possible that the library of the future will not include ILL services, or the future will not include libraries at all. Dedicated librarians, library users, and library staff with the best of imaginations find it difficult to imagine such a world. Writers and librarians alike consider it an extremely dystopian vision should all information become private property and sharing be viewed as theft, or should governmental or commercial forces control all information, hiding or shaping it for their own purposes (Pennavaria, 2002). Any shrinking of the conduits through which information travels is dangerous when information is valuable and knowledge is a human need and human right. Libraries and ILL are worth fighting for and supporting. Both librarians and library users must do all they can to ensure that none of us ever have to live in such a world.

ILL services, like libraries, even if neither can ever literally encompass all information, symbolically represent the world of information, the ordering of knowledge, answers to questions, and information access. Librarians also serve as metaphors for the opposite sides of such dichotomies as confusion and order, questions and answers, information restriction and information access (Posner, 2002). If, in the future, the more positive of these dualities are what remain in the forefront of information users' minds, it will represent real progress for libraries and the world. Appropriately supported and operated, ILL departments can contribute a great deal to such a world.

As for librarians, they need to cultivate certain habits of mind as they face the future. They need to be open-minded and flexible. They need to reject false dichotomies and strike a balance between being inclusive and specific, rational and intuitive, realistic and imaginative, practical and radical. They need achievable goals, but they also need to be open to new possibilities. They foremost need to remain engaged in the world of information and information users. They need to take advantage of automation, while providing excellent personal customer service. They need to provide a holistic information service from discovery to delivery. They need to facilitate global information access. They need to minimize costs. They need to serve current information users, think about potential ones, and provide for future ones. Traditional concerns, for example, information literacy, privacy, and preservation, also remain important.

Today, some impressively high-volume ILL departments operate like factories, with transactions as their valuable widgets. Others function more as bespoke services, getting people unique information that must be supervised in reading rooms. Most, however, do their best to lend and borrow with limited staff and budgets. Physical delivery also remains slow and/or costly. Despite current and evolving challenges, there is every reason to be optimistic about the future of libraries and ILL. Technical innovation will continue, and such developments as interoperability and circulation availability information are coming. ILL services will undoubtedly evolve as long as the goal of ILL is for anyone anywhere to access any information, despite economic, legal, technical, staff, time, and geographic barriers.

ILL departments can thrive as long as they remain flexible and librarians are willing to rethink services and able to support these with needed resources and staff. Perhaps soon, the history, services, and philosophy of library information and resource sharing will even make it into the library-school curriculum. As for ILL specialists, those who continue to succeed will be those who possess not only the detail-oriented skills to efficiently process transactions, but also a willingness to constantly learn, a strong customer service orientation to meet user information needs as they evolve, the creative skills to envision new services, the communication skills to advocate for continual positive change, the eagerness to help connect people and information despite any and all barriers, and the courage to positively shape the future.

MAKE IT HAPPEN WITH MOTIVATION AND EDUCATION

As Oberlander (2011) notes, "We must retain our strengths as successful advanced problem solvers and searchers, willing to innovate, adapt, and redesign our services around user requests" (118). Rather than being fearful or negative about their own futures, ILL specialists need to be confident. As Sarah McHone-Chase (2010) writes, "If interlibrary loan can be confident, sell its services, and show its benefits, then perhaps it can continue . . . to be the go-to source for users to access the information that they need" (205).

Once we make traditional ILL departments more efficient, getting excited about better serving patrons is inevitable. If we get needed resources to do so, we will implement new services beyond library-to-library resource sharing to facilitate information access and delivery. Such motivation, driven by education, is the clear, natural, and necessary first step, and it is available to any individual who has started to learn more about ILL from others, or in books, articles, best-practice guidelines, and other training materials. Fully understanding and using all the capabilities of any ILL software, for instance, OCLC Worldshare ILL, can be undertaken by anyone who has the will, interest, and a bit of time to discover and learn new things.

Nonetheless, even changes that can be made on one's own should generally be discussed with supervisors and others since this allows ILL staff to demonstrate their own motivation and value, as well as the potential of ILL services. The next step, once good ideas are identified and there is agreement about implementing them, is to identify and deal with barriers to implementation. Even small changes face some issues, and bigger changes, for example, new services or policies, are likely to require additional planning, budgets, and staff. For ILL departments that are currently understaffed and under-budgeted, or have been a peripheral service in the past, this can be quite daunting; however, the library world today is open to changes, so ILL specialists who are ready for opportunities to make their case are likely to get repeated opportunities to do so.

WORKING TOGETHER WITHIN, AMONG, AND BEYOND LIBRARIES

One person, working alone, is generally not sufficient to make meaningful and lasting change. ILL, by its nature, requires cooperating and working with others. Even learning with others has its benefits. So, taking training classes or asking questions of ILL colleagues is an excellent way to become both more motivated and better educated. Beyond this, ILL staff must convince others in their department and their library of what support they need—time, money, access to training, changes in policies—to do things differently and/or do more. Additional resources in one library area may mean less in another. ILL staff can help those in other departments but may need help from them. For instance, if they institute a buy versus borrow program, they will need to work with acquisitions and collection development librarians. If they want to borrow or lend rare material, they will need to work with special collections and archives.

There are other considerations, including budget, preservation, and procedural complications, that have to be worked out with other departments. Showing other department managers or library administrators what other libraries do, especially libraries serving similar communities, can be convincing. Supporting information and data are also invaluable, since library directors, in turn, might have to seek additional support from administrators who are allocating scarce resources.

Beyond their own library and organization, librarians are also fortunate to have the ability to regularly and successfully cooperate with one another through local and regional consortia, library cooperatives like the OCLC, and professional organizations. By doing so, they can learn more, become more motivated, and do more. They can discover best practices and try things that have already been done and evaluated as successful. They can also support their leaders in educating, advocating, and lobbying interests beyond libraries about how information sharing benefits the wider world. Librarians need to work with legislators, authors, and citizens on such issues as intellectual property, copyright restrictions, and the OA movement, and they must work with publishers to create reasonable pricing and purchasing models. Ongoing discussion and experiments are required to find the best balance of information creation and sharing.

THE TIME IS NOW

If librarians and library staff continually discuss just how information is created and shared, everyone will come to see that ILL is an essential part of scholarly communication and cultural progress. It is up to ILL specialists to ensure that library leaders understand the importance of ILL in the world of information sharing so that they, in turn, can carry this message beyond libraries to the rest of the world. Speaking as a dedicated ILL librarian, unless we all support library information sharing, we may find that other library services take the spotlight, or that laws and business interests that do not support information sharing may change the world where we live and work in ways that we do not want. Our jobs may become far less interesting and valuable, or we may find our jobs gone. We may not have time to do it all, and there are days when all we can do is try to keep up with our borrowing and lending requests. But we should also be secure in the knowledge that this work remains essential. We never know which ILL transaction will make a real difference in a student's education, a scholar's research, or a doctor's medical case, but we do know that we fulfill the basic purpose of libraries with every one, as does every librarian and library staff member who participates in and fights for continued and ever-increasing information sharing.

REFERENCES

Anderson, Rick (2012). "Interlibrary Loan and Stockholm Syndrome." *Library Journal*, September 20. Available online at http://lj.libraryjournal.com/2012/09/opinion/peer-to-peer -review/interlibrary-loan-and-stockholm-syndrome-peer-to-peer-review/ (accessed August 30, 2013).

Bruno, Tom (2013). "Interlibrary Loan and Document Delivery." In *Twenty-First-Century Access Services: On the Front Line of Academic Librarianship*, edited by Michael J. Krasulski Jr. and Trevor A. Dawes for ACRL, 43–63. Chicago: Association of College and Research Libraries, a division of the American Library Association.

CBC News (2012). "Library and Archives Interlibrary Loans Soon Eliminated." *CBC-News Ottawa*, November 7. Available online at http://www.cbc.ca/news/canada/ottawa/story/2012/11/06/ottawa-library-and-archives-canada-interlibrary-loans-cancelled.html (accessed September 6, 2013).

Heick, Terry (2013). "30 Incredible Ways Technology Will Change Education by 2028." Te@chthought. Available online at http://www.teachthought.com/trends/30-incredible-ways-technology-will-change-education-by-2028/ (Accessed May 15, 2014).

International Federation of Library Associations and Institutions. "Document Delivery and Resource Sharing Section." Available online at http://www.ifla.org/docdel (accessed September 6, 2013).

Jackson, Mary E. (1995). "The Future of Resource Sharing: The Role of the Association of Research Libraries." *Journal of Library Administration* 21, nos. 1/2: 193–202.

———. (2004). "The Future of Interlending." *Interlending and Document Supply* 32, no. 2: 88–92.

Lanier, Jaron (2013). "Jaron Lanier Discusses Power Laws, Centralized Publishing, and the Social Perils of Free Information." *Scholarly Kitchen*, July 29. Available online at http://scholarlykitchen.sspnet.org/2013/07/29/jaron-lanier-discusses-power-laws-centralized-publishing-and-the-social-perils-of-free-information/ (accessed September 6, 2013).

Mannion, Annemarie (2013). "Elmhurst Library Drops Out of Large Sharing Network." *Chicago Tribune*, August 26. Available online at http://articles.chicagotribune.com/2013-08-26/news/ct-tl-elmhurst-library-20130826_1_swan-library-director-mary-beth-campe (accessed September 6, 2013).

McHone-Chase, Sarah, M. (2010). "Examining Change within Interlibrary Loan." *Journal of Interlibrary Loan, Document Delivery, and Electronic Reserve* 20, no. 3: 201–6.

Mitchell, Sydney B. (1939). "Libraries and Scholarship." In *The Library of Tomorrow: A Symposium*, edited by Emily Miller Danton, 68–77. Chicago: American Library Association.

Oberlander, Cyril. (2011). "The Future of Interlibrary Loan." In *Interlibrary Loan Practices Handbook*, 3rd ed., edited by Cherié L. Weible and Karen L. Janke, 109–19. Chicago: American Library Association.

———. (2012). "What's around the Bend: Future Currents in Resource Sharing." Amigos Online Conference, November 15. Available online at http://www.amigoslibraryservices.org/resource_sharing (accessed August 30, 2013).

Pennavaria, Katherine. (2002). "Representation of Books and Libraries in Depictions of the Future." *Libraries and Culture* 37, no. 3: 229–48.

Posner, Beth. (2002). "Know-It-All Librarians." In *The Image and Role of the Librarian*, edited by Wendi Arant and Candace R. Benefiel, 111–29. New York: Haworth.

Posner, Beth, and Evan Simpson. (2011). "The Rethinking Resource Sharing Initiative: Education, Advocacy and Inspiration for Libraries." *Interlending and Document Supply* 39, no. 3: 142–47.

Radnor, Mary C., and Kristine Jo Shrauger. (2012). "Ebook Resource Sharing Models: Borrow, Buy, or Rent." *Journal of Interlibrary Loan, Document Delivery, and Electronic Reserve* 22, nos. 3/4: 155–61.

Reference and User Services Association. "STARS Rethinking Resource Sharing Policies Committee." Available online at http://www.ala.org/rusa/contact/rosters/stars/rus-starethink (accessed September 6, 2013).

Rethinking Resource Sharing Initiative. "A Manifesto for Rethinking Resource Sharing." Available online at http://rethinkingresourcesharing.org/manifesto/ (accessed August 20, 2013).

II

ADDING PERSONALIZED, HIGH-QUALITY SERVICE

6

Don't Just Say "No" When Faced with Rules and Policies

You have to learn the rules of the game. Then you have to play better than anyone else.

—Albert Einstein

I never had a policy. I have just tried to do my very best each and every day.

—Abraham Lincoln

There are interlibrary loan (ILL) rules you have to learn, but you do not have to play better than anyone else. In addition, you do need an ILL policy, but try to do your best each day and others will do the same. Interlibrary loan is the most frequently used term, but some libraries may call it document delivery, interloan, interlending, interlibrary borrowing, interlibrary lending, or resource sharing. It is the way we share our materials with another library where it is not owned or is currently unavailable. That library may be located across town or in another country. The patron may have placed a request that was reviewed by library staff or it was unmediated, but, in either case, the borrower's library is responsible for the material from the time it leaves your library until it is returned to your library. The types of materials grow and the methods evolve, but the requests continue.

MISSION STATEMENT

Look first at your library's mission statement. It provides the reasons why or principles on which your library exists. The following are examples of mission statements from a large public library, a small public library, a college library, a university library, and a medical center library. These facilities are located in New York, but look for your institution's statement and those of other nearby libraries.

Albany Public Library educates, entertains, and empowers our community.

Elting Memorial Library is a cornerstone of our community. It is one of the institutions that make our community a rich and interesting place to call home.

The Sojourner Truth Library fosters learning and supports scholarship at SUNY New Paltz, by providing an extensive array of information resources and services.

Cornell University Library promotes a culture of broad inquiry and supports the university's mission to discover, preserve, and disseminate knowledge and creative expression.

The mission of the Center for Public Health Services of the Albert Einstein College of Medicine is to enhance research, scholarship, and practice in public health to train tomorrow's leaders.

While sharing between libraries surely has a long history, the first U.S. Interlibrary Code was adopted by the American Library Association (ALA) in 1919. It states our ongoing purpose in the introduction to the Explanatory Supplement:

> Interlibrary loan (ILL) is intended to complement local collections and is not a substitute for good library collections intended to meet the routine needs of users. ILL is based on a tradition of sharing resources between various types and sizes of libraries and rests on the belief that no library, no matter how large or well supported, is self-sufficient in today's world.

The explanatory supplement to the current code states that the first responsibility of both the requesting library and the supplying library is a written policy that is available in a written format and, when possible, posted on the library's website. ILL staff members should have copies of this code, and it should be reviewed thoroughly with them. See appendixes B and C for the full text. It will be useful for preparing policies and guidelines.

POLICY AND GUIDELINE EXAMPLES

The Albany Public Library, along with its branches, is part of the Capital District Library Council. On its website it displays a policy that guides its community patrons in a straightforward way that is relevant to their needs and concerns, but it also clearly states what it will borrow and what it will lend—something that is quite useful.

Albany Public Library Interlibrary Loan Guidelines

Borrowing   Interlibrary loan (ILL) service is provided by all branches of the Albany Public Library (APL) for materials that member libraries of the Upper Hudson Library System do not own. Any customer in good standing (fines below $10.01 and no restrictive use notes) may use this service: ILL is not available to temporary cardholders. The ILL librarian reserves the right to manage the number of customer requests in light of workflow constraints.
   APL will borrow/acquire:

- books
- photocopies of journal articles less than fifty pages
- microfilm
- microfiche

The ILL librarian will have the discretion to determine if any materials are for *in-library use only*.
   APL will not borrow/acquire:

- books less than six months old
- audiovisual materials such as audiobooks, music CDs, VHS tapes, and DVDs
- textbooks

There are *no renewals* of ILL materials. Each customer must wait a minimum of three months from the date of return of any item before rerequesting the same ILL item.

The lending period of materials is set by the lending library, not APL, so customers will not be able to borrow material for the same loan periods as comparable Upper Hudson Library System (UHLS)-owned items. If a reference copy of a requested item is available locally, the item will not be requested, and the customer will be directed to the local owning library.

ILL is not a rush delivery service for books. The minimum wait period for materials is two weeks, and it is sometimes over a month. Customers will be notified by phone unless they request a mailed card, so it is essential that they provide a phone number that is able to receive and record messages.

Abuse of the privileges afforded by ILL service may result in the suspension and/or termination of a customer's ILL privileges at the discretion of the ILL librarian.

Lending libraries outside of the UHLS may also request items through ILL *APL will lend only*:

- books older than six months old
- photocopies (free of charge for fifty pages or less, $.20/page in excess of fifty pages.

Assistance: Contact (name), interlibrary loan librarian at (telephone number).

What Potential Borrowers Should Know

It is important to clearly state what ILL services you offer and who is permitted to use them. It is also necessary to mention that interlibrary loan, as seen by its name, is a transaction between two libraries, and never between a library and an individual. A loan is always requested on behalf of an individual, but the reason a librarian needs to exert control over borrowing is that it should be borne in mind that the lending of materials by a library is a favor and a courtesy. This idea is well expressed by Constance Winchell, who wrote the earliest set of guidelines for us:

> Thus, the practice of the loaning of books by one library to another has grown from an occasional favor to a more or less organized system. This, however, should not release the borrowing library from a sense of appreciation and a realization that to request a loan is still to ask a favor. (Winchell, 1930, 14)

It also must be made clear that it is the lending library that has the right to determine what it will lend and set conditions, for example, that the material must not be taken out of the building of the borrowing library or that copies cannot be made. That the safety of materials from the moment they leave the lending library until they are returned to the lending library is the responsibility of the borrowing library is clearly stated in the codes. Public libraries serve unattached scholars, students of every age and academic level, and individuals with a variety of interests residing permanently or temporarily within their geographic area. Colleges differ. See the following example:

SUNY Oswego Interlibrary Loan Service Summary

This service is available only to faculty, faculty spouse or partner, emeriti faculty, staff, and students.

What can be requested through interlibrary loan (ILL)?
- Books* (including those listed as lost, missing, or checked out in our catalog)
- Photocopies of journal articles and book chapters (in compliance with U.S. Copyright Law)
- Media materials: DVDs, CDs, VHS, audiocassettes. *Patrons may be restricted to ten active ILL media requests.*
- Music scores
- Microfilm and microfiche
- Theses and dissertations
  - Due to cost and high demand, they are extremely hard to borrow.
  - Delivery period for this type of item frequently exceeds ten to twenty days.
  - Loan periods for all ILL materials are at the discretion of the owning library and are *not* for the entire semester. Renewals are often not allowed on textbooks, and textbooks are frequently subject to recall by the owning library. Failure to return your ILL material in a timely manner results in blockage of service.
  - Textbooks are expensive. As with all ILL materials, if an item is lost either in transit or while in your possession, or damaged (which includes but is not limited to underlining, highlighting, marginalia, water or other liquid spills, torn or chewed pages or cover, etc.)

What cannot be requested through ILL?
Materials owned by Penfield Library that have a circulating capacity within or outside the library (i.e., reference material, course reserve material, IMC (Instructional Media Collection).

How is ILL material delivered and how long does it take?
- Articles are delivered electronically and generally average two to three business (M–F) days.
- Physical items are shipped to us and generally average five to seven business (M–F) days. All physical materials obtained through the Interlibrary Loan Service must be picked up in Penfield Library at the Check-Out and Reserves Desk.
- Some materials may be restricted to in-library use only by the lending library or at the discretion of the Penfield ILL librarian.
- Distance learners should see the *Services for Distance Learners Web page* regarding requesting physical ILL materials.

---

*While we do not ban requesting *textbooks*, this practice is *not* recommended:

What's my cost?

- Faculty, emeriti faculty, staff, graduate students, Upper Division Honors Track students, and McNair Scholars are subsidized up to $200 per person per academic year (including summer) or until Penfield's ILL subsidy budget is depleted for the given fiscal year. Only those requests that are research/work related will be considered for subsidy. Personal/hobby type requests will not be subsidized.
- Undergraduate students are offered the choice of paying fees, before the material is ordered, if fees are indicated.
- Any fines, fees, charges, unusual shipping requirements, or invoice(s) incurred because of late return, loss, or damage to the ILL material are the patron's responsibility and will be charged against your library account.

Due Date

- The due date is printed on the book band. *Do NOT remove the book band.*
- Material delivered electronically is yours to keep.
- Electronically delivered material is available from your ILLiad account and is limited to thirty days.

Renewal Requests

- Renewals can be submitted through the ILLiad system if your material:
- Allows renewals. Check the book band.
- Is *not* overdue.
- If this is the first renewal you are requesting for this material the lending library may opt *not* to renew or to renew for a shorter period than requested. In that case you will be advised by e-mail and need to return the material as indicated.

Responsibilities: All Patrons

- You are responsible for ensuring the material is not defaced or damaged, to return/renew the material on time, as well as for any legal consequences due to violating copyright from personal reproductions.
- ILL loan materials (physical items that need to be returned) may not be placed on reserve.
- Recalled ILL material(s) must be returned immediately [when] the lending library has advised us that they must have it returned immediately. Failure to immediately return recalled ILL material(s) will result in a block of ILL service, as well as $2.00 per day fines.
- Any fines, fees, charges, or invoice(s) incurred because of late return, loss, or damage to the ILL material are the patron's responsibility and will be charged against your library account.

- Any ILL patron who has material(s) more than two weeks overdue may be blocked from ILL service and library circulation.
- Faculty owing $50.00 or more of any ILL fines, fees, charges, or invoices will be blocked from ILL service and library circulation.
- Students and staff owing $10.00 or more of ILL fines, fees, charges, or invoices will be blocked from ILL service and library circulation.

Document Delivery
Electronic copies (scans) of articles and book chapters, as permitted by copyright and as available in paper copy in Penfield, may be requested by SUNY Oswego faculty, graduate students, and distance learners using the interlibrary loan form.

This service is offered to other libraries. Requests for items are only accepted via OCLC/ILLiad, ALA forms, or via e-mail. Penfield Library follows the most current approved ALA Interlibrary Loan Code for the United States, as well as copyright laws and CONTU guidelines. Rush requests are accommodated as time and staffing permit.

Materials Available for ILL Lending
*All circulating materials except for those listed below.

Materials NOT Available for ILL Lending
Microfilm/Microfiche: case-by-case basis; Noncirculating Media, Reference: case-by-case basis; Periodicals, Reference: case-by-case basis; Reserve, Rare Materials/Archives, and Puppets.

Charges
- Copies free for first fifty pages, may be fewer if oversized.

Loan Period and Renewal
- monographs: 35 days, 1 renewal
- browsing collection: 2 weeks, no renewals
- media: 2 weeks, no renewals

Lost Items
Material that is three months overdue is declared lost, invoiced, and no longer eligible to be returned in lieu of payment. A $25.00 processing fee is charged, in addition to the amount charged for the item. Replacement copies are not generally accepted.

INTERNATIONAL, NATIONAL, STATE,
AND REGIONAL CODES THAT GUIDE ILL

Reviewing the Interlibrary Loan Code for the United States, you will learn that its purpose is to explain the responsibilities of libraries when they borrow or lend materials. First written in 1917, and adopted in 1919 by the ALA, it serves as the basic ILL guideline. States, regions, or partner libraries can create more restrictive or more generous agreements; it is recommended that they do so, and most of them do. Check the various agreements within your area. There is no official ALA oversight of that agreement, thus libraries can simply say "no" to libraries that do not follow these guidelines, or libraries can suspend other libraries, just as libraries suspend patrons who do not follow the rules.

Having served on the STARS (Sharing and Transforming Access to Resources Section) Committee for the 2008 ALA Code revision, let me draw your attentions to some changes. Longer loan periods to cover sending, usage, and return will, it is hoped, result in due date returns. Communication is suggested in advance for special requests and afterward when problems arise or suspensions may follow. Technology advances are noted that have created unmediated requests, direct-to-user delivery, purchase on demand, and increasing full-text availability. Shipping and packaging details have greatly expanded. Reference is made to several appropriate ALA guidelines from other ALA divisions that deal with transborder ILL, confidentiality, and special collections.

It is also a "truth universally acknowledged" that a format you will not lend should not be borrowed. Do not borrow DVDs or newly published books unless you will lend DVDs and newly published books. This, however, is not stated in the Interlibrary Loan Code for the United States. It simply says in its introduction that, "the American Library Association, in its adoption of this code, recognizes that the sharing of material between libraries is an integral element in the provision of library service and believes it to be in the public interest to encourage such an exchange."

The U.S. code tells us (3.0) that it only regulates ILL in the United States. It then states that, "Interlibrary loan transactions with libraries outside of the United States are governed by the International Federation of Library Associations and Institutions' International Lending Principles and Guidelines for Procedure." See appendixes G and H for the 2009 IFLA revision, which has changed its title from International Lending to International Resource Sharing and Document Delivery but still provides the Principles and Guidelines for Procedure. Once you move beyond document delivery services and request from individual libraries abroad, review this document as you "go global," with help from chapter 10.

Most recent is the ALA Library Fact Sheet Number 8, produced in January 2013, with an incredible list of resources and guidelines that you will want to review. It was accessed on August 1, 2013, at the following location: http://www.ala.org/tools/libfactsheets/alalibrayfactsheet08. See appendix E. The fact sheet explains that ILL with Canada is "conducted on much the same basis as domestic loans, particularly with those that are members of OCLC. But many have 'slightly different mailing procedures.'" Customs regulation is one of them.

UNDERSTANDING COPYRIGHT LAW

Let us begin with the Article I, Section 8, Clause 8, of the Constitution of the United States, enacted in 1790, known as the Copyright Clause that empowers the U.S. Congress: "To promote the Progress of Science and useful Arts, by securing for limited Times to Authors and Inventors the exclusive Right to their respective Writings and Discoveries." Copyright Law has been revised several times by Congress, and it had also been tested in court. It contains the source of what is called the "First Sale Doctrine" or, in other countries, "Exhaustion of Rights." This allows the owner of a book or other physical copy of a copyrighted work to mark, resell, or, in the case of libraries, loan it. It does not permit the making or distribution of additional copies. This right originated in court cases involving secondhand bookstores, but it is encoded in Copyright Law, Title 17, U.S. Code, Section 109.

Fair use is an American term, but there are similar ones, like *fair dealing*, in other countries. This originated because we did not want the author or owner to prevent us from learning from, commenting on, or even parodying these copyrighted original works. The exclusive rights of the copyright owner, which can be the author or creator but is often the employer or publisher, are encoded in Section 106. Fair use of a copyrighted work that was enacted by Congress as Title 17 U.S. Code, Section 107, which allows for fair use of a copyrighted work, is specified as follows:

Section 107. Limitations on exclusive rights: Fair Use.

Notwithstanding the provisions of sections 106 and 106A, the fair use of a copyrighted work, including such use by reproduction in copies or phonorecords or by any other means specified by that section, for purposes such as criticism, comment, news reporting, teaching (including multiple copies for classroom use), scholarship, or research, is not an infringement of copyright. In determining whether the use made of a work in any particular case is a fair use the factors to be considered shall include:

1. The purpose and character of your use,
2. The nature of the copyrighted work,
3. What amount and proportion of the whole work was taken, and
4. The effect of the use upon the potential market for or value of the copyrighted work.

The fact that a work is unpublished shall not itself bar a finding of fair use if such finding is made upon consideration of all of the above factors.

The fourth factor is considered the most important. A person who views or borrows a book or video from a library may also want to buy it after free exposure. A library that borrows an item from another library may also want to buy it. Efforts to correlate ILL copying with a decline in journal and magazine subscriptions (print or electronic) have been unsuccessful so far. Yet, it deserves our close attention. Electronic journals and e-books are now acquired as licensed works, which are part of contract law and not subject to copyright law.

PHOTOCOPYING RIGHTS AND GUIDELINES JUST FOR LIBRARIES

Section 108 of the Copyright Law is important to libraries and their patrons. Since it is quite long, the following list is a summary:

Subsection (a) states that not all libraries qualify for these special copying rights. Public libraries, academic libraries, school media centers, and special libraries qualify if their collections or archives are open to the public or outside researchers.

Subsection (b and c) allows libraries and archives to make copies for replacement and security, or for preservation.

Subsection (d) states that reproduction and distribution rights apply to a copy . . . made at a patron's request, for scholarship, study, or research . . . of an article or a small part of another copyrighted work if certain other criteria are met such as the copy becomes the property of the patron; the library has no reason to believe that the copy will be used improperly; and copyright warnings are displayed where the copyright orders are accepted. This is also where the limit to one article from a journal is required. Notice: This material may be protected by Copyright Law Title 17 U.S.C.

Subsection (e) says that an entire work or substantial part of it may be copied . . . for individual research if, after a reasonable search, a copy cannot be obtained at a fair price. Again the criteria of 108 (d) apply.

Subsection (f) states that the only individuals protected are library employees. Individuals who make use of unsupervised reproductive equipment are not covered by Section 108, but libraries are protected if the unsupervised equipment displays the copyright notice. Be sure to do so.

Subsection (g) allows isolated and unrelated reproduction of the same material on the same or separate occasions as long as interlibrary arrangements do not have as their purpose "aggregate quantities as to substitute for a subscription or purchase of such a work."

Subsection (h) says that reproductions do not apply "to musical works, a pictorial graphic, or sculptural work . . . or a motion picture or other audiovisual work other than an audiovisual work dealing with news."

ARE CONTU GUIDELINES A SUGGESTION?

Because Section 108 of the Copyright Law required more guidance on the portion of subsection (g) within the aforementioned quotes, a Commission on New Technological Uses of Copyrighted Works was appointed by Congress in 1976. The resulting guidelines are summarized as follows:

1. Periodicals published within the past five years are the focus of the guidelines and have become known as the "rule of five." Periodicals older than five years are still not open to unlimited copying under Section 107.
2. During one calendar year no more than six copies may be requested and reproduced from a single journal title. The sixth request shows the library should enter a subscription. The usual response is to pay copyright fees or purchase from a vendor for the sixth and the others.
3. The library may request an article it owns or will own but not available without counting it.
4. The borrowing library request form must state CCG to show it complies with CONTU Guidelines. Lending libraries need not keep copyright records but should look for the CCG on the lending request form.
5. The borrowing library must maintain records of all requests for those copies that were filled for the recent three calendar years.

A better term than the word *suggestion* might be a *safe harbor*. The meaning comes from a ship that is safe in a harbor during a storm or war. Another definition is any place or situation that offers refuge or protection. The alternative is going to court. Remember that five was really a compromise. According to Laura Gasaway (1996), librarian and law professor, "Publishers favored permitting libraries to borrow only two items within the most recent ten years of a journal, while libraries wanted to be able to borrow ten items per year from the most recent two years of the journal" (15).

CONCLUSION

Once the rules and guidelines are in place, consider the different ways patrons and their requests can be handled. ILL began as a special service in the reference department; then, as a result of online discovery of various materials, it overwhelmed what were very small departments. Many libraries that are part of consortia saw ILL as a circulation department function, and ILL was added as a partner unit. Budget cuts affected collection development, leading to a review of ILL requests for purchase decisions. Read on to learn about some of the reasons for library reorganization of space use and staff functions and the effect this has had on ILL units in many facilities.

REFERENCES

Gasaway, Laura N. (1996). "Copyright and Interlibrary Loan: The Uneasy Case for the Digital Future." *Colorado Libraries* 22, no. 3: 14–17.

Parry, Michelle (2013) E-mail by head of ILL to author approved use of "SUNY Oswego Interlibrary Loan Summary." August 16.

Winchell, Constance (1930). *Locating Books for Interlibrary Loan: With a Bibliography of Printed Aids Which Show Location of Books in American Libraries.* New York: H. W. Wilson Company.

7

Showing Users What
They Missed in the Library

ILL as Reference

The best inventions of America are librarians on the one hand and a martini on
the other hand.

—Louis Stanley Jast, public librarian in Britain, 1868–1944

Louis Stanley Jast was a pioneer in the development of the British public library
system and inventor of the bookmobile, although he called it a bibliobus. He became chief librarian of the Manchester Public Library and president of the Library
Association in Britain. Little of what he wrote or spoke was published or is available
online. Biographical entries call him witty; the aforementioned quote appears on
the Internet in different versions, without authentication. In her April 23, 2009,
blog, *Indicommons*, Deborah Wythe, head of Digital Collections and Services at the
Brooklyn Museum, posted the question, "Why isn't everything digitized yet?" Her
answer was as follows:

> In our small archives . . . we have 1,600 feet of documents . . . just about any format
> you can imagine, covering the museum's history. . . . Here's the math—an estimated
> 3,000 documents per foot, that's 4.8 million items. Even if you could scan, describe,
> and process 30 per hour (highly unlikely), that's 160,000 hours of work, or 20,000
> eight-hour workdays.

A librarian at a reference desk can guide someone in search of materials located
in your local collection, your special collections, and your archives. To find the local items, help from the circulation staff will also be useful. And for items on order
but not yet added to the local collection, the acquisitions staff should be contacted.
But to obtain items in other libraries, the interlibrary loan (ILL) staff is needed. Of
course the ILL staff could do it all—find it, request it, or buy it. Our special skills

come to the fore when we need to discover the contact person at Manchester Library special collections or the British Library Association archive when a copy of the original paper or article about Jast's witticisms is required.

LIBRARY AS PLACE

The current trend in libraries is a return to the view of S. R. Ranganathan, the librarian from India, famed for his faceted classification scheme similar to that used by Google today. His basic principle was that work of the library should be approached from the view of the patron. We have lived through an explosion in population and publication, with a resulting growth in library collections and library staffs. We continue to face this explosion of users and their information needs, but we also face severe budget cuts. Public, academic, special, and medical libraries are learning that their purpose is as a place to serve the user.

From the 1960s through the 1990s, libraries focused on place as a storehouse of collections selected primarily by librarians aided by professional and trade selection reviews. As collections grew, the debate centered on compact storage units versus off-site storage, and others supported deselecting. The library building as place was seen as doomed because all future resources would be digital, and users did not need to visit a library to use its services or its resources. The virtual library would be popular and easy to use. Library staff understood what was actually happening, but leadership did not. Prediction was far ahead of reality.

Reference service changed as users needed help with technology, and they came in growing numbers to the circulation desk or information desk for that help in all types of libraries. Technology in the library was often better than that at home or in the dorm room. Library staff gladly passed on everything they themselves were learning from technical staff the library hired or they themselves had recently learned in library training programs. But there was more to understand, and our administrators finally abandoned the top-down approach and "got it." Students wanted a place to interact, as well as to receive technical support for their research, in academic libraries. Public libraries realized that attendance did not increase just to check out media. The public library is also a community space where people can linger comfortably.

A decade or more after predictions of the end of libraries, the role of the library throughout history as a place to collaborate and experience community has been recognized once again. Also understood is that the user cannot depend upon the digital environment for the equipment to be used and the wide information coverage that was expected. The desired result is a hybrid of digital and analog materials in a quiet place to work alone or interact with others. Roger McNamee, a venture capitalist involved in new media and information technology, was the first to use the term *new normal* to describe business conditions after the dotcom bust in 2001. Susan Montgomery and Jonathan Miller (2011) consider this a "useful way to think about librarianship in the second decade of the twenty-first century" due to the "period of fiscal constraint" we are experiencing.

WALLS TUMBLING DOWN

Joseph E. Straw, professor of library administration at the University of Illinois at Urbana-Champaign, asserts that, "dissolving of walls is one of the main themes of library history." Current efforts to reorganize library staffing structures and change the educational role of librarians are the result of our "electronic environment" (Straw, 2003, 263). When the American Library Association (ALA) was established in 1876, one of the first committees formed was to promote cooperation between libraries. An area of continuing ILL concern is delivery and can it all be electronic? One of the first questions the committee raised was how to develop interlibrary lending. Some interlibrary borrowing and shared cataloging was tried amongst a few large institutions, which led them to create indexes and bibliographic guides (Kraus, 1975).

The U.S. Postal Service (USPS) only delivered letters during the nineteenth century. Packages were shipped by such private carriers as American Express and Wells Fargo. The development of ILL required more favorable postal treatment, as stated in this 1910 editorial in *Library Journal*:

> Anything in the nature of a parcel's post is fiercely opposed by the express companies and by other allies of the railroad interest, and to a large extent by local merchants, who have an undue fear of mail-order houses. Librarians and other friends of a parcel's post should be as active in favor of it as these opponents are against it, and whenever the subject is up in Congress, the chairman of the Post Office Committee should hear from librarians [throughout] the country. (Symposium. . . . 1910, 102)

By the early years of the twentieth century, libraries were able to contact one another by telephone to verify requests. In 1913, the USPS started parcel post so libraries no longer had to use private companies. Relief efforts during the Depression led to the development of many union lists so that, "at the end of the 1930s, [more than] 700 such tools had been published." Efforts by the Library of Congress (LC) in cooperative cataloging resulted in the publication of the Union List of Serials in 1927.

The LC began its union catalog project in 1901, in an attempt to locate a copy of every important book in the United States. The catalog grew to 11 million cards and was then issued as the LC Catalog of Printed Books. To simplify research, it was decided in the 1960s to publish all the references to pre–1956 imprints in a single alphabetical listing. During the next fourteen years, about five 600-page volumes were published each month, for a total of 754 volumes. The *National Union Catalog of Pre-1956 Imprints* is best known as Mansell, after its publisher.

REFERENCE, FIRST HOME OF ILL

This effort to develop cooperation between libraries did not create a heavy flow of materials between libraries. Manuscript materials, rare books, current periodicals, audiovisual materials, and so on were not lent. If you lived within fifty miles, you were expected to visit the library and take notes. Remember, Xerox did not invent the copy machine until 1959. Heaviest borrowing was for nonfiction and technical books. Even college libraries did not average more than a hundred loan requests a year. ILL was considered the "stepchild of reference work" for two reasons. First, people came to the reference desk for help in finding materials and for reader's advisory assistance. Second, each request required help in stating what was needed in library terms (Katz, 1969). And the ALA placed ILL in the Reference Services Division, thinking it would be comfortable there.

Where the ILL function belongs has long been questioned. In the 1960s, the editor of the *Library Journal* wrote:

> True, the interlibrary loan procedure is often handled by reference librarians in the larger libraries. True, it often involves evaluation at some stage, and some bibliographic checking or searching. But these factors alone do not make it a reference service. . . . By its very name and nature, interlibrary loan seems to us a circulation function or service. . . . In the majority of libraries . . . interlibrary loan has to be handled by other than reference staff, because there are no such animals in sight. ALA's reference survey, published in 1961, demonstrated that, even among medium-sized libraries, only 37.4 percent have a full-time professional working in reference. (Moon, 1964, 1698)

During the 1990s, library articles discussed the reference model, traditional reference as dead, new directions for reference, teaching information literacy, and even ILL as the new reference. None of the articles discuss how and when the increased librarian reference desk coverage developed. Some staffing has resulted from assigning every librarian a reference desk shift, but I suspect that it came from the impact of the Online Computer Library Center (OCLC) on the jobs of original catalogers.

Cataloging has been compared to biology and botany as a descriptive science. Reference still lacks a philosophy. One version "concerns the instruction of the public in the use of reference works." Albany University library school professor, William Katz (1969) explains it this way:

> The analogy of the automobile mechanic is often used to explain this paradox. When the student takes his car to a garage, he does so because he cannot repair it himself. He goes to the garage because he knows little or nothing about how his car functions. What is more, he even cares less. He depends upon the skills of the mechanic to put the car back into operation. But what will be the reaction if, when the car is driven into the shop, the mechanic takes the driver aside, gives him a manual and a wrench, and tells him he will instruct him in how to repair his own car. (Katz, 1969, 28)

MEDIATION, WHY AND WHERE

Reference librarians are trying to create a single service point offering face-to-face reference, receiving telephone calls, and handling virtual interactions, guiding use of print, as well as various electronic information sources. Help comes from trained student assistants, and help is sought from technical staff when a device does not do what is expected. An ALA town hall summary in 2009 included a discussion by library-school educators and doctoral students about the multitasking problem faced in both college and public libraries. One of the participants said, "If you're on the desk, you're also answering the phone. You may be doing chat while you're also having to monitor e-mail . . . and there's no opportunity to handle just one patron at a time."

Those who monitored both the ALA focus groups and town hall meeting came to the following conclusion:

> While librarians might be called upon less for assistance in the mechanics of basic information searching, they are now needed more than ever for expertise in teaching users about the nature of modern information, for sharing their knowledge of the wide range of available information resources, for collaborating with users during the various stages of the search and research process, and for evaluating information quality. (Agosto et al., 2011, 242)

The first concern raised by reference librarians is the need to educate patrons about how to use local and consortium collections before turning to ILL. When ILL borrowing requests were mediated by librarians, they noticed that additional and better sources could be available in the local collection. Now that "direct request" is available through the OCLC, libraries can create profiles that only check for ownership of that item, and then the unmediated request is sent directly to the first of a group of libraries that match that profile. The only requests mediated are those that meet no match. Should reference librarians become part of this process?

THE TEACHABLE MOMENT

Can we redirect what Cyril Oberlander (2002) calls the "teachable moment" to the reference desk? He writes that library users frequently talk to circulation and ILL staff about the "challenges they encounter when looking for books or articles" (666). In fact, faculty and students develop more rapport with them than with reference staff. In many libraries, these two are joined in what is called "Access Services."

As Oberlander notes, some typical topics raised with circulation staff are new-user orientation, locating materials, looking up items in the online catalog, reserve items, copyright provisions, and items not found. With ILL staff, copyright questions are frequent, as well as how to cite items for ILL requests and find full-text articles. Research projects and special needs are also often discussed. Should both units ask such questions as, "Did you find everything you were looking for? Is there a way to pass this information on through written surveys at the circulation desk? Should ILL refer users to the reference librarian to review a reference strategy?" (Oberlander, 2002).

The question, "Where is your interlibrary loan department," was asked on the ILL-L listserv in September 2002. The following is a summary of the seventy responses that were given in the United States:

26   circulation or access services
14   independent ILL departments
12   reference
7   technical services
5   collection development
4   public services
2   serials

An increase in ILL borrowing requests and unchanged staffing have caused the streamlining of workflow and dependence on systems improvements. Technical support and additional ILL staff with further training is still needed. As part of Access Services, the response can be to provide "cross-utilization of staff resources" to assist borrowers with their needs, and circulation is a pickup point for ILL loans, as well as local items "on call" for patrons (Cheung et al., 2003).

COMBINED SERVICE POINT

The "teachable moment" for librarians at the reference desk may require another approach. Combining Circulation and Reference at a single service desk could be the answer, and many facilities are in the process of doing just this. A posting by Rachel Naismith on the LIBREF-L and CIRCPLUS listservs, as well as telephone interviews, resulted in the following guidelines:

• Having one service point can work well for a library, especially one with staff who have good relationships and a good customer service attitude.
• If there are territoriality problems, this change may not ameliorate the problems.
• Connecting two operational desks (research function on one side and circulation/reserves on the other) works well for many libraries, with staff "crossing over" if they are needed or when it gets busy.
• Putting one person in charge of the desk is generally a good idea.
• Good training is important, but so is monitoring quality.
• Since some reference staff are not keen on some circulation duties and some circulation staff may not be comfortable answering research questions, it is important that people be comfortable referring patrons to another staff person.

- Work out the "rules" carefully, and make sure everyone knows what their role is, how and when to refer, how to communicate, etc. (Naismith, 2000, 17–18)

A combined service point may bring reference librarians in contact with faculty for comments about their research through conversations about their ILL requests and the success of the current library visit. A 2009 research survey by ITHAKA, which incorporated JSTOR and PORTICO, mailed to 35,184 faculty, asked if they began their research "in the library building," at the Reference Desk. The favorable response was that about 5 percent did so, so the report concluded that the library was being "disintermediated from the discovery process." Since we know that they never began their research projects by face-to-face consultation with reference librarians, let ILL staff send them to you for their ILL questions, and maybe you will hear about their research project for that "teachable moment." Despite a history of more than one hundred years, formalized by the initial efforts of ALA and now promoted as one of the primary services of the OCLC, ILL and document delivery must be accepting of continuous change.

WHERE IS ILL GOING?

Previously seen as a doomed service to be replaced by direct request, ILL has become a basic service that is enhanced by technology and supports a new library philosophy of access versus ownership. This is demonstrated by the continuous growth of both lending and borrowing transactions. An excellent example of this is the increased workload shown in the *ARL Statistics 2012–2013*. Between 1990 and 2012, there was a 295 percent increase in interlibrary borrowing and a 126 percent increase in interlibrary lending in the Association of Research Libraries (ARL). In addition, Google is not posing the implied threat to ILL; instead, it is exposing users to more unusual sources that they expect to receive easily via ILL. Thus, Google is joining, not replacing, WorldCat and other databases as the catalyst for user information needs.

In 2004, Mary Jackson, director of Collections and Access Programs at the ARL, in Washington, DC, identified ten key resource-sharing trends in her presentation to the International Federation of Library Associations and Institutions (IFLA), although she said she would look no more than five years ahead. They are summarized as follows:

1. User expectations will increase. Users will want materials delivered to their homes in hours, not days, for free, with no limits, as part of a core service, personalized to needs of every patron, user, or customer. Just like Amazon.
2. Mediated interlending will not disappear. Internal workflow improvements, plus management software using ISO ILL protocol-based systems, will facilitate the increased traffic.

3. User-initiated searching and requests will be sent directly to potential suppliers. The National Information Standards Organization (NISO) Circulation Interchange Protocol will also increase direct consortial borrowing.
4. Access to electronic journals, databases, or Web resources through consortia will increase.
5. Licenses will become the preferred contract for electronic journals and other electronic content. U.S. Copyright Law may become restrictive from the Sony Bono Copyright Term Extension Act.
6. Portals (web-scale discovery systems) for user searching of catalogs, websites, and print and electronic journals may link the user to the full text and slow ILL increases.
7. Enhancements to centralized online catalogs related to portals will present a list of publications with availability and ranking for relevance, plus links to other content.
8. The line will become blurred between ILL requests and collection development. Buy or borrow?
9. Technical standards will provide the infrastructure that permits catalog records to be created, remote catalogs to be searched, and ILL requests to be exchanged. The ISO ILL protocol that previously only supported mediated requests now also supports user-submitted requests. The NISO Circulation Interchange Protocol Z39.83 governs communication between two circulation applications or between a library's circulation and ILL applications. This standard has the ability to turn a mediated ILL transaction into a circulation transaction. The Open Archives Initiative Protocol for Metadata Harvesting permits portals to discover content that may have been hidden in repositories or archives. Finally, the OpenURL will address the "appropriate copy" problem, helping the user to determine whether the library has a print or full-text copy, whether the item is available from a commercial document supplier, or whether another library might own the title.
10. Increased globalization will be made possible by these international technical standards, and globalization will increase as holdings are discovered and libraries change their policies. The IFLA will address a method of sending and receiving that is understandable to both parties, the high cost of physical delivery and lack of universal electronic delivery, and the methods of payment. The OCLC's Global Sharing Program will increase international holdings. Ariel is so ubiquitous and international that document delivery traffic could be characterized as truly global. (88–93)

Some of Jackson's speculations are only coming into effect now, for example, the discovery portals, and Ariel has been dropped by many libraries, but without a bad report after ten years.

ACQUISITIONS AND ILL AS PARTNERS

Acquisitions receives an annual budget, while ILL does not. Bibliographers at colleges and librarians in branches and in the central public library create collection development policies that guide purchases. Decisions must be made in a timely manner in academic libraries to meet classroom needs, and in public libraries for books that will soon be on best-seller lists, but they do not usually face as time sensitive a schedule as does ILL, which needs backup staff. Libraries can no longer purchase every wanted item, and many libraries have tried purchase-on-demand (POD) programs. This creates a greater quandary for academic libraries than public libraries, which have long argued that what interests or absorbs patrons should be considered when building a library collection.

David Tyler (2011) provides a lengthy chronological review and summary of the case studies of POD programs and their findings. The books, dissertation, media, and e-books added to the collection circulated at a higher rate than librarian-selected items, some of which did not circulate at all. Little impact was caused by rush cataloging, and books from Amazon came faster than those on loan. Some reports show that POD purchases cost more due to lack of vendor discounts, although cost calculations per loan transaction produced a lower average. Prices through Alibris and Better World Books were modest. Some felt that patrons made excessive requests, abusing POD. Others preferred the librarian selection process, although that same criticism has been raised in the past regarding blanket orders.

Some POD programs created better staff morale and increased efficiency; however, most of the programs have not lasted in spite of declining budgets. Combining and cross-training ILL and acquisitions may establish the value of POD and develop best practices. After twenty years of experiments, it is time to put this program in place so that it can prove its value and guidelines can be refined. Combining these staffs can lead to a sharing of skills and the development of the big picture so that together they can become even more important to the library operation.

It may also be time to develop a closer relationship with serials staff in Technical Services. Kristin Calvert, Rachel Fleming, and Katherine Hill (2013) believe that journal cancellations have little effect on ILL, a sentiment that needs further study, since embargoed electronic journals do create ILL requests. In addition, the limited retention of certain print journals leads to ILL frustration. Working together to improve local serials holdings records (print, electronic, and aggregated), as well as understand that deflection policies set by the library, license permissions, and embargoes of vendors that have an impact on ILL, would be of benefit.

CONCLUSION

Would it be cost effective to shift staff from areas that are no longer as active as they once were to support ILL now that it is a core service? Is ILL a backroom operation, or is it a reference service that needs to meet with its users? What is your organizational plan? Another approach might be to review the ALA's Core Competences of Librarianship, created in 2008 and adopted in 2009. "This document defines the basic knowledge to be possessed by all persons graduating from an ALA-accredited master's program in library and information studies." The core competencies are as follows:

1. foundations of the profession
2. information resources
3. organization of recorded knowledge and information
4. technological knowledge and skills
5. reference and user services
6. research
7. continuing education and lifelong learning
8. administration and management

Reviewing this document, I find five is obviously reference, three is cataloging, and two is collection development. Could six, which has the shortest list of components, be the future home of ILL? We can work on that later. Next let us review how ILL fits in with collection development.

REFERENCES

Agosto, Denise E., Lily Rozaklis, Craig MacDonald, and Eileen G. Abels (2011). "A Model of the Reference and Information Service Process." *Reference and User Services Quarterly* 50, no. 3: 235–44.

American Library Association (2009). "Core Competencies of Librarianship." Available online at http://www.ala.org/educationcareers/sites/ala.org.educationcareers/files/content/careers/corecomp/corecompetences/finalcorecompstat09.pdf.

Calvert, Kristin, Rachel Fleming, and Katherine Hill (2013). "Impact of Journal Cancellations on Interlibrary Loan Demand." *Serials Review* 39, no. 3: 184–87.

Cheung, Ophelia, Susan Patrick, Brian D. Cameron, Elizabeth Bishop, and Lucina Fraser (2003). "Restructuring the Academic Library: Team-Based Management and the Merger of Interlibrary Loans with Circulation and Reserve." *Journal of Interlibrary Loan, Document Delivery, and Information Supply* 14, no. 2: 5–17.

Jackson, Mary E. (2004). "The Future of Interlending." *Interlending and Document Supply* 32, no. 2: 88–93.

Katz, William A. (1969). *Introduction to Reference Works: Reference Services and Reference Processes.* Vol. 2. New York: McGraw-Hill.

Kraus, Joe W. "Prologue to Library Cooperation." *Library Trends.* 24, no. 2: 169–81.

Montgomery, Susan, and Jonathan Miller (2011). "The Third Place: The Library as Collaborative and Community Space in a Time of Fiscal Restraint." *College and Undergraduate Libraries* 18, nos. 2/3: 228–38.

Moon, Eric. "Reference Vagaries." *Library Journal.* 89, no. 8: 1698.

Naismith, Rachael (2004). "Combining Circulation and Reference Functions at One Desk." *Journal of Access Services* 2, no. 3: 15–19.

Oberlander, Cyril (2002). "Access Services and RILI: Great Partnership Opportunities." *C&RL News* 63, no. 9: 666–67.

Straw, Joseph E. (2003). "When the Walls Came Tumbling Down: The Development of Cooperative Service and Resource Sharing in Libraries, 1876–2002." *Reference Librarian* 40, no. 83/84: 263–76.

"Symposium of Library Coordination and Inter-Library Loans." 35: 101–02.

Tyler, David C. (2011). "Patron-Driven Purchase-on-Demand Programs for Printed Books and Similar Materials: A Chronological Review and Summary of Findings." *Library Philosophy and Practice* (June): 108–27.

Wythe, Deborah (2009). "Why Isn't Everything Digitized Yet?" *Indicommons*, blog post, May 15. Available online at http://blog.witness.org/2009/05/why-isnt-everything-digitized -yet/ (accessed May 22, 2014).

8

Buy or Borrow?

Getting What the Patron Needs

> Be not superior and reserved. Remember that he who to the popular eye wears
> much the air of wisdom is never wise. See that your library is interesting to the
> people of the community, the people who own it, the people who maintain it.
> Deny your people nothing [that] the bookshop grants them.
>
> —John Cotton Dana, ALA presidential address (1896)

If you are part of the interlibrary loan (ILL) staff, you know that you are not in a
traditional library department. Your unit probably began during the late 1970s or
early 1980s, with the emergence of the World Wide Web and the realization by patrons and librarians that all sources of information could not be found in the library.

Thus began the first principle of ILL: Get the patron what he or she needs. Academic libraries first tolerated this ILL policy because the items were returnables, not
to be added to the collection, even though this service seemed too close to public
library behavior. Budget limits were the next hurdle, and ILL gained support because
it allowed academic libraries, as well as public libraries, to continue building housed
collections based on their carefully developed collection development policies. Both
patrons and librarians were satisfied. Pay attention to the change that is coming!

Those in charge of libraries want to predict the future of library buildings, the
future role of library professionals, and the future building of the library collection.
Rick Anderson (2011, 211), associate dean of the Willard Marriot Library at the
University of Utah, laments that the "future of the library collection is not a collection." In spite of the efforts of library staff to build a collection of "very good books,"
they "yet fail to contain the *specific individual titles* that library patrons actually need
(while at the same time including many titles that those patrons do not need)." What
haunts Anderson is the inability to make even a ten-year prediction of the impact of

97

technology on libraries. While he would still like to see universities building "monumental collections," (213) he fears that the library collections will be patron-driven.

Of course, the monumental collections that the Library of Congress and Harvard University have, and the University of Utah aspires to have, have actually been in the process of being built virtually by the Online Computer Library Center (OCLC), the world's largest cooperative, for more than thirty years. By getting libraries nationwide, and now worldwide, to cooperate by listing and then sharing their holdings as part of the OCLC WorldCat online catalog, they have helped patrons in public, school, college, medical, and special libraries to access the titles they need for study, for help in their everyday lives, or just for enjoyment.

UBIQUITOUS INFORMATION

The Web greatly altered the information discovery process. As a result, by the late 1980s, ILL staffs were functioning at 100 percent capacity. Studies focused on ILL costs and automation efforts to increase ILL staff productivity. Why did libraries focus so much on ILL costs? The Pennsylvania commissioner of libraries, Sara Parker, in her annual address in 1991, stated her view that, "Money spent for books yields a capital asset in a community" (quoted in Perdue and Van Fleet, 1999). She went on to say that each ILL transaction only satisfies a single library patron and does not benefit the library collection.

The Bertrand Library at Bucknell University, in rural Pennsylvania, responded by initiating one of the first ILL book purchasing programs. The program ran from 1990 through 1994. The library made the decision to purchase all books requested through ILL that were available in print, with the hope that this would reduce ILL staff workload, OCLC processing, and ILL shipping costs.

As a follow-up, they compared the circulation records of these purchases with those placed through their usual collection development process. Of course, every ILL request circulated once to the requestor. During the program period, 39 percent of collection development orders did not circulate at all, while the others averaged 2.4 circulations. The ILL purchases averaged 4.5 circulations. As a result, they moved ILL from reference to acquisitions. The Bucknell venture was only partly successful because some orders were delayed, as there were not yet any online vendors; however, this cooperation did cause out-of-print (OP) requests to be referred to ILL for the immediate satisfaction of a patron at the same time as they were sent to OP dealers (Perdue and Van Fleet, 1999, 20).

A PILOT PROJECT WELL PUBLICIZED

In 2000, Purdue University created a six-month pilot project to separate out recently published books requested by ILL patrons and purchase them from Amazon, the discount internet supplier that began service in 1995. They would then add them to the collection after the initial loan. The following parameters were set:

- scholarly works with publication dates within the past five years
- English-language only
- paperbacks preferred
- price limit of $100
- shipping date in five days or less

A follow-up survey showed that patrons were so enthusiastic that the pilot project was continued for two more years. Most books acquired were in the social sciences and literature. The staff was concerned that few scientific and technical books were available for the price limit set, available from that vendor, and received in the stated time frame (Ward, 2002).

Subject bibliographers analyzed the Purdue Books on Demand program purchases. The usual distribution of ILL requests was 30 percent faculty/staff and 70 percent student. This average also carried over to departmental affiliations, except that faculty requested 62 percent of the titles that fell into the history category. Bibliographers wondered why the books were not already in the collection and discovered the following reasons:

- So new the bibliographer was not aware of them
- They were taken from a publisher from whom they do not receive catalogs
- Many came from university presses
- They contained interdisciplinary topics that did not fall into a subject area
- They had narrow topics
- They involved newer and non-Western studies
- There was a lack of funds to purchase everything of interest

A further review showed that about half of the titles were requested by patrons not affiliated with that subject department, which added insight into their interdisciplinary interests. There were also some titles that would not have been considered by bibliographers—textbooks, handbooks, and popular works—but, in most cases, they agreed that these titles were appropriate (Anderson et al., 2002).

The Purdue Books on Demand program articles have been widely cited and instrumental in convincing many libraries to try this approach. In 2009, with the program still functioning, they again looked at the nearly 10,000 titles that had been added to the collection based on ILL patron requests. Criteria had been modified to include DVDs, non-English titles, and a maximum cost of $150. Most titles (82 percent) requested were in the liberal arts, and 13 percent in the science/technology areas. Since only 65 percent of the requestors were from the liberal arts, it was clear that liberal arts requests were coming from other areas, again promoting the interdisciplinary aspect of current educators (Anderson et al., 2010).

Nancy Lichten Alder (2007), the ILL librarian at Brigham Young University and one of those influenced by the Purdue program, asserts that "buy or borrow" is the "most discussed" ILL topic, and she recommends buying patron-requested books because the "process is often faster, and, sometimes cheaper, than interlibrary loan." She also contends that the "patron cares little about how books are acquired." Their workflow places the purchase decisions in ILL, routes them for expedited purchase in acquisitions, and sends prompt patron notification of purchase instead of routing requests to the subject selectors. In this Utah library, they include only faculty ILL requests and exclude popular or juvenile books, and requests cannot exceed a cost of $80 (Alder, 2007, 9).

COLLECTION BUILDING CONCERNS

An essay by William H. Walters (2012), dean of Library Services at Menlo College, in Atherton, California, criticizes patron-driven acquisition (PDA), which allows patrons to select and purchase books for the library collection without librarian subject selector mediation or oversight. He emphasizes that librarians are responsible for book selection in most academic libraries. Even when faculty selectors help build the collection, librarians regulate the process and ensure that the selected titles meet the broader needs of the library and university. Walters's particular concern is focused on efforts to give students a more prominent role. He asserts that, "PDA is likely to diminish collection quality unless librarians implement safeguards to maintain their central role in book selection" (Walters, 2012, 199).

Reviewing recent articles about thirteen PDA programs established at eleven universities since 2000, Walters does raise some interesting points. Most programs using patron's ILL requests as purchase recommendations can be considered unlimited. Some only purchase if they meet established criteria relating to cost, language, format, and date of publication. Most articles note the use of online vendors that provide quick delivery. Walters states concerns found in journal articles that present complete descriptions of thirteen PDA programs at eleven universities: Ohio State University; Purdue University; Southern Illinois University; University of Denver; University of Florida; University of Iowa; University of Mississippi; University of Nebraska; University of Texas; University of Vermont; and University of York, England.

Bibliographers can also benefit from direct interaction with faculty and students at the reference desk, in the classroom, and during office hours. An example involving graduate students in advanced information literacy courses at the University of California, Santa Barbara, shows that moving students from preparing a bibliography while learning how to approach library research became exciting when each was given a specific dollar amount to spend on books and media (not journal subscriptions) that would actually be purchased and added to the collection. As a result, this subject bibliographer felt better prepared when attending the next book fair. On the other hand, this project was not well received by library colleagues, who saw this person as having "too much money" and as letting "random students spend it how they wished" (Barnhart, 2012).

Librarian selectors rely on book reviews, publisher reputation, and professional intuition to guide them in the selection of books for their patrons. Early studies showed that users of major academic library collections checked out an astonishingly low percentage of these largely librarian-selected books. A frequently cited study revealed that 20 percent of the collection receives 80 percent of the use (Trueswell, 1969). Retrospective analyses of use for collection building of multiple-filled ILL transactions miss the "moment of need." Studies of patron selections showed surprisingly high usage (Nixon, Freeman, and Ward, 2010).

PUBLIC LIBRARY FOCUS

The Washoe County Library System, in Reno, Nevada, was among the libraries that responded to the Patron-Focused Services workshop at the American Library Association (ALA) meeting in Atlanta, on June 16, 2002. During the meeting, three academic librarians and one public librarian proposed a new relationship between acquisitions and ILL. Still archived in ALA Reference and User Services archives, to find it go to http://archive.ala.org/rusa/mouss/archives/ill/ill02_files/frame.htm.

In the ILL model, a book is borrowed, used for a few weeks, and then returned. The new model is to purchase the book if it meets library collection policy. The benefits are that unfilled ILL requests can be filled, the collection is enhanced, and patron satisfaction is improved. The following criteria were used for their yearlong 2003 trial: 1) the item is too new to borrow, 2) there is no potential lender of the item, 3) there are multiple requests for the item, 4) the item was published within the last five years, and 5) the item is readily available from a library vendor. As a result, 105 books were purchased at an average cost of $12.53 per book, with a 30 percent library discount and an added estimate of $6 for processing.

Thus, the $18.53 per book was slightly more than the Association for Research Libraries (ARL) 1995 cost study for ILL borrowing transactions of $18.35. That the ARL's cost might be higher in public libraries is raised in this analysis, as colleges use many student workers. Circulation of these books averaged seven times, all at least once, and one for nineteen times within two years. The writer was upset that after promising patrons to purchase titles, six of them were not available from the vendors used. Learning how to avoid this problem led to purchases in areas where the collection should buy more for foreign languages, pure sciences, and religion—which signified topics represented by ILL article requests. The conclusion was that, "books purchased following the established criteria are more cost-effective than interlibrary loan" (Campbell, 2006, 35).

In public libraries, the proportion of ILL requests is small in comparison to circulation. At the Baltimore County Public Library in 1990, it was six thousand ILLs to 8 million circulations. They also receive 26 percent more ILL requests than they send; requests they do not send are for general books, and books that they do request are on specialized topics. The best-seller issue is controversial, as they buy multiple copies so that people do not have to wait months for a popular book. Nora Rawlinson, then-head of materials selection, says that otherwise there would be no differences between public and academic libraries. Her library spends 20 percent of its budget on "high-demand" materials, which is the highest percentage of any library system in the country. This library also does not want to waste high-maintenance space on warehousing. It focuses on popular reading and the business collection, and invests in the latest technology to allow users access to information. Rawlinson went on to become editor of the *Library Journal* and later *Publisher's Weekly*. It was her idea to republish the ALA speech of John Cotton Dana, from which the opening quote is taken (Rawlinson, 1990).

BUDGET CONCERNS

"At what point is it more cost-effective to buy instead of borrow?" was the question asked at Brigham Young University. ILL transaction costs have been carefully measured in college-wide studies by Mary Jackson, the latest in 2004, when the cost to borrow an item dropped to $17.50, which is still seen by library administrators as expensive; however, few libraries measure all the costs involved in adding titles to their collections (Jackson, Kingma, and Delaney, 2004). Gerrit van Dyk (2011) writes that libraries, when comparing whether to buy or borrow, do not include the overhead costs of adding a book to the collection. He complains that the "only time in which purchasing a book is less expensive than a single ILL borrowing transaction is when the library buys a cheap, used copy of a title and simply gives the book to the patron."

Studies show that ordering costs (not including librarian selection efforts) range from $8.50 to $11.31 per title, and for cataloging $8.87 to $16.25, so that the minimum to add a book to the collection would be $17.37 ($8.50 + $8.87). This also does not include the cost of shelving and circulating a title. He contrasts that with automated ILL, which gets borrowing costs closer to the circulation costs of $9.27 per item. If the library purchases a patron-initiated title, the costs of processing, cataloging, and storage will be added. Dwelling on ILL cost is "misleading," as the author suggests (van Dyk, 2011, 85).

A "patron-centric" pilot program at the University of Florida was initiated in 2006, because the collection budget had been flat for several years, in spite of the creation of new academic degree programs. During the same period, ILL requests from both on and off campus increased, so they turned to the literature on purchasing ILL requests, which suggests it is often cheaper to buy than borrow. They proposed a pilot project with a $15,000 budget that was patron centered. Of great interest is the comment that the project was "met by enthusiasm by the collection management librarians." They viewed "this program as a supplement to their collection development activities" (Foss, 2007, 312). They also turned to the Purdue University model for guidance and used their criteria for purchasing books. Unable to secure a credit card, the project used online purchase via OCLC IFM, which currently only involves Alibris for the purchasing of books, although there are plans to add more publishers to a program like "Get It Now" for book purchases (Foss, 2007).

In the thirty-six Washington and Oregon state libraries that comprise the Orbis Cascade Alliance, faculty use their budget allocations to make most library selections. Librarians know that gaps exist, so they support the purchase of ILL requests with library general funds as a way to analyze and evaluate their collections. Only seven members have purchase-on-demand (POD) programs, and four have plans to establish them. The Orbis group shares a joint library catalog, and they have used a consortial approach to obtain e-book purchasing. They are also open to including DVDs and music scores as recommendations from ILL as long as the following criteria are met (Houle, 204, 2):

- the item is unavailable in the consortium
- the request is from faculty or graduate students
- the item has a recent publication date
- the item's purchase price is within the stated limit (Fountain and Frederiksen, 2012)

WORKFLOW CHANGES

Workflow is the second POD roadblock in the seven Orbis libraries with POD programs. ILL reviews requests against POD criteria (7), acquisitions reviews and places order (5), or routes to liaison review and purchase decision (2). Received item is circulated to the patron before (2) or after rush cataloging (5), patron notified and then checked out (7), cataloging follows review to add item to the permanent collection (2) (Fountain and Frederiksen, 2012).

ILL departments request from Alibris (ALBRS), but no longer Better World Books (QUICK), which allows payment through OCLC IFM (ILL fee management). The OCLC has sought to add to this list of IFM vendors, but some fear being confused with lending libraries. Most want to receive payment when the request is changed to "shipped" instead of waiting until updated to "received." Those who are assigned credit cards or use those in acquisitions choose Amazon or Yankee Book Publishers (Baker and Taylor). Several of these programs have similar e-book purchasing programs that allow patron-initiated purchasing of e-books that were developed by E-book Library, ebrary, and NetLibrary. ILL departments often find it difficult to obtain a credit card. Thus, workflow problems arise when they must use the credit card assigned to another unit.

The Interlibrary Loan Department at the University of Minnesota Law Library is authorized (like other campus libraries) to make immediate purchasing decisions for inexpensive items to speed delivery of requested materials to patrons and enhance patron satisfaction. Access to a credit card allows them to create a comprehensive list of vendors. The creative librarian suggests those listed at AddAll.com, which has a comprehensive list of vendors, including Amazon, Alibris, Abe Books, Half-Price Books, and others. Since media is a fast-growing portion of ILL request, CDs and DVDs can also be ordered from this site (Zopfi-Jordan, 2008).

A fascinating story from the Schulich Library, on the downtown campus of McGill University, which serves twelve science programs at all academic levels, challenges many of our assumptions. In 2001, they decided to turn all ILL monographs and conference and technical report requests into rush acquisitions. Aware that "many firm orders by bibliographers or approval plans never circulate," they would now be assured at least one circulation. Selection criteria list no publication date or cost limits. This ILL department sends anything other than science ILL requests to the main library to reduce their workflow.

Now they work closely with acquisitions to obtain these titles within seven days, although only 34 percent met that goal. Ph.D. students made the most requests (43 percent), followed by master's degree students (24 percent), staff (13 percent), faculty (11 percent), and undergraduates (8 percent). Unexpectedly, requests based on publication dates of these science titles were 21 percent (2000+), 43 percent (1990s), and 17 percent (1980s), with 19 percent that included books even dating back to the nineteenth century. The average cost of a book was $136.55, including shipping and taxes, but costs ranged from a 1977 electrometallurgy book at $22.87 to a 2002 chemistry title at $1,057.11 (in Canadian dollars) (Houle, 2004).

SURVEY FEEDBACK

The University of Florida used three criteria to evaluate their Books on Demand pilot project. The first was the response to a short questionnaire that was included with each book, as had been done by Purdue. The questionnaire gauged patron satisfaction with the library purchase, the turnaround time, the usefulness of the item, and comments. The second was the number of circulations in a two-year period. The third studied who used the service and why. The majority of the requests came from graduate students. Undergraduates were included, and the majority of their requests were for titles missing from the catalog. Analysis of department requests showed that changing directions in departmental research resulted in titles that bibliographers would not have selected. Also significant was the need to raise the $150 limit to include science titles (Foss, 2007).

Online surveys are also a popular way to learn which other libraries are participating in a new program. Thus, Washington State University contacted the thirty-six public and private academic libraries in the Orbis Cascade Alliance to learn if they had implemented patron-initiated collection development programs. The twenty-nine responses (76 percent response rate) revealed that only seven had current POD programs, but four more had plans to start within six months. Seventeen libraries (61 percent) had no POD plans. The biggest roadblock to participation is funding. Three libraries used general funds, two created a special allocation, and one used gift funds. None of these libraries tapped into academic subject allocations (Fountain and Frederiksen, 2012).

Oregon State University is one of the Orbis libraries, and their one-year POD project during 2009 was permanently adopted after patron surveys showed a high level of satisfaction. Other projects have stated this, but few have actually done a survey. What they learned was that turnaround time is most important, and having the item permanently available for future use came in second. Having reviewed numerous POD articles, librarians know that program budget, user population, selection criteria, and workflow were the necessary components of POD implementation.

These purchases circulated an average of three times, and the average cost per circulation of $31 was not much greater than the ARL transaction cost. While POD is only one part of collection development, it utilizes expert help more than the traditional input bibliographers receive from faculty and graduate students. These POD requests represent "cutting-edge information need" not met by such traditional just-in-case tools as approval profiles, publisher catalogs, and faculty request forms. Oregon noted that it was looking at the GIST (Getting It System Toolkit) software, which gives patrons choices (buy, borrow, undecided), while also showing WorldCat holdings and Amazon pricing and reviews (Hussong-Christian and Goergen-Doll, 2010).

CONSORTIAL BUY OR BORROW

Recent developments in resource sharing have fundamentally changed the accessibility of academic library collections. Traditionally, ILL served faculty and students at the fringes of their work—a last resort for a small percentage of items that must be consulted but were not available on campus. A wait of two to three weeks for a few items was not problematic, and this leisurely and often quite personal service was generally much appreciated. But with growing reliance on instantaneous access to electronic information, rising costs of labor-intensive services, and the buying power of each library decreasing, a group of librarians challenged the expectations about speed and costs of access to physical collections.

Beginning in 1999, seven Ivy League colleges (Brown, Columbia, Cornell, Dartmouth, Pennsylvania, Princeton, and Yale) explored the concept of fast, inexpensive access to one another's collections that allowed their patrons to borrow circulating materials directly without using the same circulation system. Instead, they used an Informix RDMS (relational database management system) with a SQL client interface. Patron requests are unmediated, which accounts for the 85 percent fill rate. With UPS delivery accounting for most of the $10 per transaction cost and the four-day delivery requirement met, patron satisfaction is high. Ironically, the smaller collections in the current partnership are strong net lenders, and some of the larger collections are net borrowers. Unfilled requests are automatically referred for purchase (Nitecki and Renfro, 2004).

After ten years, the shared access to returnables is still increasing. Lack of renewals is the one disappointment users feel. One library studied consortial requests and found that 54 percent were items owned by the library but not currently available, while ILL requests were for only 10 percent of items owned. Furthermore, 66 percent of the borrow-direct items were published within the past ten years, while this applied to only 10 percent of the ILL requests. Distances between the consortial libraries varies from 41 to 304 miles (Nitecki, Jones, and Barnett, 2009).

BUILD FOR THE FUTURE

Leslie J. Reynolds (2012), associate dean for User Services at Texas A&M University, in her Special Libraries Association PowerPoint, sees "[c]ollections in transition" due to "increasing customer expectations, technological advances, fiscal realities, and internal funding models." She is ready to move from "librarian-mediated to customer-initiated" purchase requests. "Give them what they want, now," and "if they ask for it, they'll use it," so "get them what they need," and we will "build for the future scholars," she says.

SUNY Geneseo developed the GIST software, which integrates with the ILLiad ILL management software. When a user places an ILL request or book purchase request, GIST collects information from both the user and external sources to provide decision-making data, for example, whether the title is held locally, whether a free Internet version exists, whether the user has a format or edition preference, and how much the title costs. Working together, GIST and ILLiad simplify the complex ILL and acquisitions processes by allowing loan and purchase requests to pass between the two departments. "GIST is an innovative tool designed to reconcile formerly disparate workflows and enable effective collection decision making" (Pitcher et al., 2012, 222).

For the thousand libraries that use ILLiad as their ILL management software, this is a big step forward; however, it still requires an interface with the software of use in the acquisitions department, which is necessary if ILL staff need to check on the status of referred requests.

Public librarians have long been provocatively arguing that patrons' tastes and interests should shape their libraries' collections. During the latter half of the twentieth century, numerous academic librarians were vocally arguing that ILL requests—either alone or in combination with acquisition and circulation data—are a better predictor of what patrons will want than are librarians, book-jobbers, or professor's intuitions. Librarians have seemed loath entirely to trust patrons and share collection development responsibilities. Nevertheless, there does seem to be a shift occurring in the library field from "librarian-mediated to patron-initiated collection development" (Hodges, Preston, and Hamilton, 2010, 208).

CONCLUSION

Use of the library building is considered important, so the space for library services and collection storage is thought to be extremely expensive. Thus, the space must be repurposed for the users we serve; therefore, what we collect now should meet their needs, and ILL is the easiest way to determine this. However, our policies differ, our software is not mutually accessible, and ILL is still considered a guest user of the acquisitions budget. While collection collaboration is possible, we are not there yet, and there are even more confusing questions and problems to be faced. We call them conundrums in the next chapter.

REFERENCES

Alder, Nancy Lichten (2007). "Direct Purchase as a Function of Interlibrary Loan: Buying Books versus Borrowing." *Journal of Interlibrary Loan, Document Delivery, and Electronic Reserve* 18, no. 1: 9–15.

Anderson, Kristine J., Robert S. Freeman, Jean-Pierre V. M. Hérubel, Lawrence J. Mykytiuk, Judith M. Nixon, and Suzanne M. Ward (2002). "Buy, Don't Borrow: Bibliographers' Analysis of Academic Library Collection Development through Interlibrary Loan Requests." *Collection Development* 27, nos. 3/4: 1–11.

———. (2010). "Liberal Arts Books on Demand: A Decade of Patron-Driven Collection Development, Part I." *Collection Management* 35, nos. 3/4: 125–41.

Anderson, Rick (2011). "Collections 2021: The Future of the Library Collection Is Not a Collection." *Serials* 24, no. 3: 211–15.

Barnhart, Anne C. (2012). "Want Buy-In? Let Your Students Do the Buying! A Case Study of Course-Integrated Collection Development." *Collection Management* 35, nos. 3/4: 237–43.

Campbell, Sharon A. (2006). "To Buy or to Borrow, That Is the Question." *Journal of Interlibrary Loan, Document Delivery, and Electronic Reserve* 16, no. 3: 35–39.

Dana, John Cotton (1990). "Hear the Other Side." *Library Journal* 115, no. 11: 68–71. Originally printed in 1896.

Foss, Michelle (2007). "Books on Demand Pilot Program: An Innovative 'Patron-Centric' Approach to Enhance the Library Collection." *Journal of Access Services* 5, no. 3: 305–15.

Fountain, Kathleen Carlisle, and Linda Frederiksen (2010). "Just Passing Through: Patron-Initiated Collection Development in Northwest Academic Libraries." *Collection Management* 35, nos. 3/4: 185–95.

Hodges, Dracine, Cyndi Preston, and Marsha J. Hamilton (2010). "Patron-Initiated Collection Development: Progress of a Paradigm Shift." *Collection Management* 35, nos. 3/4: 208–21.

Houle, Louis (2004). "Convergence between Interlibrary Loan and Acquisitions: A Science and Engineering Library Experience." *IATUL Annual Conference Proceedings* 14, paper 28. Available online at http://docs.lib.purdue.edu/iatul/2004/papers/28.

Hussong-Christian, Uta, and Kerri Goergen-Doll (2010). "We're Listening: Using Patron Feedback to Assess and Enhance Purchase on Demand." *Journal of Interlibrary Loan, Document Delivery, and Electronic Reserve* 20, no. 5: 319–35.

Jackson, Mary E., with Bruce Kingma and Bruce Delaney (2004). *Assessing ILL/DD Services: New Cost-Effective Alternatives.* Washington, DC: Association of Research Libraries.

Nitecki, Danuta A., and Patricia E. Renfro (2004). "Borrow Direct: A Case Study of Patron-Initiated Interlibrary Borrowing Service." *Journal of Academic Librarianship* 30, no. 2: 132–35.

Nitecki, Danuta A., Carol Jones, and Jeffrey Barnett (2009). "Borrow Direct: A Decade of a Sustained Quality Book-Lending Service." *Interlending and Document Supply* 37, no. 4: 192–98.

Nixon, Judith M., Robert S. Freeman, and Suzanne M. Ward (2010). "Patron-Driven Acquisitions: An Introduction and Literature Review." *Collection Management* 35, nos. 3/4: 119–24.

Perdue, Jennifer, and James A. Van Fleet (1999). "Borrow or Buy? Cost-Effective Delivery of Monographs." *Journal of Interlibrary Loan, Document Delivery, and Information Supply* 9, no. 4: 19–28.

Pitcher, Kate, Tim Bowersox, Cyril Oberlander, and Mark Sullivan (2010). "Point-of-Need Collection Development: The Getting It System Toolkit (GIST) and a New System for Acquisitions and Interlibrary Loan Integrated Workflow and Collection Development." *Collection Management* 35, nos. 3/4: 222–36.

Rawlinson, Nora (1990). "Give'em What They Want!" *Library Journal* 115, no. 8: 45–47. Originally printed in 1981.

Reynolds, Leslie J. (2012). "Collections in Transition." SLA Annual Conference, August 7. Available online at www.sla.org/pdfs/sla2012/CollectionsinTransLReynolds.PDF.

Rottman, F. K. (1991). "To Buy or to Borrow: Studies of the Impact of Interlibrary Loan on Collection Development in the Academic Library." *Journal of Interlibrary Loan, Document Delivery, and Information Supply* 1, no. 3: 17–27.

Trueswell, Richard L. (1969). "Some Behavioral Patterns of Library Users: The 80/20 Rule." *Wilson Library Bulletin* 43, no. 5: 458–61.

van Dyk, Gerrit (2011). "Interlibrary Loan Purchase-On-Demand: A Misleading Literature." *Library Collections, Acquisitions, and Technical Services* 35, nos. 2/3: 83–89.

Walters, William H. (2012). "Patron-Driven Acquisition and the Educational Mission of the Academic Library." *Library Resources and Technical Services* 56, no. 3: 199–213.

Ward, Suzanne M. (2002). "Books on Demand: Just-in-Time Acquisitions." *Acquisitions Librarian* 27, no. 14: 95–107.

Zopfi-Jordan, David (2008). "Purchasing or Borrowing: Making Interlibrary Loan Decisions That Enhance Patron Satisfaction." *Journal of Interlibrary Loan, Document Delivery, and Electronic Reserve* 18, no. 3: 387–94.

9

Conundrums

Confusing and Difficult Problem or Question

"The time has come" the Walrus said,
"To talk of many things:
Of shoes—and ships—and sealing wax—
Of cabbages and kings."

— Lewis Carroll, *Through the Looking Glass* (1872)

When the STARS Committee met in 2007, to revise the ALA Interlibrary Code for the United States and Explanatory Supplement, we discussed the many challenges facing interlibrary loan (ILL). Journal cancellations created challenges to workflow, with no increases in staff. Change involved more automation, but also a return to poor citations. Clients were asked not to see us since they can get their loans at the circulation desk, where, for confidentiality, books can be shelved backward, or to get answers about ILL request status at the reference desk, which wanted more user contact. Collaboration with acquisitions to buy, not borrow, raises the controversy of differing service policies. Then, of course, always raised in libraries is the cost of ILL. Our answer was that ILL can do it all, and we know that clients rank us highly on library surveys.

CANCELLATIONS IMPACT INTERLIBRARY LOAN

For years during the serials crises of the 1980s and 1990s, concern developed in collection development departments that the percentage allocated to monographs was under siege and would soon be consumed. While library budgets were in decline, salaries stagnated, and then subscriptions were cancelled by libraries and individuals. Journal prices were higher than inflation in the 1980s and rose about 10 percent a year during the 1990s, with annual increases of 4 to 5 percent in the next decade (Bosch, Henderson, and Klusendorf, 2011).

University of Florida librarians, armed with usage statistics and criteria guidelines from their literature review of earlier cancellation projects, met with departmental faculty. Librarians presented journal costs and usage statistics, accepted arguments for retention, and offered ILL as the cancellation alternative. Since faculty doing research already had close relationships with ILL, and with the removal of any previous financial cost for requests provided, consensus was reached. Before and during the early days of online databases, undergraduate use of ILL was discouraged and required faculty intervention. Reviewing ILL requests during the next two years, they found only a 2 percent increase, resulting in thirty-eight requests for articles from twenty-four of the 1,377 titles cancelled in 1993. ILL lending had doubled in the state during the past five years, but no connection was seen. Noted with concern was the failed effort to coordinate cancellations at all Florida University units. Since some cancelled titles were no longer available anywhere in the state, smaller college libraries and public libraries dependent on free articles were adversely affected (Crump and Freund, 1995).

With no similar studies for a decade, Calvert, Fleming, and Hill (2013) decided to repeat a study of journal cancellation impact upon ILL. In 2012, cancellation of 799 journals, 25 percent of subscriptions, took effect at Western Carolina University. With low use of these titles and overlap within online database packages, it was believed that access would not be lost; however, 11 percent of the journals were newly embargoed, and two journal titles were cut from databases after library decisions. Then notice came from ILL that total requests had increased by 11 percent between 2011 and 2012, the same time period as journal cuts. Analysis showed that only a 2 percent ILL increase was due to the cuts. Cause and effect is difficult to determine. For example, a discovery service was installed the same year as the journal cancellations. What was the impact there?

Other Reasons

While ILL staff continue to connect journal cancellations to increased ILL workflow pressure, we can find many other reasons why ILL requests are not declining as predicted. Two technological innovations, the use of Web forms in place of paper forms, and the use of electronic transmission and delivery systems instead of faxing and mail, have become part of the "want it now" attitude of patrons. Other suggestions for maintaining interlibrary demand are the researching of obscure subjects; new and interdisciplinary topics; embargoed text or text that has not yet been digitized; having patrons who are willing to wait for that special article; personal service; as well as "no cost and no limit," which removes the confinement of a traditional library collection (Rheiner, 2008, 384).

A survey of vendors and publishers reveals that they do not support cancelling subscriptions in favor of aggregator databases. Chambers and So (2004) conclude that libraries "engage in a gamble" when they cancel subscriptions (190).

CHALLENGING SURVEY

A recent ILL study presumes the "underlying question" to be whether ILL could become a central library function, whether it would cease to exist, or whether it would just be reduced in importance "due to the impact of new technology" (Williams and Woolwine, 2011. 166). After finding only local and regional studies, the same questions were asked nationally of 1,433 academic libraries listed in the Online Computer Library Center (OCLC) database, of which 442 responded. A Survey Monkey questionnaire asked for data from 1997 through 2008, and OpenStat, similar to SPSS, was used for analysis. These results, which are as follows, are important to us:

1. The library lending fill rate has been dropping since the late 1990s. Such explanations as licensing issues are suggested, but further research is needed.
2. Borrowing dipped between 2003 and 2005, but continues to grow. Fulfillment rates are also dropping, but not as much as lending. (Williams and Woolwine, 2011)

According to Williams and Woolwine (2011, 166), "This may indicate that the national interlibrary loan system is coming under increased strain and the primary issue is not lack of requests or need, but rather an inability to fill requests at the same level as previous decades." ILL is a time-sensitive service, but unlike similar services, circulation and reference, there is seldom backup staff provided.

1. There is a positive correlation between the size of an institution's monograph collection and its ILL activity. It is somewhat stronger for lending.
2. There is a stronger positive correlation between the size of an institution's print journal collection and its greater amount of ILL activity. It is even stronger for lending.
3. The number of databases at an institution results in more ILL, but this is weakening, although it is more correlated with print monographs and print journal holdings. The presence of a link resolver (sending requests directly to the Web form) is a stronger correlation, with increased ILL activity.
4. Only ninety-nine responding libraries reported having at least one full-time MLS librarian in the department. Such departments appear to find ways to fill lending while complying with licensing requirements. A positive correlation exists with borrowing as well.

The presence of licensed databases with full-text content does not lower ILL activity in U.S. academic libraries. Since findings support ILL as an important function, the declining rate of fulfillment is what requires further research. Survey results also indicate that "having a librarian as head of a department correlates positively with interlibrary loan activity" (Williams and Woolwine, 2011, 80). These conclusions also support Margaret Butler's concern about ILL job descriptions that do not require academic qualifications (2009). It is important to have a librarian actively involved in both the day-to-day work as well as continuous assessment and improvement of the operation. Otherwise, fill rates may continue to fall.

CHANGES NEEDED

Our patrons have high expectations and want fast turnaround times for articles and book chapters. The Information Delivery Services (IDS) Project in New York sets forty-eight hours as the standard, as does OhioLink, RapidILL, and the Association of Southeastern Research Libraries, known as Kudzu. A wait of a week is ideal for other formats. To operate an efficient, time-sensitive ILL operation, we must focus on equipment, managing, staffing, holdings records, deflection, embargoes, and database licensing.

It is important that a technology librarian, Natalie Sturr, and a resource-sharing librarian, Michelle Parry, of the State University of New York at Oswego, have worked together to focus on successful practices. From a review of the literature, they concluded that hardware (computers, monitors, and scanners/photocopiers) should be replaced every three to five years. As important is ILL management software (Clio, ILLiad, Relais, SHAREit, and WorldShare) that allows unmediated requests and requires fewer times that a staff member must become involved. Periodically consider fee-based services and software that provides electronic delivery of copies. The following is Sturr and Parry's (2010) updated list of recommended software:

Ariel   http://www.infotrieve.com/ariel
ALIAS   http://idsproject.org/tools/ALIAS.aspx
Article Exchange   http://www.oclc.org/resourcesharing/features/articleexchan gen.html
Clio   http://www.cliosoftware.com/
Effective Data   http://www.effective-data.com/
eSerials Holdings   http://www.oclc.org/eserialsholdings/default.htm
Get It Now   http://www.copyright.com/content/cc3/en/toolbar/productsandso lutions/getitnow.html
IDS Project   http://idsproject.org/
ILLiad   http://www.oclc.org/illiad/
Kudzu   http://www.aserl.org/
OCLC Batch Processing   http://www.oclc.org/batchprocessing/default.htm
Odyssey   http://www.atlas-sys.com/products/odyssey
RapidILL   http://rapidill.org/
Relais ILL   http://www.relais-intl.com
SHAREit   http://www4.auto-graphics.com/products-shareit-inter-library-loan -ill.asp
True Serials   http://trueserials.com
WorldShare Interlibrary Loan   http://oclc.org/worldshare-ill.en.html/ (116, 123)

Training in the use of equipment and software, plus Word, Excel, and e-mail attachments, is needed, as well as knowledge of the local circulation system, the online catalog, and the library organization scheme. ILL update training is needed, with face-to-face training preferred, but the usual today is interactive or recorded training sessions. If they come from a commercial service, cost is involved, but if they come from the OCLC, they are free; however, staff interest fades quickly in all sessions. One reason is that much of what is presented does not apply to the duties of each person watching, and they will not send this in a comment.

The IDS Project has regional update sessions to which all ILL departmental members are invited. Many check e-mail or Facebook during a presentation, except for those who are extremely conscientious or it just happens to match their need. The IDS Project also has mentors who will answer questions on the phone or even make a special visit. The OCLC free teleconferences are good, but one can even tire of them after too many. And then there are the software updates that always have lots of bugs, referred to as permanent beta.

AN INTERESTING TALE

Grace Murray Hopper graduated from Vassar College in 1928, and returned there to teach after being the first woman to receive a Ph.D. in mathematics at Yale University. She taught at Vassar until 1943, when she volunteered to serve in the U.S. Navy, which she did until the age of seventy-nine. She developed COBOL, one of the first programming languages, and taught hundreds of service men and women computer programming. While a computer added incorrectly, a dead moth was found "trapped between the metal contact points" inside the computer and taped into the log book. The term *debugging* was coined to blame the computer and not a person for system failure. Dr. Hopper used it to tell a great story and the log book is now in the Smithsonian. Her goal was to make life easier for users of computer programs, something ILL staff still wish for (Zuckerman, 2000).

HOLDINGS HELP NEEDED

Local holding records in OCLC WorldCat are important to successful ILL service. These data show which library has the article needed. There are four levels of holdings data (see table 9.1). Level 4 and 5 holdings can be created and updated by the Connexion Browser, but level five, which is to include a barcode, is still pending. The OCLC offers free batch processing services. While many libraries do maintain holdings for their print journals, few do this for their online subscriptions or aggregated holdings. The OCLC has a free service for e-holdings, but it does not go beyond level one.

Table 9.1.   The Four Levels of Holdings Data

Level 1	OCLC holdings symbol only.	ABC
Level 2	OCLC symbol with some information.	BCD For microfilm see #999999
Level 3	MARC field 866 text that displays this.	CDE v.9 (1989)—current
Level 4	MARC 853/863 field is more detailed.	DEF v.1- 1970- v. 14, no. 2 1984

True Serials is an electronic resource management service. When a library chooses to provide serials access through aggregated database subscriptions, they become the primary source for full-text articles, but many holdings have embargo periods of six months, a year, or longer. Databases like EBSCO often state that they cannot "guarantee that a full-text journal will be available in future years" (Sturr and Parry, 2010). ILL requests for online articles will be sent to a group of libraries without knowing if any of them can supply the article in the OCLC. If only we could compete with DOCLINE on this. Another approach has been purchasing articles from journal websites, but a credit card is needed, the cost can be high, and directions vary from site to site.

CITATION PROBLEMS RETURN

Citation Definitions

Librarians cannot understand why patrons have such problems with citations. Yet, if you look in a dictionary for the word *citation*, a noun, a definition similar to the one that follows will appear:

1. An official order to appear before a court of law.
2. A formal public statement that praised a person for doing something good or brave.
3. A line or short section taken from a piece of writing or a speech.

Metadata is now a popular library term. We even hire metadata catalogers. Maybe we should promote that term, which is defined in Webopedia as follows:

Data about data. Metadata describes how and when, and by whom, a particular set of data was collected, and how the data is formatted. Metadata is essential for understanding information stored in data warehouses [many databases] and has become increasingly important in XML-based Web applications.

Information source is a better description of what is needed from a patron. Information can come from observations, people, speeches, pictures, documents, publications, organizations, or websites, and it is provided in a variety of formats. There is confusion about primary, secondary, and tertiary information sources and which ones are scholarly and how to describe them.

Among the formats we acquire for patrons are books, book chapters, dissertations, documents, journals (entire issues or articles), music, movies, newspapers, photographs, theses, and so forth. Librarians fuss about citation styles, while students do not. We state our belief that proper citation is basic to good research. A better argument is that someone else will want to find the source used, and to do so they will need enough information to find it themselves, or for an ILL librarian to join in the hunt. Reference libraries now provide guides to citation styles on Web pages or, in the recent years, through citation management software. The most popular are RefWorks, EndNote, and Zotero, although some faculty prefer Mendeley, as it allows collaboration.

Constance Winchell, one of our foremothers, wrote a book in 1930 entitled *Locating Books for Interlibrary Loan*, which is primarily a bibliography of printed aids to show where books could be found in American libraries. She begins her preface with a quote from John Kepler, a seventeenth-century scientist known for his laws of planetary motion and numerous books: "It may well wait a century for a reader, but sooner or later some scholar will want it, whatever it may be, and will inquire for it in a library." That is the real reason for citing a source.

In those days, the biggest problem for ILL was locating a book or journal you did not own, and the development of a union catalog by the Library of Congress was still many years away. Note that Winchell's Columbia University ILL borrowing statistics, which appear in table 9.2, have a high fill rate.

Verification Required

Verification importance was stressed. Although accuracy was increasing, the lending requests received by Columbia during 1929–1930 were "approximately 60 percent incomplete and inaccurate."

For instance, a library asked to borrow Van Dyck, *Ottoman capitulations*, cited in a footnote on page 34 in *The eastern question, a study in diplomacy* by Stephen Pierce Duggan (N.Y. 1902). Upon verification, the work proved to be a government document: U.S. 47th Congress, Special session, senate ex. doc. 3; 47th Congress, 1st session, senate ex. doc 87. The government list of depository libraries included the name of the library which sent the request, and made it unnecessary to send the book. (Winchell, 1930, 38)

Table 9.2.   Constance Winchell's Columbia University ILL Borrowing Statistics

	1927–1928	1928–1929	1929–1930
Number of requests	305	378	482
Located through records at Columbia	167	223	316
Located by letter	103	223	122
Not located	35	82	44
Total located	270	296	438

She goes on to show examples of requests that could not be verified by smaller libraries.

- *Der Ritter mit dem Schwan* is a subtitle of *Lohengrin*.
- *Gregory on landing Basil* is *In laudem Basilii* by Gregorius.
- Several titles with only year of publication turned out to be periodical articles. (Winchell, 1930, 15–16)

Partial Solution

Online databases with link resolvers to Web forms put the needed information into the proper slots. When patrons manually enter a request, more citation mistakes occur. They include the mistakes already noted, plus mistakes in titles or author's names, or after remembering journal information mentioned in class, given by a friend, taken from footnotes, or found on the Internet, sometimes in preliminary versions. Abbreviated journal titles are a bother; many databases enter them into Web requests. One Internet site providing help that covers numerous subjects is journalseek.net. A bigger problem is when patrons guess what the letters represent and enter that. Encourage more use of the note field in an ILL request form so you will get everything the patron learned about a source, and then you can follow up with them rather than just rejecting the request.

Electronic databases cover increasing amounts of overseas research and believe that they aid researchers by translating foreign-language titles of articles, especially in the sciences, into English. Sometimes there is no indication of this in the database or it is buried it the text. This is a frequent problem for undergraduates, but even for others, and it creates additional work for ILL, as the patrons must be contacted to learn if they know that the article is in Russian, or Hungarian, or Japanese, and so on.

An even greater problem is when a librarian isn't involved at all. Kit Condill and Lynne Rudasill ask the following questions:

> Is it clear enough for ILL staff to interpret [the citation] correctly? Are ILL staff at the user's library able to match the request to the correct item or items in WorldCat? Is the material included in a series or subseries that could be cataloged in multiple ways, generating different titles for the same item? Are there broader issues of cataloging, staffing, or others at the lending library that make it difficult for ILL staff to locate the requested material? With nonmediated interlibrary loan requests becoming more common, who, if anyone, is verifying [these] citations before the request is sent? (2009, 55, 57)

CLIENTS WE SERVE WELL

"Customer service goals first, technology second" is what Harry Kriz learned while developing ILLiad at the West Virginia Tech library. "Discovering what services are needed and desired is the first order of business. Searching for a means, or a technology, to fulfill those goals is secondary order. This simple rule is so often forgotten both by librarians and technologists" (Kriz, 2002, 24–25).

I thought his message had been heard by everyone when the "library as place," both collaborative and community space, in all types of libraries was proclaimed, but it is a time of fiscal constraint that is being called the "new normal." We are remodeling libraries to create a more welcoming and attractive place away from home or work. But it was the people who "voted with their feet" and showed us that they wanted the places that already existed, where they can be alone in a quiet place with friendly staff who can help them when needed. The "new normal" is calling for continuous change in staff assignments and what is collected. For ILL, the "new normal" calls for collaborating with your library colleagues, just as we do with other libraries to benefit clients (Montgomery and Miller, 2011, 228).

Lending Is Important

Lending is an area of concern for ILL departments because of dropping fill rates. It should be of concern to administrators because libraries are dependent on one another. A good lending fill rate is 75 percent, since lenders have only one chance to fill a request, while a borrowing request can go to several libraries before it is counted as filled. The item to be loaned could be checked out, in use, noncirculating, missing, or just not found. The journal from which an article is needed could be in use, but a holdings problem is more likely and should be reported. The most common reasons for article cancellations include not found as cited, lack of volume/issue, holdings end before the volume, or holdings begin after the volume. It is important to train student assistants to find items and use a report form for later review. It is also important to encourage student assistants and clerks to ask questions so that problems can be corrected (Gibson, 2008).

During weeding periods and journal cancellations, it is important that records are updated in WorldCat as soon as they are updated in the local catalog. During a local cancellation project, the year's lending fill rate dropped to 30 percent. If a title is never to be loaned, deflection should be entered into the catalog record. There are also libraries that cancel requests from libraries outside their consortium at busy times to meet turnaround times within that group. Concern for one's lending statistics means that we hope others will do the same for us. Work closely with serials staff to correct errors, enter detailed holdings, and keep holdings records current. This should be done, but it is not even attempted with electronic holdings.

Faculty Talk with Us

Working with clients in ILL is very rewarding. A faculty member recently wanted a novel in Finnish entitled *Sotaromaani*, about the life of an unknown soldier in World War II. It had been published in five editions since 1954, until finally being published uncensored from the original manuscript in 2000, but it was only located in eight U.S. libraries. He got it quickly through personal contact with us about his project and by us personally contacting the lending library. He picked it up at the circulation desk. After returning from his conference presentation, he found his way to the recently moved ILL, now a back-office location, and proceeded to talk about his research. This happens in our office frequently. They can still find us.

Moving us and asking faculty and students to take their questions to the reference desk will relieve us of heavy workloads, we are told. Another plan, raised at a conference, was to move ILL into the reference office so that reference librarians could become more familiar with the research of the faculty of the departments for which they are liaisons and teach information literacy courses. ILL moves, and the faculty (and students) follow. Reference librarians could help us handle ILL requests. Then faculty might talk to them about their research interests.

Can We Help Unattached Scholars?

The clients that lack college or university connections find ILL to be an increasingly hidden service. The alternative is digitized collections and consortial borrowing within their associated libraries, as promoted by the Boston area public libraries (Preece, 2008). School libraries are also rarely participating in ILL because, like public libraries, they are not well funded. There are examples of school library collaboration with public libraries and academic libraries, but they are few in number (Gee, 2011). Librarians in both types of libraries find the ILL process confusing, and their superiors see it as expensive. But most libraries have Internet connections, and they can receive or send ILL requests using online programs, e-mail, fax, or even postal mail. Many academic libraries have "Friends of the Libraries" membership programs to which you can refer adult patrons or parents to gain direct collection access, but not usually ILL.

CONTROVERSY INVOLVES US

How does ILL cope with licensing agreements? We have different approaches that result from either our involvement or noninvolvement in the negotiating process. When libraries subscribed to print journals, the "first sale" right (U.S. C. Title 17, Section 109) allowed us to lend, sell, or dispose our holdings. With the development of photocopiers, the ILL and archival rights were stated in U.S. C. Title 17, Section 108 and the number of copies managed by the CONTU guidelines set for borrowing libraries. Libraries tried to own electronic formats but lost out when the Digital Millennium Copyright Act was passed. Thus, we have contracts covering electronic databases, e-journals, and e-books governed by state contract laws that are imposed upon the lending libraries. These contracts are usually made by consortia or university administrations.

Some libraries avoid the problem by not filling any ILL requests from their licensed materials; therefore, they do not borrow formats they cannot supply. Janet Brennan Croft calls this "avoidance approach." Developing lists of licensing terms leads to what she calls the "reactive approach" (2005, 46). Many libraries create local lists of database licensing terms to which ILL departments can refer when they receive a request for an electronic resource. The IDS Project uses librarians from seventy-five of its member libraries to study licensing terms to be entered in ALIAS (Article License Information Availability Service), a project developed working with ATLAS that allows ILLiad to construct a lender string of permitted article requests that are sent straight into the OCLC.

Croft lists several project and commercial services that also do this. Another way is the "proactive approach," where libraries refuse to sign contracts unless their terms are met. There are classes on license negotiation offered by national and regional library associations. Efforts have led to the development of model agreements and the recommendation that vendors should rarely refuse to negotiate their terms.

Format Issues

E-books are usually licensed, not sold to libraries, and many are prohibited from being used for ILL. It is more likely that ILL will receive a request for a print copy of an e-book for which the library provides access. Local user requests are often received for articles in print journals. This leads to the suggestion that rather than reject the request, we should scan and send them the article. Media is a problem for ILL, as the volume of requests for sound or video recordings has risen to a third of our borrowing requests. Of course, to borrow we must lend similar items. The primary concern here is the fragile nature of CDs, videotapes, and DVDs, but also efforts to deflect requests for those DVDs for which we purchased performance rights. Special packaging and insurance or using such shipping services as UPS and Federal Express help us to avoid damage to both what we borrow and what we lend.

Students are unhappy about the high cost of textbooks, so they send requests to ILL. If the library owns a copy, a student has already checked it out. If you order a copy for another student, there is a good chance you will receive it. The problem is that it will become overdue and is not returned until the end of the semester. Several libraries, including mine, have provided required textbooks on reserve. Like us, they have acquired copies from faculty or past students to put on reserve. Those that have purchased them, like the University of Illinois at Urbana-Champaign, found that it was popular with the students but considered too expensive by the library (Crouse, 2007).

Some ILL departments reject textbook requests when they can identify them. This has been much discussed on the ILL-L listserv. The ALA Code, which mentions textbooks, takes no stand for or against them. The recommendation is that borrowing libraries should request a longer loan period in advance (Blackburn and Tiemeyer, 2013).

Open Access

Open-access (OA) materials include journal articles, research publications, as well as author's and academic online archives. A way to look for these is a search in Google Scholar or the Directory of Open Access Journals. WorldCat is also useful for locating OA repository materials since it connects to OSIster, which includes metadata for a wide range of materials, but it limits access of the past five years to subscribers. For more information about the OA movement, review the Budapest Open Access Initiative of 2002 (Martin, 2010). Beware that electronic collections can create new walls. Universities collect theses, dissertations, and faculty articles and then charge for access off campus or for ILL. Some cannot lend these electronic publications due to intellectual property rights, copyright law, and publisher practices.

WHAT IS COSTLY?

Two library science professors, Carol Tenopir and Donald King, were "setting the record straight on journal publishing" during the serials crisis of the 1980s and 1990s. It was connected to inflation, with journals raising prices to personal subscribers, who then kept only a few subscriptions, dropped the rest, and began to use the library periodical collections more. Surveys from 1977 to 1993 of university scientists using library periodicals showed that usage increased from 25 percent to 54 percent. Faculty began to photocopy articles. The number of subscribers determines journal price. Thus, a journal with five thousand subscribers charging $110 for article review, refereeing, subject and copy editing, preparation, paper, printing, binding, and mailing would have to increase the price to $830 if the number of subscribers dropped to five hundred.

Next publishers turned to libraries to recover costs after their studies showed that price increases had little impact on library demand. Libraries, with shrinking funds, reacted strongly by calling publishers "greedy." Interlibrary loans of costly, little-read journals was the temporary answer, even though studies showed that ILL costs were at more than $20 per item. Electronic publishing was the future (Tenopir and King, 1996).

Today library focus is on staffing as the major cost of ILL. Cyril Oberlander (2011) estimates the cost of reviewing, selecting, purchasing, and processing a book to be $95 (price not included) in his presentation on GIST (Getting It System Toolkit), which sends ILL requests for current books to purchase to cut collection-building costs. Catalogers dropped in numbers when the OCLC made it possible to simply attach your symbol if a book had already been entered into WorldCat. Original cataloging back then was estimated to be just under $45 per item (Leung, 1987).

Reference librarians find that most questions are directional or involve computers and printing. Much attention was given to a *Library Journal* article that tallies data and determines the price to be the "staggering sum of $108 and some cents per question" (Wisner, 2008, 41). While questions were similar in another study, each cost only $7.09 (Merkley, 2012). Does one pay a living wage and the other not? Are these the kind of statistics we should keep? That was the question asked about ILL studies that concentrate on wage costs per transaction (Morris, 2005).

Another Thought

The standard for ILL cost has been set by the Association of Research Libraries (ARL) data, with the latest 2002 costs averaging $17.50 for the borrowing side and $9.27 for the mean mediated cost of lending. Staff account for 58 percent of borrowing and 75 percent of lending (Jackson, 2004). The most recent multilibrary cost study of ILL lowered the mean average cost of borrowing to $9.62, which, combined with the lending mean net cost of $3.93, totals $13.55. The emphasis here is that costs have changed, although the concern is still that staffing is considered high, with borrowing at 55 percent and lending at 63 percent. Is unmediated ILL really the best way to handle all ILL requests? The authors of this study call on ILL librarians to "contribute to a community effort" based on our "tremendous track record of sharing" to become more efficient and collaborate more with other departments (Leon and Kress, 2012).

ANOTHER DIRECTION

"What kept you up at night?" was the headline on the cover of the OCLC's *NextSpace* newsletter for November 2013. The answer was "first and foremost customer service." For ILL librarians, discovery services have meant "going global," because that is what our users are doing in their databases. Getting materials from our neighboring countries, north and south, as well as Europe, Asia, and beyond, may be easier than you think, and it could be, according to that headline, "what motivates you to get up in the morning" and keeps you "focused and optimistic."

REFERENCES

Blackburn, Gemma, and Robyn Tiemeyer (2013). "Textbooks and Interlibrary Loan." *Journal of Interlibrary Loan, Document Delivery, and Electronic Reserve* 23, no. 1: 5–18.

Bosch, Stephen, Kittie Henderson, and Heather Klusendorf (2011). "Under Pressure, Times Are Changing." *Library Journal* 136, no. 8: 30–34.

Bowersox, Tim, Cyril Oberlander, Kate Pitcher, and Mark Sullivan (2011). "Getting It System Toolkit: GIST, A Remix." ILLiad Conference, March 24. Available online at http://www.atlas-sys.com/ILLiadConf/Presentations/GISTGettingItSystemToolkit.pdf (accessed March 21, 2014).

Butler, Margaret (2009). "Job Descriptions for Interlibrary Loan Supervisors: Core Functions and Best Practices." *Journal of Interlibrary Loan, Document Delivery, and Electronic Reserve* 19, no. 1: 21–31.

Calvert, Kristin, Rachel Fleming, and Katherine Hill (2013). "Impact of Journal Cancellations on Interlibrary Loan Demand." *Serials Review* 39, no. 3: 184–87.

Chambers, Mary Beth, and Soo Young So (2004). "Full-Text Aggregator Database Vendors and Journal Publishers: A Study of a Complex Relationship." *Serials Review* 30, no. 3: 183–93.

Condill, Kit, and Lynne Rudasill (2009). "GIVES: Interlending and Discovery for Non-English Resources." *Interlending and Document Supply* 37, no. 1: 49–60.

Croft, Janet Brennan (2005). "Interlibrary Loan and Licensing: Tools for Proactive Contract Management." *Journal of Library Administration* 42, nos. 3/4: 41–53.

Crouse, Caroline (2007). "Textbooks 101: Textbook Collection at the University of Minnesota." *Journal of Access Services* 5, no.3: 285–93.

Crump, Michele J., and LeiLani Freund (1995). "Serials Cancellations and Interlibrary Loan: The Link and What It Reveals." *Serials Review* 21, no. 2: 29–36.

Gee, C. William (2011). "Connecting K–12 School Media Centers to University Library Resources through Interlibrary Loan: A Case Study from Eastern North Carolina." *Journal of Interlibrary Loan, Document Delivery, and Electronic Reserve* 21, no. 3: 101–16.

Gibson, Tess (2008). "Cancelled Requests: A Study of Interlibrary Lending." *Journal of Access Services* 5, no. 3: 383–89.

Jackson, Mary, with Bruce Kingma and Tom Delaney (2004). *Accessing ILL/DD Services: New Cost-Effective Alternatives*. Washington, DC: Association of Research Libraries.

Kriz, Harry M. (2002). "Customer In-Reach and Library Strategic Systems: The Case of IL-Liad." *Public Services Quarterly* 1, no. 1: 19–26.

Leon, Lars, and Nancy Kress (2012). "Looking at Resource-Sharing Costs." *Interlending and Document Supply* 40, no. 2: 81–87.

Leung, Shirley W. (1987). "Study of the Cataloging Costs at the University of California, Riverside." *Technical Services Quarterly* 5, no. 1: 57–66.

Martin, Rebecca A. (2010). "Finding Free and Open Access Resources: A Value-Added Service for Patrons." *Journal of Interlibrary Loan, Document Delivery, and Electronic Reserves* 20, no. 3: 189–200.

Merkley, Cari (2009). "Staffing an Academic Reference Desk with Librarians Is Not Cost Effective." *Evidence Based Library and Information Practice* 4, no. 2: 143–47.

Montgomery, Susan E., and Jonathan Miller (2011). "The Third Place: The Library as Collaborative and Community Space in a Time of Fiscal Restraint." *College and Undergraduate Libraries* 18, nos. 2/3: 228–38.

Morris, Leslie R. (2005). "Random Comments on 'Accessing ILL/DD Services: New Cost-Effective Alternatives,' by Mary Jackson, with Bruce Kingma and Tom Delaney." *Journal of Interlibrary Loan, Document Delivery, and Electronic Reserve* 15, no. 4: 97–100.

Preece, Barbara G. (2008). "'Free to All' Made Possible by an Academic/Public Library Collaboration." *Against the Grain* 20, no. 1: 26–28.

Rheiner, V. Renee (2008). "How Electronic Full-Text Journals Impact Interlibrary Loan Article Requests at a Small, Liberal Arts University." *Journal of Interlibrary Loan, Document Delivery, and Electronic Reserve* 18, no. 3: 375–86.

Sturr, Natalie, and Michelle Parry (2010). "Administrative Perspectives on Dynamic Collections and Effective Interlibrary Loan." *Journal of Interlibrary Loan, Document Delivery, and Electronic Reserve* 20, no. 2: 115–25.

Tenopir, Carol, and Donald W. King (1996). "Setting the Record Straight on Journal Publishing: Myth vs. Reality." *Library Journal* 121, no. 5: 32–35.

Williams, Joseph A., and David E. Woolwine (2011). "Interlibrary Loan in the United States: An Analysis of Academic Libraries in a Digital Age." *Journal of Interlibrary Loan, Document Delivery, and Electronic Reserve* 21, no. 4: 165–83.

Winchell, Constance (1930). *Locating Books for Interlibrary Loan.* New York: H. W. Wilson Company.

Wisner, William H. (2008). "$108 . . . and Some Cents." *Library Journal* 133, no. 16: 41.

Zuckerman, Laurence (2000). "If There's a Bug in the Etymology, You May Never Get It Out." *New York Times*, April 22, B11.

10

Going Global

It's Easier Than You Think

There is no delight in owning anything unshared.

—Lucius Annaeus Seneca, Roman philosopher, mid-1st century AD

We all know that no library can own all the published materials. Yet, it is so easy for our patrons to learn about the articles, books, music, movies, and more produced throughout the world. They wonder, "Who has it?" and "Is it possible for me to get it?" It is also easy for them to submit the requests through manual, and especially through various automated, systems of academic, public, school, and special libraries so those questions are passed on to the staff at those institutions.

We interlibrary loan (ILL) librarians strongly advocate for access to information no matter where it is located or in what format. So what do you do when you think that request will not be easy to lend or borrow, nor will it be fast or cheap? You can just say "no," or you can take the time to learn the necessary steps. You may fail, but you will succeed more often than you are unsuccessful.

HISTORICAL NOTES

For many years, manuscripts never left the library, and they were often chained to a shelf. It is told that an exchange of materials took place between Athens and Alexandria to allow for copies. Manuscripts were also informally copied and shared between Islamic libraries (Aman, 1989) and Chinese libraries (Fang, 2007). In 1634, a French nobleman, Nicololas Claude Fabri de Periesc, tried to arrange a formal exchange agreement between the Royal Library in Paris and the Vatican Library in Rome. It was unsuccessful, but he is credited with the first effort to establish a "formal lending system" (Gravit, 1946).

Informal sharing continued through the nineteenth century, when the idea of lending for a stated period was widely discussed and the term *interlibrary loan* came into usage by librarians. Melville Dewey proposed a standard request form in 1888, when he wrote the following in his phonetic way: "Interlibrary-loans which wer a litl while ago almost unknown ar now of daily occurrence" (405).

Richard R. Bowker, an American editor and publisher, addressed attendees at an American Library Association (ALA) meeting, recommending the following: "We should develop some system that will enable a library first of all to know where a book ought to be found, and, secondly, if there is no special place for it, some means of asking who has it" (1909, 156).

WORLDCAT REGISTRY

Now you can find information about libraries and consortia throughout the world by going online to the WorldCat Registry, at http://www.worldcat.org/registry/ institutions. It does not include as much information about each library as the Online Computer Library Center (OCLC) policies directory, but one day it may. Looking for my community of New Paltz, you will find addresses for Elting Memorial Library, Historic Huguenot Street (HHS), New Paltz High School, New Paltz Middle School, SUNY at New Paltz, Samuel Dorsky Museum of Art, and Ulster School Library System, which has its main office here. Only the State University at New Paltz and the Ulster County School Library System have entered policies and will accept online ILL requests. The others list an OCLC symbol for regional use and an address, while Elting shows its telephone number. HHS lists a telephone number; e-mail address; and URLs for its home page, library, and underground archives.

If you look on the Web for more information about Elting Memorial Library, you will learn that it is a public library with an excellent historical collection that is thoroughly described. Elting, like the facilities that are not OCLC members, cannot, at present, expand its registry record. The OCLC displays nonsubscribing libraries so its member libraries can see some basic information about libraries throughout the United States and worldwide. Look up your community or type in the name of a community in another country. You may agree that we live in a small world.

ESTABLISHED POLICY DOCUMENTS

Most libraries have both a regional and statewide ILL policy, but look first at the ALA Interlibrary Loan Code for the United States, first created in 1917, last revised in 2008, and found online at http://www.ala.org/rusa/resources/guidelines/ interlibrary.cfm. You will receive encouragement when you read the following three sentences in the introduction, which summarize our purpose:

In the interest of providing quality service, libraries have an obligation to obtain material to meet the informational needs of users when local resources do not meet those needs. Interlibrary loan (ILL), a mechanism for obtaining material, is essential to the vitality of all libraries. The effectiveness of the national interlibrary loan system depends upon participation of libraries of all types and sizes.

The basis for the provision of ILL between countries lies in the International Resource Sharing and Document Delivery document, first accepted by the International Federation of Library Associations and Institutions (IFLA) in 1954, last revised in 2009, and also found online at http://www.ifla.org/files/assets/docdel/documents/international-lending-en.pdf. Its principles are clearly stated in the first three sentences of its introduction.

The shared use of individual library collections is a necessary element of international co-operation [sic] by libraries. Just as no library can be self-sufficient in meeting all the information needs of its users, so no country can be self-sufficient. The supply of loans and copies between libraries in different countries is a valuable and necessary part of the interlibrary loan process.

Before implementing your workflow, step back and review your library's policies. If you want to borrow internationally, you will be expected to provide materials as well. This is not an enforceable requirement, yet it is strongly encouraged that you should be willing to lend the types of materials you want to borrow.

Before starting the international search, check your OCLC policy to see that your address and contact information are current. List what materials you will provide, your methods of delivery, and how much you charge and your acceptable payment options for the overseas areas. Read the listings for a few other similar libraries for suggestions. If you are not an OCLC member, you probably borrow and lend as part of a regional system, but you can expand your current policies to move outside those limits.

INTEGRATED WORKFLOW

These national and international resource-sharing documents also provide procedures for both lending and borrowing. You already have a workflow, so just integrate international ILL into what you already have with any ILL software, or even manually. Even though your patrons might think of an item provided by a library in Hong Kong or the Netherlands as a very special event, it should follow the usual ILL cycle, somewhat modified.

1. The borrowing request is received from the patron.
2. Local, regional, and national holdings are checked.
3. A multinational or another country catalog search locates the item.
4. The patron is notified of the steps taken and the probable time frame.

5. The payment method is indicated (IFM, invoice, credit card, or IFLA voucher).
6. The request is sent electronically, via e-mail or IFLA form, sent by fax or postal mail.
7. The request is received overseas and the item found and sent.
8. If the item is unavailable, the patron is notified and further options are explained.
9. Once the requesting library receives the item, the patron is notified and the patron checks it out.
10. If the item is not returnable, the process ends here. If the item has been loaned, the item is returned promptly by the due date.
11. The lending library receives the item, and the request is finished. (Fredericksen, Bean, and Nance, 2012)

It is assumed that there are questions on your patron request form asking the date needed by, language other than English accepted, and source of the citation. These should be reviewed carefully before going overseas. Extra queues and special e-mails are necessary to track international ILL and keep a patron aware of the progress being made and the time involved in international requests.

FINDING A LENDER

You start your search in the OCLC's WorldCat, at http://www.worldcat.org. If you find a foreign lender that receives requests electronically and whose symbol is uppercase (currently lending), check the OCLC policies directory to learn what they expect from you and what they will supply. Two useful online sources for European materials are the British Library Document Supply Service (BLDSS) and the Bavarian State Library (GEBAY). Since articles will be supplied electronically by them, fees are the concern. If you request a loan, shipping procedures and other costs will be added.

If you cannot find what was requested even after doing an Internet search, go back to the patron for more information. Another international catalog to try is the German Visual Catalog (Karlsruher Virtueiller Katalog KVK), the largest European catalog (http://www.ubka.uni-karlsruhe.de/kvk_en.html). It includes many non-OCLC libraries. The library listings include contact information. For more information about each library, copy the description into Google Translate and you can read it in English.

For more international searching, look at ShareILL (http://www.shareill.org), an ILL Wiki maintained by librarians. You will find union catalogs and archives from throughout the world at http://www.shareill.org/index.php?title=National_librar ies_and_archives. Government documents are best searched online by title so that you can provide the URL to the patron, who can then download the text. If that does not work, go to the agency or organization website. Helpful for United Nations documents is http://documents.un.org/, and for nongovernmental organizations, a useful site is WANGO (http://www.wango.org) (Fleming, 2012).

NONSYSTEM REQUESTS

The IFLA request form for loans or photocopies can be sent to any library that does not use the OCLC for lending transmission or that does not have its own form for use. IFLA forms are available for download or printing at http://www.ifla.org/files/assets/docdel/documents/il-form.pdf. Instructions require four copies, typed or completed in legible ballpoint pen, dated, and including a responsible library employee's signature. You may assign a tracking number in the upper right-hand corner of the form if you wish. One of the four copies is kept at your library, and one is returned to you with the item requested. It is helpful to include a mailing label with the request.

IFLA guidelines recommend that loans received in response to international ILL should be returned by the fastest mailing method available. Whether you send the IFLA form or use e-mail for your request, the IFLA guidelines require the following information:

- All the bibliographic information that you have, including the source of the reference.
- Format required, need by date, and your max cost.
- Name and date to indicate library's responsibility and copyright compliance.
- Library's full address, plus any variation for delivery or billing.
- Name of the lending library (but it is up to them to complete their address).

You will expect the following from them, as they will expect the same from you when you receive an international request:

- A prompt reply regarding the item needed and the willingness to answer more questions and listen to any concerns so the request can go to another library if it cannot be filled there.
- That they have a policy, or one in process, on international lending and a listing of countries or regions that may be served on a case-by-case basis, free or at some cost.
- That decisions on availability and condition of material, to loan or copy, have been made. Any copyright or licensing restrictions and method of shipment are also needed.

TRANSLATOR TOOLS

If the response to your request is not in English or you wish to translate your overseas notes, try Google Translate, a free online language translation service, and only one of several that are browser supplied. Make your message simple, to the point, and polite. To ensure that you said what you desire to say, translate your message back into English. Some changes may be needed before you actually send the message.

SHIPPING AND CUSTOMS

Shipping internationally will cost more than shipping nationally, so start by interacting with our neighbors in Canada and Mexico for loans before moving on to Europe. Asia is more of a challenge and will take longer, but materials will be sent. The U.S. Postal Service (USPS) is the most common way to send library materials, but always ship first class to Canada or Mexico, and use air mail to Europe or Asia. Use a tracking number or pay a little extra for delivery signature, guaranteed delivery, or insurance. On customs forms, always declare "no value" and write "Content: Library materials books/ photocopies" on packages. Doing so should avoid duty payments and delays at borders

PAYMENT METHODS

Other than IFM, the most common form of international payment is by invoice, which is paid by a check from your institution or a credit card. Credit cards handle money conversion easily. The invoice process will have to be explained to you by your institution. A problem sometimes arises when the invoice is in a foreign currency and the payment is by check in dollars. One approach is to ask your payment office if you can provide the amount requested in U.S. dollars. If they agree, you need only use an online currency converter. Some foreign institutions will not be pleased because their banks will charge a conversion fee, so they may indicate this.

I.F.L.A. INTERNATIONAL LOAN/PHOTOCOPY REQUEST FORM FORMULAIRE DE DEMANDE DE PRET/PHOTOCOPIE INTERNATIONAL COPY B EXEMPLAIRE B	Request ref no/Patron identifier No de commande/identité de lecteur	
Borrowing library's address Adresse de la bibliothèque emprunteuse	Needed by Demande avant	Quote if cost exceeds Prix si plus que
	Shelfmark Cot de placement	
	Request for: ☐ Loan ☐ Photocopy ☐ Microform Commande de: Pret Photocopie	
	Report/Reponse	

Books, Author, title - Livres, Auteur, titre/Serials, Title, article title, author - Périodiques Titre, titre de l'article, auteur

☐ Part not held/Volume /fascicule non detenu

☐ Title not held /nous n'avons pas ce titre

☐ Not traced/Ne figure pas dans cette bibl.

☐ Not for loan/Exclu de prêt

Place of Publication Lieu de publication	Publisher Editeur

☐ Copyright restrictions

Year-Annee	Volume-Tome	Part-No	Pages	ISBN/ISSN

☐ Not immediately available. Reapply in......weeks Non disponible actuellement. Renouvelez la

Edition	Source of verification/reference Référence bibliographique/Verification

demande dans............semaines

☐ Lent until/Prêté jusqu'au...................

Lending library's address/adresse de la bibliothèque prêteuse

☐ Use in library only/A consulter sur place uniquement

I declare that this publication is required only for the purpose of research or private study. Je déclare que cette publication n'est demandé qu'à des fins de recherche ou d'étude privée.

Signature..................................

Date. ....

Figure 10.1.   IFLA Interlending Form

Figure 10.2. IFLA International Payment Voucher

IFLA vouchers are an internationally recognized and convenient way to pay for foreign requests. They come as full vouchers for $12 and half vouchers for $6 each. They can be sent along with the request, with the returned loan, or separately through the USPS since the vouchers require physical transfer. That the Library of Congress requires three vouchers to lend a book and two vouchers to provide an article photocopy is a possible guide for others. Vouchers can be purchased in the United States from the OCLC and charged to the monthly OCLC bill. Forms can be downloaded at https://www.oclc.org/forms/ifla-vouchers.en.html.

Even simpler is the use of an OCLC blank online ILL request form. Enter VOUCH as the lender and "IFLA vouchers needed" as the title. The IFM box must be checked and a dollar amount listed as your MAXCOST. The borrowing note should state, "I want to purchase (number) IFLA vouchers." The number requested should equal the amount put in MAXCOST.

RECORD KEEPING

Make your international ILL requests part of your usual online or manual record keeping no matter how the request is sent. In your online ILL management software (e.g., ILLiad, Clio, or WorldShare), create a dummy symbol for a foreign library nonlender. Then input contact information from the OCLC policies directory or the WorldCat Registry into you nonlender record. Enter two letters from the country name, followed by an underscore, and then the OCLC symbol to identify your library.

An example is BNMEX for the Biblioteca Nacional de México. The OCLC policies directory provides an address but no further contact information for them; however, TROEL for Alliant International University does provide a street address and e-mail address. Since both are in Mexico City, the latter might help you with access to the former. ILL is all about people and connections. Be sure to follow the same pattern for your country prefix and also tag the requests as international for statistical purposes. They will add an interesting dimension to your annual report.

1. Put this symbol in the ILL software lending string. Generate an e-mail to send the request as an e-mail to their ILL department.
2. Include your payment terms.
3. Put "request sent" in the queue created for these requests.

E-MAIL OR FAX REQUEST DETAILS

Template 1: Request for an Article (Based on IFLA Guidelines)
From:
Date: Supplied by system if e-mail
To:
Subject:

Dear Colleague:
Are you able to supply the following journal article to our patron?
Journal title, year, volume, part, page number:
Article title and author:
Call number/shelf mark:
Verification source:
This would be CCG or CCL for copyright compliance.
Patron:
We prefer to pay with IFLA ILL Vouchers. Max cost is _____ IFLA ILL vouchers. Or we prefer to pay with invoice. Max cost is U.S. $_____.
Billing address:
Urgent request: Needed before _____
Please send the item to: Name of library and full address.

Thank you.
Your name and title
Your e-mail
Your fax

Template 2: Request for a Loan (Based on IFLA Guidelines)
From:
Date: Supplied by system if e-mail
To:
Subject:

Dear Colleague:
According to your catalog, you hold:
Bibliographic description:
Call number/shelf mark:
Verification source:
Would you be willing to lend?
We prefer to pay with IFLA ILL Vouchers. Max cost is _____ IFLA ILL
vouchers. Or we prefer to pay with invoice. Max cost is U.S. $_____.
Billing address:
Urgent request: Needed before _____
Please send the item to: Name of library and full address.

Thank you.
Your name and title
Your e-mail
Your fax

CONCLUSION

Live and function in the present while we hear the many conflicting statements about our library future. Enjoy the challenges. Resource sharing is increasing. Resource sharing is decreasing. We're busier than ever. No one uses the library anymore. Global library service is attainable. ILL will cease to exist. Information wants to be free. Everything has a price (Fredericksen, Bean, and Nance, 2012).

What keeps me up at night is thinking about the books, journals, newsletters, newspapers, records, films, music, and documents that are in my region in various libraries. How can I gain access to them? I can request most of them on ILL through the OCLC or our regional system, but I like to browse in libraries and then take them with me. Open Access provides this option at the local community colleges, but not at the local private colleges. In the next chapter, we will discuss consortial arrangements that include groups of different libraries and even what worked better with an ALA form in the past and may work again one day.

REFERENCES

Aman, Mohammad M. (1989). "Document Delivery and Interlibrary Lending in the Arab countries." *Interlending and Document Supply* 17, no. 3: 84–88.

Bowker, Richard R. (1909). "Remarks." *ALA Bulletin: Papers and Proceedings, 31st Annual Meeting of ALA* 3: 156.

Dewey, Melville (1888). "Inter-library Loans." *Library Notes* 3: 405–7.

Fang, Conghui (2007). "The History and Development of Interlibrary Loans and Document Supply in China." *Interlending and Document Supply* 35, no. 3: 145–53.

Fleming, Robyn (2012). "Demysitifying International ILL." Illiad International Conference, Atlas Workshop, March 23. Available online at http://www.atlas-sys.com/conference2012/presentations/Demystifying%20International%20ILL.pdf (accessed February 4, 2013).

Fredericksen, Linda, Margaret Bean, and Heidi Nance (2012). *Global Resource Sharing*. Oxford, UK: Chandos Publishing.

Gravit, Francis W. (1946). "A Proposed Interlibrary Loan System in the Seventeenth Century." *Library Quarterly* 16, no. 4: 331–34.

11

On-the-Spot Interlibrary Loan

Come take choice
Of all my library,
And so beguile
Thy sorrow.

—William Shakespeare, *Titus Andronicus*

Some people know exactly what they want and, like a friend of mine, will wait months to get it. When she learned that I was planning to write about resource sharing, she contacted me to tell me that she adores interlibrary loan (ILL). That was after she asked me, "What is resource sharing?" She said, "I've had books on Amerindian history turn up eighteen months after I requested them at my public library, and it was worth the wait." Some of my faculty colleagues will also wait. The longest wait was for a May 1932 complete issue of the British edition of *Good Housekeeping*, located in an English library that had placed it in storage for the summer while undergoing renovation. My friend was studying the placement of stories and continuation pages in magazines. Photocopies of the stories themselves would not meet her need.

Today there is a network of library collections in libraries close to each and every one of us, and thousands more throughout the world. The largest network of library content, known as WorldCat, is located on the Web, and it is where most people start their search for information. If you are looking to check out books, music, or media, or research articles and such recorded items as audiobooks to borrow or download, you can search numerous libraries at once and locate what you are looking for at a library nearby (http://www.worldcat.org/wcpa/content/whatis).

Patrons regularly contact libraries to ask if an item is there, assuming that means they have access to it. Membership is needed to check out an item and, in some cases, even to enter that library. Public-library cards often give patrons the ability to borrow books and media from any system library, as well as request that the item be delivered to their home library, and sometimes their office or home.

SPECIAL ARRANGEMENTS

We need to become increasingly flexible and collaborative to provide user-centered library services. Students leave during the summer but continue working for professors or, increasingly, take classes online. Retired faculty who move to new locations hope to continue their area of research but will not be recognized by the local college or university library. They become like the unattached scholars, who write books or articles or do research as part of their work but sometimes lack the library connections they need to do so.

In the 1980s, the Archives Libraries Committee of the African Studies Association produced a guide called *The Lonely Africanist* to allow access to the major collections on Africa throughout the United States. The premise was that faculty at colleges without departments or programs on Africa lacked resources needed for their research but should be recognized and aided, as many were their former graduate students. With on-site access to collections and Africana bibliographers, although without checkout privileges, they were better prepared for the use of ILL upon return to their home library.

Some public libraries in tourist areas allow visitors to borrow books and media. This is a concept that could be more widely explored by local governments, chambers of commerce, and tourism websites. Could libraries play a more visible role as a point of interest for tourists? Libraries are a vibrant dimension of the local culture, and the people working in them are a wonderful source of community information.

I first came in contact with this premise while living in South Africa. Although my family and I had become members of the local library in Grahamstown, it was upon a visit to East London, situated by the "Sunshine Coast" on the Indian Ocean, that I learned about a willingness to check out books to visitors staying there for only a few weeks. The visitor was expected to have a library card from within the country or overseas, but no effort was made to verify their connection. From discussion I learned that while a few books were lost or returned late by mail, the local government strongly supported this service and enhanced their library budget.

SYSTEM BORROWING

The State University of New York (SUNY) system, which covers sixty-four campuses plus Empire State College (tutored and online study), has a policy of opening its library resources on every campus to all students, faculty, and other employees with the presentation of a valid ID card from one's home campus. Registration is required, which means that a complete record will be created at the circulation desk for each visitor. Those records remain in the system indefinitely, even if the person never visits one of the libraries again. If they do return, the record must be updated upon presentation of their current ID card. After registration is completed, any materials may be borrowed or used there, depending upon policies, and reference or other services received as if one belonged to that campus.

In this open-access agreement, overdue notices are sent by the lending library circulation department directly to the user, who is liable for the same overdue fines or charges, or lost or damaged items, as levied at the lending campus. If there is no response, staff at the borrower's library are expected to help "with general advice or to answer specific inquiries," but not to take responsibility for the unresponsive student or faculty member, or pay for the lost item. Each circulation department is expected to create its own "directory of addresses and phone numbers of other libraries in the SUNY system." With open access, the lending library is working on its own; however, borrowed items left with us will be returned to any SUNY libraries. Circulation just uses the ILL delivery system.

Grumbling is heard from circulation departments in SUNY when an open-access loan is lost and there is not the desired level of cooperation from another campus's circulation department. Consortium borrowing lacks the network of trust and co-operation that has resulted not just from the national and international ILL agreements, but also from the understanding that develops when all libraries realize that they cannot be self-sufficient. Similar arrangements exist in other circulation-based borrowing arrangements; however, unlike ILL, where the loan is between libraries, the borrower's library does not take responsibility.

THE INTERLIBRARY LOAN CODE

The Interlibrary Loan Code for the United States, first adopted by the American Library Association (ALA) in 1917, and last revised in 2008, states that the same conduct is expected from each participating library. The regional, state, and international codes all repeat the following statement. Some library personnel balk when they first read it, but everyone soon realizes that it is the key to continued access. Remember that Collette Mak says in the introduction to this book, "As I have told many a library user, until the book arrives, we're working for you; as soon as that book arrives, we're working for the library that lent it to us." Per the Interlibrary Loan Code for the United States,

> Assume responsibility for borrowed material from the time it leaves the supplying library until it has been returned to and received by the supplying library. This includes all material shipped directly to and/or returned by the user. If damage or loss occurs, provide compensation or replacement, in accordance with the preference of the supplying library.

Developing a relationship between librarians responsible for ILL seems easy. An international directory of more than 7,000 libraries exists for ILL staff that describes libraries of all types (https://illpolicies.oclc.org). While providing descriptions of available collections, the greatest value lies in the names, addresses, telephone numbers, and e-mail addresses of the people to contact. We meet the needs of our patrons through the help of other libraries because we all know that no one library can have everything our patrons need. The Interlibrary Loan Code for the United States explains in its introduction the basic premise of ILL:

> In the interest of providing quality service, libraries have an obligation to obtain material to meet the informational needs of users when local resources do not meet those needs. Interlibrary loan (ILL), a mechanism of obtaining material, is essential to the vitality of all libraries. The effectiveness of the national interlibrary loan system depends upon participation of libraries of all types and sizes.

BLURRING THE LINES

Students currently enrolled at any of Massachusetts' twenty-nine public institutions of higher education may borrow from any other campus library through the "Walk-in Interlibrary Loan" (W.I.L.L) program. They must show a valid student ID that shows proof of enrollment to check out materials. Use of the term *interlibrary loan* appears to indicate that the library will take responsibility for what the student borrows if there is not adequate response to a lending library circulation department overdue notice or lost loan invoice; however, the administrators who initiated this agreement did not include any statement of the borrower's library responsibility, and problems have resulted.

Patrons sometimes complain upon hearing that a book or DVD they need is out on ILL. Learning that "not available" in the code allows that the item can be requested from another library usually satisfies the patron, who probably has benefited in the past from ILL. Cooperative and consortial resource-sharing arrangements are blurring the lines between circulation and ILL.

My local public library is part of the Mid-Hudson Library System, along with ninety other public libraries located in several neighboring counties. I can, with my library card, check out items at any of these libraries and then return them through my local public library. Of course, to avoid fines, I must honor due dates. I can also check out items in four public libraries in a different system, because they are located in my county. Several of the other fifty-nine public libraries in that system are closer than some in my system, but I cannot use my card at those sites.

In all open-access borrowing arrangements, loaned items can be returned to any library, and they will usually be sent home through the delivery system used for ILL. Libraries also find books in return bins that are not from any system or consortial library. Wherever they belong, ILL staff will return them to the owner library, knowing that they would receive the same courtesy.

BORROWING PROGRAM CHANGES AT MAJOR UNIVERSITIES

ILL SHARES began as a collaborative effort within the ARL that formed the Research Libraries Group (RLG) to create their online catalog, the Research Libraries Information Network (RLIN). The New York Public Library and the university libraries at Harvard, Columbia, and Yale joined with Stanford University to adopt their online processing system called BALLOTS, which evolved into RLIN. In 2006, RLG merged with the OCLC.

This access program was a remake of the ARL reciprocal borrowing program that allowed students, faculty, and staff at the 193 member universities to gain temporary on-site access and borrowing privileges at any of the libraries of the consortium. The OCLC continued the program, but only for ARL institution faculty. Before visiting one, a Reciprocal Faculty Borrowing Program Card had to be requested at the home library circulation desk. Bringing this to the circulation department of the library being visited determined whether the card would be accepted for on-site use and/or borrowing. Exact policies varied from library to library and had to be checked before visiting. It was the responsibility of faculty to do the following:

- Present identification when requesting the Reciprocal Faculty Borrowing Program Card
- Observe the regulations of the lending library
- Return materials in person or by mail within the loan period prescribed by the lending library
- Return materials immediately in person or by express mail if recalled by the lending library
- Pay any and all fines or other charges incurred due to late return of materials or damages to materials

Some open-access circulation agreements do not last, even when set up with the best of intentions at a high level of library organization. The ARL/OCLC ILL SHARES now enables participating institutions to agree on prices, procedures, and policies; monitor their own performance; and manage work flow to support increased lending activities. This has become an international sharing partnership—together with technology supplied by OCLC Research—that expands and enhances local collections with materials owned by partners throughout the world.

ILL SHARES is now an "interlending and document supply" program. The home page presents an enhanced ILL program and generous on-site access plan for SHARES participants (http://www.oclc.org/research/activities/shares/procedures

.html?urlm=160231). "On-site access privileges through SHARES partnership permit faculty, emeritus, faculty, students, and academic and professional library staff of partner institutions to use the collections and services at other SHARES libraries." The following policies are abridged:

- Visitors must present a current, valid institutional ID with photo or with other photo ID.
- In-library use is permitted, but not borrowing privileges. Stack access is the same as peers and advance arrangement for special or restricted collections.
- Access does not include alumni, all retired faculty, spouses, docents, or other nonmembers.
- Local protocols take precedence.
- Visitors can expect reference consultation, local rate copying, local database access rate, and other services to comparable host groups.
- Visitors cannot bring an ALA request form and expect to check out the requested item.
- Access is available during regular business hours of the library. Check in advance.

On the OCLC page discussing the benefits of SHARES participation, there is a quote from a Princeton University participant not identified. That this person could return to his or her university and request a number of items relevant to a research project is wonderful. That the liberal ILL SHARES ILL agreement allows unlimited numbers of volumes and microfilm reels supplied within ten days is impressive as well. But why not on-site ALA forms? According to the OCLC Research website,

> SHARES on-site access is essential. For long runs of items, it is often easier and more practical for the researcher to go to the holding library, particularly if relatively local. Also, researchers do not always have the time to wait for interlibrary loan. For the serious scholar, being able to actually browse a collection has enormous value.

PREPARATION FOR ON-SITE ACCESS

The Interlibrary Loan Code for the United States is already prepared for on-site access, demonstrated on section 4.9, which says that as part of ILL, libraries should "[a]ssume full responsibility for user-initiated transactions." To implement this as the basis for on-the-spot ILL between libraries with no consortia or system relationship, two steps are needed.

1. An introduction to indicate a patron in good standing who needs access to a collection.
2. A method for recording the on-site transaction between the lending library and the borrowing library.

Browsing and seeking the aid of librarians in another library collection will always be needed, even though libraries are promoting digitization of materials, e-books, and streaming video to make it possible never to leave your home.

ON-THE-SPOT ILL

A signed referral card from a public, school, academic, or special library accepted by ILL departments is the way to gain access to a library. You only need to demonstrate the need for this access for your patron in good standing. We are already learning that the library is their second "living room" and a place they all want to come. More than a year ago I started a discussion on the ILL-L listserv using the term *on-the-spot ILL*, a term coined by local regional systems librarian Judy Fischetti. I posted the following:

> I am interested in promoting people visiting collections and gaining checkout privileges. Sometimes visiting another library is useful. In days past, we would see patrons from public, school, academic, and special libraries in our region come with several ALA forms already signed for a patron it would benefit. They would bring selected books and completed forms to ILL staff to process. A copy would go with the book, a copy was mailed to the borrower's library, and the original stayed with us. Wonder how we could do this in the electronic age? Any ideas?

I received several responses. Kate Irwin-Smiler, of Wake Forest University, said,

> Consortia are great but are limited to libraries you know your patrons are going to visit. We have a lot of students who leave over the summer but continue working for professors (or, increasingly, take classes online) in faraway locations. Something like this through interlibrary loan could be a great benefit.

There are consortial agreements that involve unaffiliated public libraries and unaffiliated college libraries. One that has worked for a decade is in Iowa, where Robyn Clark-Bridges, of Mount Mercy University, says she can use her ID to "check out items from libraries at Coe College, Cornell College, Kirkwood Community College, [as well as] Cedar Rapids, Hiawatha, [and] Marion public libraries—all within an hour of [her] home." That this was reciprocal for all of the libraries mentioned is noted.

WALKING ILL

For decades a referral card has been used in the eight-county region where I live. It serves as an introduction for a patron from a school, public, special, or college library to a library where needed materials can be found. In the past, when combined with signed ALA forms, it also allowed for what we called a "walking interlibrary loan." The patron brought the completed forms to the ILL department, where minimal processing allowed the patron to borrow the items. A copy of the form was given to the visitor, a copy was filed, and a copy was sent to the library that took responsibility for the patron by signing the ALA forms.

Local discussion for what is now called "on-the-spot ILL" still involves bringing the items needed to the ILL department. Seated at a computer, the patron can complete his or her online ILL form and then submit it for processing at the home library, with a note designating where to send the request. A telephone call is usually needed to draw attention to this request and accelerate the process. Another method we have suggested is to fax the signed ALA forms (yes, they are still used) and ask the lending library to enter the request to our library into ILLiad, the same ILL management system that we use, or one that is ISO compatible.

Let us develop technology to support resource sharing for patrons "on the spot" by using the well-developed networks and policies that have been put in place throughout time by ILL librarians. Trust is the key and the basis for almost a century of ILL code-supported sharing between libraries. Patrons still try to contact libraries directly to borrow items, but it never works. Referral by ILL staff who know the patron is the best answer.

Paul B. Drake, of the University of Guam, recalled during the listserv discussion a few types of situations when he worked in Rhode Island, with patrons who tried to initiate "on-the-spot ILL" on their own. It turned out that the patron was not currently in good standing, not enrolled, or no longer employed. Verification of library records was necessary.

FINDING A BALANCE

In 1935, L. A. Burgess questioned ILL loans by asking, "First, are they economical?" and "Second, are they ethically justified?" His article, entitled "Co-operation Again," was reprinted in 1992, and it remains timely, as it raises the same concerns that are present today. Sending loans is expensive, some will want the materials for months, and it may not always be ethical to lend rare and valuable items or proper to request contemporary fiction and textbooks (Burgess, 1992, 43).

Thomas H. Ballard, a public library director, feels that "bibliographic networking is merely a return to the closed-stack concept." He asserts that "people want to browse among books," and that if people want ILL, they want to do it in the least costly way (1985, 257). Costs of consortia (Miller, 2010) and the "fear and loathing" of change proposed for collection development (Collins, 2012) may mean that local libraries should just buy what they believe suits the majority of their patrons.

CONCLUSION

Let us send those with special interests our blessing, a referral card, and several ALA request forms for the library they choose. Collections in local libraries offer great

Southeastern Referral Card
Southeastern New York Library Resources Council
P.O Box 879, Highland, New York 12528

Patron's Name:_____ Date: _____

Requests Access To:_____
(Name of Institution and Library)

Address: _____

For on-site use of the following materials (include Author and Title or Subject):_____

_____

Arrangements Made By: _____
(Name) (Title)

Library Making Referral:_____ Telephone: _____

VERSO

Procedures for Issuing a Southeastern Referral Card

TO THE USER: 1. This card permits on-site use of the material cited on the front of this card.

2. This card does not entitle you to borrow material.

3. This card does not guarantee that the material you wish to use will be available.

4. Policies of the local library supersede Referral Card policies.

Special Arrangements (if any):_____

HOST LIBRARY: Please return to SENYLRC

1. Was the user able to locate the items in your collection? Yes [ ] No [ ]

2. Did the user browse the subject area and find other materials? Yes [ ] No [ ]

General Comments:

Figure 11.1.   Southeastern Referral Card

ALA Interlibrary Loan Request Form 2002

Request date _____
Need before _____
Request number _____
Client information ....

Borrowing library name and address

Citation Information
Book author ....
Book title _____
Publisher _____ Place _____ Date _____
Series _____
This edition only _____ ISBN _____

Serial title _____
Volume / issue _____ Date _____ Pages _____
Author of article ....
Title of article _____
ISSN _____

Audiovisual title _____
Date of publication _____

Verified in and / or cited in _____
Other bibliographic number _____
Lending library name and address

Lending library phone _____
Lending library fax _____
Lending library email _____
Lending library electronic delivery address _____

Notes _____
_____

Request complies with
[   ] 108(g) (2) Guidelines (CCG)
[   ] other provision of copyright law (CCL)

Authorization _____
Phone _____
Fax _____
Email _____
Electronic delivery address _____

Type of request:
[   ] Loan
[   ] Photocopy
[   ] Estimate
[   ] Locations
Charge information
Account number _____
Maximum willing to pay _____
Have reciprocal agreement _____
Payment provided _____
Lending library report
Date of response _____
Date shipped _____
Shipped via _____
Insured for _____
Return Insured [   ]
Packing Requirements _____
Charge _____
Date due _____
Use restrictions
[   ] Library Use Only
[   ] Copying not permitted
[   ] No Renewals
[   ] _____
Not sent because
[   ] At bindery
[   ] Charge exceeds limit
[   ] Hold placed
[   ] In process
[   ] In use
[   ] Lacking
[   ] Lacks copyright compliance
[   ] Locations not found
[   ] Lost
[   ] Non-circulating
[   ] Not found as cited
[   ] Not on shelf
[   ] Not owned
[   ] On order
[   ] On reserve
[   ] Poor condition
[   ] Prepayment required
[   ] Request on _____
[   ] Volume / issue not yet available
[   ] _____
Estimate for
Loan _____
Copy _____
Microfilm _____
Microfiche _____
Borrowing library report
Date Received _____
Date Returned _____
Returned via _____
Insured for _____
Payment Enclosed [   ]
Renewals
Date Requested _____
New Due Date _____
Renewal Denied [   ]

Figure 11.2.   ALA Interlibrary Loan Form

variety, and these libraries provide librarians to aid your special interests. In the next chapter you will learn about efforts to place all the materials available in a region in the local library.

REFERENCES

Ballard, Thomas H. (1985). "Dogma Clouds the Facts." *American Libraries* 16, no. 4: 257–59.

Burgess, L. A. (1992). "Co-operation Again." *Journal of Interlibrary Loan and Information Supply* 2, no. 4: 39–46.

Clark-Bridges, Robyn (2012). E-mail to author, May 17.

Collins, Peter (2012). "Fear and Loathing in Cooperative Collection Development." *Interlanding and Document Supply* 40, no. 2: 100–104.

Drake, Paul B. (2012). E-mail to author, May 17.

Irwin-Smiler, Kate (2012). E-mail to author, May 17.

Miller, William (2010). "Libraries and Consortia: What Will Libraries Pay For?" *Journal of Interlibrary Loan, Document Delivery, and Electronic Reserve* 20, no. 4: 221–26.

12

Enhancing Discovery

Taking Responsibility at the Local Level

Every library should try to be complete on something, if it were only the history of pinheads.

—Oliver Wendell Holmes Sr. *The Poet at the Breakfast Table* (1872)

In its May 1, 2010 issue, *Library Journal* draws attention to the results of a country-wide faculty questionnaire in an article that claims that libraries are facing "potential irrelevance" (Oder, 2010, 12). According to its website, "ITHAKA was formed in 2003, as a not-for-profit organization dedicated to helping scholars take full advantage of rapidly advancing information and networking technologies." In 2009, ITHAKA absorbed JSTOR (short for Journal Storage), a nonprofit organized in 1995, to meet the concerns of librarians about the costs of scanning and maintaining collections of back issues of digitized journals for the long term. The three previous faculty surveys received little attention, but now when ITHAKA speaks, the library world listens. The 2009 report, compiled by Roger C. Schonfeld and Ross Housewright, summarizes its findings on libraries as follows: "Basic scholarly information use practices have shifted rapidly in recent years, and, as a result, the academic library is increasingly being disintermediated from the discovery process, risking irrelevance in one of its core functional areas."

In my published response to this survey, I challenged the view that librarians are no longer part of the discovery process. We continually adapt to the changing interests and requirements of our users. In fact, we experience patron needs that continue to grow, defying predictions, and maintain electronic networking that is global, involving libraries of all types. The challenge we should accept is not just to locate the needed information, but also to keep it where it can be found again, to enhance delivery (Nyquist, 2010).

UNIQUE HOLDINGS

In 1985, our chemistry department held an international conference on polymers. I knew nothing of this until I received a request for one of the presented papers. Curious and willing to make the effort, I tracked down the faculty organizer. Gathering papers for publication was still in process, and this was the first of several annual conferences, so my interlibrary loan (ILL) request was seen as an interruption to the organizer's work and also a deterrent to future attendance. Since campus support was involved, an informal agreement was made that resulted in the library receiving copies of the published proceedings. Thus, that first request was finally filled, as were many later requests as we promptly received each published volume for the four conferences that followed. I learned that attendance did not suffer. I also learned that the keyword was "plastics," as did Benjamin in the movie *The Graduate.*

We recently received a request for an article published in *Imhotep: Journal of Afrocentric Thought.* After locating it at Temple University, where it was an Africana studies graduate student journal, an ILL request was sent. It came back unfilled, as it was not listed in the main library catalog. Following an e-mail, a colleague went, as instructed, to the Africana library, where it was assumed they had the publication in their stacks. He made a photocopy, which he then scanned and sent to us, which was forwarded to the requester. We discovered that Temple now lists this in their catalog to make it more available.

We also received a news feed by e-mail that focused on published articles about our university system, known as SUNY, or the State University of New York. It noted an article interview with Vladimir Feltsman, "one of the greatest pianists for our time," who happens to be a faculty member on our campus. No longer able to perform in the Soviet Union because he applied for an exit visa, he was eventually rescued through the efforts of many Americans, including our former campus president, Alice Chandler, and even President Ronald Reagan. The article was in the April 2012 issue of the *Chronogram*, and the next day I could walk to one of many local shops or offices and find copies to read or take home.

The magazine is free, large, in color, and chock full of articles about people, places, events, and issues in the Hudson Valley, along with local advertisements. Published regionally since 2007, registered with the Library of Congress (LC), and listed in WorldCat with zero holdings, some of the articles can be found online on the magazine's website. There will be requests for this publication in the future. Published in Kingston, New York, the public library there now acquires and records one of the free copies they receive. In 2010, the SUNY University Press published *Learning to Be Human: Selections from Over Thirteen Years of "Esteemed Reader" Columns in Chronogram Magazine,* by Jason Stern, cofounder of the magazine. That book has been added to a few libraries.

THINK GLOBALLY, ACT LOCALLY

"Think globally, act locally" is a phrase that has been used in a variety of contexts. It encourages us to consider the entire planet as we are involved in activities in our own communities. While the Online Computer Library Center (OCLC) is using cloud computing to provide library cooperation and collaboration for access to the materials gathered by libraries throughout the world, the communities surrounding each of us have more to offer than is currently available in even those libraries, let alone the thousands of libraries not yet participating in the OCLC.

Campuses have conference proceedings, student newspapers, literary magazines, theses, dissertations, and locally produced media. Communities have newsletters and magazines, as well as books that are self-published locally. This archival role need not be limited to colleges, public libraries, local governments, and organizations. It is also suited to schools where the student's first contact with primary sources might be their school newspaper, yearbooks, trophies, and/or programs or media copies of school performances and athletic events.

PRIMARY SOURCES

We often forget the simple description of a primary source: It is the original material produced at the time. Did the school paper note any cast changes in a play that are not in the printed program? Both the program and the newspaper article are primary sources, even if they do not agree. If a school librarian found a collection of old school-theatre programs, a teacher could ask a grade school class to compare these programs with those produced today, look for other sources, or ask questions to learn more. There are multiple directions in which such a project could lead them, but best of all, it would prepare them for future research.

On numerous occasions while working at a college reference desk, I have been asked to help find a primary source for a research paper, only to discover that students equate this term with such important documents as the Declaration of Independence or scholarly research articles. Students need to build skills that prepare them for our complex world, which is overflowing with information. It is easier to go from the simple to the complex than vice versa.

Carleton Mabee, a Pulitzer Prize–winning historian at my college, asked for my help when he was writing a book on Sojourner Truth, for whom our library is named. He told me that he would need at least five newspaper accounts of each talk she gave, preferably published in the areas where the speeches took place, so that he could compare the accounts for use in his book. Later historians interested in the same topic read my colleague's book and then returned to those newspaper accounts for new insights. Newspaper accounts are primary sources, but they are not scholarly and sometimes not even reliable, but we do assume that the reporter had personal knowledge about what was written.

COLLECTION RESPONSIBILITIES

I have often wondered why the *New York African Studies Association Newsletter*, which receives annual dues from its members, also receives annual subscription payments from one overseas university library, in Germany, that collects it as part of a national plan for its world coverage. Association members teach about Africa and the Diaspora at college and university campuses in New York, and some campuses in neighboring states. Content includes annual conference summaries and articles by members, as well as association business and stories of those receiving our awards. The newsletter began on my campus and continues to be produced here, so I can see that copies are added to our catalog and kept in this library's special collection. We occasionally receive and fill requests for these articles.

Not too long ago, we received a borrowing request for an article from the *CEA Critic: An Official Journal of the College English Association.* With a large membership from throughout the United States, one would think that copies of this publication would reside in the college library in Ohio, where the request was submitted, or the college library in Colorado, where the journal's current editor is located. The WorldCat MARC record lists no American locations, but it does list two in Germany. Using contact information from the College English Association's website to request this article with the hope that someone was currently maintaining it led to the receipt of an article from that issue when the request was passed on to someone still collecting back issues.

We did the same thing for an academic newsletter with no MARC record but with a website listing officers and their institutions. It took more than a week to locate the current president, who referred us to a past president and their unofficial archivist, and another week to obtain the article. The next time we took the easy approach and sent the request electronically to the Bavarian State Library with the symbol GEBAY, for which we paid $12.00 electronically and received the article the same day. What we have here appears to be a variation on the "think global, act local" idea. Are these German libraries stepping forth to collect what we overlook?

EVEN HARDER TO FIND

Newsletters and association journals usually register for copyright and an ISSN (International Standard Serial Number). They need only provide one copy to the LC, state their intention to publish indefinitely, and show how they designate issues numerically so that they can be checked in. Self-published authors usually seek protection of intellectual property through copyright and thereby receive a MARC record. The LC does not catalog all of its deposits. Another category of materials that is even more difficult to find and deliver is what librarians call grey (or gray) literature. Small print runs and formats lacking such basic information as author, publication date, or even the responsible publishing organization make collecting and organizing such materials difficult. Yet, many people want them.

Grey literature is usually distinguished from ephemera, an item that is generally thrown away after one use. Those school programs discussed earlier are both primary sources and ephemera. The word derives from the Greek, meaning things lasting no more than a day. They can also be called collectables, the kind of things we save for memories and that some libraries collect as history. The Bodleian Library, in Oxford, has such an archive of more than sixty-five thousand images in the John Johnson Collection; two thousand of these items are searchable online at http://www.bodle ian.ox.ac.uk/Johnson.

The Fourth International Conference on Grey Literature (GL '99), held in Washington, DC, in October 1999, defined grey literature as follows: "That which is produced on all levels of government, academics, business, and industry in print and electronic formats, but which is not controlled by commercial publishers." Add nonprofit organizations to that list.

A COMPLETE COLLECTION

In 1980, I was asked to prepare a publication titled *A Community Resource Manual* to accompany the *Handbook on Human Rights and Citizenship*, developed by the State Education Department to support human rights curriculum units for New York state schools. As the director of the World Study Center at my college, I was familiar with the major international covenants on human rights, and somewhat familiar with the international legal institutions in place to handle violations of human rights. At that time, the U.S. Government had not ratified any of the United Nations covenants on human rights, but with direction from President Jimmy Carter, it was one of our foreign-policy goals.

By consulting the fifth edition of Lee Ash's *Subject Collections: A Guide to Special Book Collections and Subject Emphases as Reported by University, College, Public, and Special Libraries and Museums in the United States and Canada*, I learned that there was a Center for Human Rights nearby at Columbia University. Visiting with J. Paul Martin, the librarian in charge, I encountered a collection of publications that was astounding. They came from throughout the world from all kinds of sources in a wide variety of formats. I focused on those applicable to my project, from nonprofit organizations that were based in the United States.

There were reports, pamphlets, newsletters, journals, meeting proceedings, occasional papers, brochures, and even self-published books. These publishing activists included lawyers groups, every church denomination, peace groups, reporter committees, academic associations concerned with each overseas area, and humanitarian organizations. They were gathering and disseminating information to document violations of human rights to their membership and the general community, but not to librarians, unless you were added to each mailing list. Although I visited several other collections, this was the basis for the *Community Resource Manual.*

FINDING GREY LITERATURE

So now you know that generally speaking, grey literature is "material that is not readily available through normal channels." Libraries, publishers, professional associations, government agencies, or other normal suppliers cannot provide it. It is either issued in limited amounts or was considered ephemeral and few kept it. Grey literature is also cited in various ways by articles, in personal communication, or on the Web. Portland State University librarians handling ILL conducted a study of cancelled requests in 2003–2004 and found that of the 2.5 percent of cancelled requests, 85 percent of them (672 requests) had no suppliers. They were labeled as grey literature.

The three main reasons why requests are usually cancelled are as follows:

1. There is no OCLC supplier.
2. No alternative sources can be found.
3. No back issues are available from the publisher.

Librarian responses to the 672 hard-to-fill requests were as follows:

- Contact the user for a copy of the original citation.
- Confer with a subject specialist for additional help.
- Review grey literature publisher pathfinders. (Auger, 1994; Matthews, 2004)
- Contact an outside source, for example, the article author or publisher.
- Suggest other titles or refer the patron to a subject specialist for a reference interview.
- Suggest that the user attend a bibliographic instruction session to learn new research strategies.

Their current e-mail cancellation notice, which I also use, is to recommend that the patron contact the author, and the e-mail address is provided. Their other message is referral to the library subject specialist, who, in my library, is the liaison librarian (Buchanan, Jackson, and Oberlander, 2004, 6–7).

I mention in an earlier chapter that ILL librarians believe that we can do it all. But how far should we go, and do we have the time needed? Should we send the request to the author on behalf of the patron? Does providing the e-mail address for the author promote communication, or is it a dead end? To what extent should we involve others inside (reference, liaisons) or outside of the library (area special collections) in the quest?

Ironically, my library experiences have sometimes given me wrong choices. While working in a public library in Skokie, Illinois, I thought patrons did not need "hand holding," but I was wrong and was told to guide every patron to the needed item. I was wrong again when I started work in a college library. I was scolded for leading a patron into the stacks to find a book. Have you read the Brothers Grimm fairy tale *Hans im Glück* (*Hans in Luck*)? He always tried to do the right thing but usually made the wrong choice. Now colleges follow the public library approach with patrons. So what is our role in ILL? What choices do we make?

WHY CARE ABOUT SPECIAL NEEDS?

Cross-training within the library and developing connections between library staff members from different types of libraries in the region is important. Special collections make your library special, but only if they are "properly cataloged for discovery and then made available for use" (Pritchard, 2009). "Hidden collections," as they are now called in Association of College and Research Libraries (ACRL) discussions, are needed for research, and ILL wants to abide by the Five Laws of S. R. Ranganathan.

Some call them the Five Laws of Library Science, since they were part of a theory proposed by Ranganathan, a university librarian and professor of mathematics in India. He was president of the Indian Library Association in the 1950s and is honored by library associations for his fundamental thinking about librarianship. In India, his birthday is celebrated every year on August 12, as National Library Day. The laws are as follows, as modified by others:

1. Books [and other resources] are for use.
2. Every reader his [or her] book [or information].
3. Every book [journal or media] its reader [user].
4. Save the time of the reader [patron].
5. The library is a growing organism.

The Rethinking Resource Sharing Initiative (RRSI) manifesto, issued in 2007, encourages libraries to get users what they want "without undue hurdles from the library community" in the "delivery format" of their choice, allowing "global access to sharable resources . . . including those in special collections. No material that is findable should be totally unattainable."

APPROPRIATE RESPONSES

What is the appropriate response to requests for material in special collections? Start the discussion with the individuals involved in digitizing or collecting at your institution. There are differing views on who should have access to original materials, locally or on ILL. Should all access wait until items are digitized with high-quality scanning and complete metadata for planned use by patrons? Some other collections focus only on people who visit the special collections. By making others aware of the requests received in ILL, your library may decide to collect more items produced on your campus, in your school, or in your community. Many library staff are unaware of efforts made by the working group of the Association of Research Libraries (ARL) that produced a report on interlibrary access entitled *Special Collections in ARL Libraries: A Discussion Report from the ARL Working Group on Special Collections* (2009). This was followed in 2013 by joint ARL and ITHAKA online report on how are digital collections being sustained. It is titled "Searching for Sustainability: Strategies from Eight Digitized Special Collections."

A major concern on the part of special collections is that items taken to ILL for scanning are often left on carts in the ILL office, sometimes overnight, or in circulation to wait for reshelving. On the other hand, administrators should be made aware of ILL requests so that libraries can "design flexible new services around those parts of the research process that cause researchers the most frustration and difficulty" (Bourg, Coleman, and Erway, 2009, 1). Every library has unique material and should make it available.

SOME DIGITIZATION MAY BE PERMANENT

There are numerous guides online and in journal articles leading you and your patrons to the sources of gray (the United Kingdom uses grey) literature and rare or special materials. Most useful are the guides created by Brian Matthews, and the article he published in *C&RL News* in 2004 is now claimed to be permanently available on the Wayback Machine, a digital archive of the World Wide Web (http://archive.is/XZ71X). This is something that could preserve the numerous items being digitized.

The archive site was named as a reference to an animated cartoon series called *The Rocky and Bullwinkle Show*. In it, a time machine appears called WABAC (pronounced as Wayback). The device appears to "witness, participate in, and, more often than not, alter famous events in history"; it is an approach to archiving the Internet (Kahle, 1997, 83). Until we know that digitization can be permanent, let us learn the story of microfilm. That was when they destroyed books to save them by cutting off the bindings to make it easier to microfilm the pages when placed flat (Baker, 2001). Microfilm was first presented as providing a library in a shoebox (Herring, 2007). Does it cost more to rent space for a book or keep it online?

CONCLUSION

Maybe this is the curatorial role mentioned for librarians that I questioned in the ITHAKA report. And maybe the discovery that many library schools, although still not teaching resource sharing, are developing archival programs tells us that special collections will continue to be developed, giving us a unique discovery approach. At my library we are developing a collection on Sojourner Truth. She is the first black woman to be honored with a bust in our nation's capital, and, as previously mentioned, my library is named after her. There is a photograph of her with President Lincoln. She did meet him, but the photo is a composite fake. Whether you go to library school or not, become involved in the discussion of the library, past, present, and future.

REFERENCES

Association of Research Libraries (2009). *Special Collections in ARL Libraries: A Discussion Report from the ARL Working Group on Special Collections*. Washington, DC: Association of Research Libraries. http://www.arl.org/storage/documents/publications/scwg-report mar09.pdf

Auger, C. P. (1994). *Information Sources in Grey Literature*, 3rd ed. London: Bowker-Sauer.

Baker, Nicholson (2001). *Double Fold: Libraries and the Assault on Paper*. New York: Random House.

Bourg, Chris, Ross Coleman, and Ricky Erway, with input from the RLG Partnership Research Information Management Roadmap Working Group (2009). "Support for the Research Process: An Academic Manifesto." Available online at http://www.oclc.org/content/dam/research/publications/library/2009/2009-07.pdf?urlm=162924 (accessed December 1, 2013).

Buchanan, Sherry, Rose M. Jackson, and Cyril Oberlander (2004). "Can Cooperative Service Solve the Grey Literature Challenge?" *Oregon Library Association Quarterly* 10, nos. 2/3: 5–9.

Fourth International Conference on Grey Literature: New Frontiers in Grey Literature, Grey Literature Network Service. (1999). Washington, DC, October 4–5.

Gee, C. William, and L. K. Gypsye Legge (2012). "Unthinkable Horror or Emerging Best Practice? Exploring Access to Special Collection Materials through Interlibrary Loan." *North Carolina Libraries* 70, no. 1: 2–14.

Herring, Mark (2007). *Fools Gold: Why the Internet Is No Substitute for a Library*. Jefferson, NC: McFarland.

ITHAKA S+R and Association of Research Libraries (2013). *Searching for Sustainability: Strategies from Eight Digitized Special Collections*. Washington, DC: Association of Research Libraries. Available online http://www.arl.org/storage/documents/publications/searching-for-sustainability-report-nov2013.pdf (accessed May 15, 2014).

Kahle, Brewster (1997). "Preserving the Internet." *Scientific American* 276, no. 3: 82–84.

Matthews, Brian (2004). "Grey Literature Resources for Locating Unpublished Research." *C&RL News* 65, no. 3: 125–28. Also available at http://archive.is/SZ71X (accessed December 12, 2013).

Nyquist, Corinne (2010). "An Academic Librarian's Response to the ITHAKA Faculty Survey 2009." *Journal of Interlibrary Loan, Document Delivery, and Electronic Reserve* 20, no. 4: 275–80.

Oder, Norman, Lynn Blumenstein, Barbara Genco, Barbara Hoffert, and Rebecca Miller (2010). "Faculty Survey: Libraries Face Potential Irrelevance." *Library Journal* 135, no. 8: 12.

156 Chapter 12

Online Computer Library Center (2009). "Treasures on Trucks and Other Taboos: Rethinking the Sharing of Special Collections." *OCLC Research*, June 5. Available online at http://www5.oclc.org/downloads/programsandresearch/parcasts/20090528Schaffner&Massie.mp4 (accessed December 12, 2013).

Pritchard, Sara (2009). "Special Collections Surge to the Fore." *Libraries and the Academy* 9, no. 2: 177–80.

Rethinking Resource Sharing Initiative. "A Manifesto for Rethinking Resource Sharing." Available online at http://rethinkingresourcesharing.org/manifesto/ (accessed December 12, 2013).

Schonfeld, Roger C., and Ross Housewright (2010). "U.S. Faculty Survey 2009: Key Insights for Libraries, Publishers, and Societies." *ITHAKA*. Available online at http://www.sr.ithaka.org/research-publications/us-faculty-survey-2009 (accessed December 12, 2013).

Appendix A

Code of Ethics of the
American Library Association

As members of the American Library Association, we recognize the importance of codifying and making known to the profession and to the general public the ethical principles that guide the work of librarians, other professionals providing information services, library trustees, and library staffs.

Ethical dilemmas occur when values are in conflict. The American Library Association Code of Ethics states the values to which we are committed and embodies the ethical responsibilities of the profession in this changing information environment.

We significantly influence or control the selection, organization, preservation, and dissemination of information. In a political system grounded in an informed citizenry, we are members of a profession explicitly committed to intellectual freedom and the freedom of access to information. We have a special obligation to ensure the free flow of information and ideas to present and future generations.

The principles of this Code are expressed in broad statements to guide ethical decision making. These statements provide a framework; they cannot and do not dictate conduct to cover particular situations.

1. We provide the highest level of service to all library users through appropriate and usefully organized resources; equitable service policies; equitable access; and accurate, unbiased, and courteous responses to all requests.
2. We uphold the principles of intellectual freedom and resist all efforts to censor library resources.
3. We protect each library user's right to privacy and confidentiality with respect to information sought or received and resources consulted, borrowed, acquired, or transmitted.
4. We respect intellectual property rights and advocate balance between the interests of information users and rights holders.

5. We treat coworkers and other colleagues with respect, fairness, and good faith, and advocate conditions of employment that safeguard the rights and welfare of all employees of our institutions.
6. We do not advance private interests at the expense of library users, colleagues, or our employing institutions.
7. We distinguish between our personal convictions and professional duties and do not allow our personal beliefs to interfere with fair representation of the aims of our institutions or the provision of access to their information resources.
8. We strive for excellence in the profession by maintaining and enhancing our own knowledge and skills, by encouraging the professional development of coworkers, and by fostering the aspirations of potential members of the profession.

Adopted at the 1939 Midwinter Meeting by the ALA Council. Amended June 30, 1981; June 28, 1995; and January 22, 2008. Used with permission from the American Library Association, www.ala.org.

Appendix B

Interlibrary Loan Code
for the United States

Introduction

The Reference and User Services Association, acting for the American Library Association in its adoption of this code, recognizes that the sharing of material between libraries is an integral element in the provision of library service and believes it to be in the public interest to encourage such an exchange.

In the interest of providing quality service, libraries have an obligation to obtain material to meet the informational needs of users when local resources do not meet those needs. Interlibrary loan (ILL), a mechanism for obtaining material, is essential to the vitality of all libraries. The effectiveness of the national interlibrary loan system depends upon participation of libraries of all types and sizes.

This code establishes principles that facilitate the requesting of material by a library and the provision of loans or copies in response to those requests. In this code, "material" includes books, audiovisual materials, and other returnable items, as well as copies of journal articles, book chapters, excerpts, and other nonreturnable items.

1.0 Definition

1.1 Interlibrary loan is the process by which a library requests material from, or supplies material to, another library.

2.0 Purpose

2.1 The purpose of interlibrary loan as defined by this code is to obtain, upon request of a library user, material not available in the user's local library.

3.0 Scope

3.1 This code regulates the exchange of material between libraries in the United States.

159

3.2 Interlibrary loan transactions with libraries outside of the United States are governed by the International Federation of Library Associations and Institutions' *International Lending: Principles and Guidelines for Procedure.*

4.0 Responsibilities of the Requesting Library
4.1 Establish, promptly update, and make available an interlibrary borrowing policy.

4.2 Ensure the confidentiality of the user.

4.3 Describe completely and accurately the requested material following accepted bibliographic practice.

4.4 Identify libraries that own the requested material and check and adhere to the policies of potential supplying libraries.

4.5 When no libraries can be identified as owning the needed material, requests may be sent to libraries believed likely to own the material, accompanied by an indication that ownership is not confirmed.

4.6 Transmit interlibrary loan requests electronically whenever possible.

4.7 For copy requests, comply with the U.S. copyright law (Title 17, U.S. Code) and its accompanying guidelines.

4.8 Assume responsibility for borrowed material from the time it leaves the supplying library until it has been returned to and received by the supplying library. This includes all material shipped directly to and/or returned by the user. If damage or loss occurs, provide compensation or replacement, in accordance with the preference of the supplying library.

4.9 Assume full responsibility for user-initiated transactions.

4.10 Honor the due date and enforce any use restrictions specified by the supplying library. The due date is defined as the date the material is due to be checked-in at the supplying library.

4.11 Request a renewal before the item is due. If the supplying library does not respond, the requesting library may assume that a renewal has been granted, extending the due date by the same length of time as the original loan.

4.12 All borrowed material is subject to recall. Respond immediately if the supplying library recalls an item.

4.13 Package material to prevent damage in shipping and comply with any special instructions stated by the supplying library.

4.14 Failure to comply with the provisions of this code may be reason for suspension of service by a supplying library.

5.0 Responsibilities of the Supplying Library

5.1 Establish, promptly update, and make available an interlibrary lending policy.

5.2 Consider filling all requests for material regardless of format.

5.3 Ensure the confidentiality of the user.

5.4 Process requests in a timely manner that recognizes the needs of the requesting library and/or the requirements of the electronic network or transmission system being used. If unable to fill a request, respond promptly and state the reason the request cannot be filled.

5.5 When filling requests, send sufficient information with each item to identify the request.

5.6 Indicate the due date and any restrictions on the use of the material and any special return packaging or shipping requirements. The due date is defined as the date the material is due to be checked-in at the supplying library.

5.7 Ship material in a timely and efficient manner to the location specified by the requesting library. Package loaned material to prevent loss or damage in shipping. Deliver copies electronically whenever possible.

5.8 Respond promptly to requests for renewals. If no response is sent, the requesting library may assume that a renewal has been granted, extending the due date by the same length of time as the original loan.

5.9 Loaned material is subject to recall at any time.

5.10 Failure to comply with the provisions of this code may lead to suspension of service to the requesting library.

For more detailed information about the provisions of this code, see the explanatory supplement in appendix C.

Used with permission from the American Library Association, www.ala.org. Prepared by the Interlibrary Loan Committee, Reference and User Services Association (RUSA), 1994, revised 2001. Revised 2008, by the Sharing and Transforming Access to Resources Section (STARS).

Appendix C

Interlibrary Loan Code for the U.S. Explanatory Supplement

Note: For Use with the Interlibrary Loan Code for the United States (May 2008).

This Explanatory Supplement is intended to amplify specific sections of the Interlibrary Loan Code for the United States, providing fuller explanation and specific examples for text that is intentionally general and prescriptive. Topical headings refer to the equivalent sections in the code. Libraries are expected to comply with the code, using this supplement as a source for general direction.[1]

Introduction
The U.S. Interlibrary Loan Code, first published in 1917, and adopted by the American Library Association in 1919, is designed to provide a code of behavior for requesting and supplying material within the United States. This code does not override individual or consortial agreements or regional or state codes which may be more liberal or more prescriptive. This national code is intended to provide guidelines for exchanges between libraries where no other agreement applies. The code is intended to be adopted voluntarily by U.S. libraries and is not enforced by an oversight body. However, as indicated below, supplying libraries may suspend service to borrowing libraries that fail to comply with the provisions of this code.

This interlibrary loan code describes the responsibilities of libraries to each other when requesting material for users. Increasingly libraries are allowing users to request material directly from suppliers. This code makes provision for direct patron requesting and at the same time affirms the responsibility of the patron's library for the safety and return of the borrowed material, or for paying the cost of a nonreturnable item sent directly to the patron.

Technology has expanded access options beyond traditional library-to-library transactions. Unmediated requests, direct-to-user delivery, purchase-on-demand options, and increasing full-text availability are exciting developments in resource sharing. At present, the Interlibrary Loan Code reflects established practices. However, libraries and other information centers are encouraged to explore and use nontraditional means where available to ensure maximum accessibility and convenience for users. More information for libraries interested in new ideas for resource sharing can be found at http://www.ala.org/ala/rusa/rusaourassoc/rusasections/stars/starssection.

1. Definition
The Interlibrary Code for the United States covers transactions between two libraries. Transactions between libraries and commercial document suppliers or library fee-based services are contractual arrangements beyond the scope of these guidelines.

The terms "requesting library" and "supplying library" are used in preference to "borrowing" and "lending" to cover the exchange of copies, as well as loans.

2. Purpose
Interlibrary loan (ILL) is intended to complement local collections and is not a substitute for good library collections intended to meet the routine needs of users. ILL is based on a tradition of sharing resources between various types and sizes of libraries and rests on the belief that no library, no matter how large or well supported, is self-sufficient in today's world. It is also evident that some libraries are net borrowers (borrow more than they lend) and others are net lenders (lend more than they borrow), but the system of interlibrary loan still rests on the belief that all libraries should be willing to lend if they are willing to borrow.

3. Scope
The conduct of international interlibrary loan is regulated by the rules set forth in the IFLA document International Lending: Principles and Guidelines for Procedure.[2]

Although the United States shares a common border with Canada and Mexico, it is important to remember that these countries have their own library infrastructures and ILL codes. The IFLA Principles and Guidelines regulate the exchange of material between institutions across these borders. Further, U.S. librarians would be wise to inform themselves of customs requirements that take precedence over library agreements when material is shipped across these national borders, e.g., as described in the Association of Research Libraries' Transborder Interlibrary Loan: Shipping Interlibrary Loan Materials from the U.S. to Canada.[3]

4. Responsibilities of the Requesting Library
4.1 Written Policies
A library's interlibrary loan borrowing policy should be available in a written format that is readily accessible to all library users. Whenever possible the borrowing policy should be posted on the library's website, as well as be available in paper copy at public service desks or wherever other library user handouts are provided.

4.2 Confidentiality

Interlibrary loan transactions, like circulation transactions, are confidential library records. Interlibrary loan personnel are encouraged to be aware of local/state confidentiality rules and laws as they relate to interlibrary loan transactions. Appropriate steps, such as using identification numbers or codes rather than users' names, should be taken to maintain confidentiality. However, it is not a violation of this code to include a user's name on a request submitted to a supplier. Policies and procedures should be developed regarding the retention of ILL records and access to this information. ILL personnel should also be aware of privacy issues when posting requests for assistance or using the text of ILL requests as procedural examples. ALA's Office for Intellectual Freedom has developed a number of policies regarding confidentiality of library records.[4]

ILL staff should adhere to the American Library Association's (ALA) Code of Ethics,[5] specifically principle III, which states: "We protect each library user's right to privacy and confidentiality with respect to information sought or received and resources consulted, borrowed, acquired, or transmitted."

4.3 Complete Bibliographic Citation

A good bibliographic description is the best assurance that the user will receive the item requested. Rather than detail these descriptive elements, the code requires the requesting library to include whatever data provides the best indication of the desired material, whether an alphanumeric string or an extensive bibliographic citation. The important point is that this description be exact enough to avoid unnecessary work on the part of the supplier and frustration on the part of the user. For example, journal title verification rather than article level verification would be sufficient.

4.4 Identifying Appropriate Suppliers

Requesting libraries should use all resources at their disposal to determine ownership of a particular title before sending a request to a potential supplier. Many libraries contribute their holdings to major bibliographic utilities such as DOCLINE and/or OCLC and make their individual catalogs freely available via the Internet. The interlibrary loan listserv (ill-l@webjunction.org) or other ILL-related lists are also excellent sources for the requesting library to verify and/or locate particularly difficult items.

The requesting library is encouraged to use resources such as the OCLC Policies Directory to determine lending policies, including any applicable charges, before requesting material.

The requesting library should clearly state on the request an amount that meets or exceeds the charges of suppliers to which the request is sent. The requesting library is responsible for payment of any fees charged by the supplying library that are less than or equal to the amount stated on its request. Libraries are encouraged to use electronic invoicing capabilities such as OCLC's Interlibrary Loan Fee Management (IFM) system or the Electronic Fund Transfer System used by medical libraries.

4.5 Sending Unverified Requests

Despite the requirements in Sec. 4.4 and 4.5 that an item should be completely and accurately described and located, the code recognizes that it is not always possible to verify and/or locate a particular item. For example, a request may be sent to a potential supplier with strong holdings in a subject or to the institution at which the dissertation was written.

4.6 Transmitting the Request

The code recommends electronic communication. For many libraries, sending requests electronically means using the ILL messaging systems associated with DOCLINE, OCLC, other products that use the ISO ILL Protocol, or structured e-mail requests.

Lacking the ability to transmit in this fashion, the requesting library should send a completed ALA interlibrary loan request form via fax, Internet transmission, or mail; use a potential supplier's Web request form or otherwise provide the necessary information via e-mail message or conventional letter. Whatever communication method is used, the requesting library should identify and use the appropriate address or number for ILL requests.

The requesting library should include a street address, a postal box number, an IP address, a fax number, and an e-mail address to give the supplying library delivery options. Any special needs, such as for a particular edition, language, or rush delivery, should be included on the request.

In addition, because the primary purpose of interlibrary loan is to provide material for relatively short-term use by an individual, the requesting library should communicate with the supplying library in advance if the material is needed for other uses (such as course reserves, classroom or other group viewing of audio-visual material, or for an extended loan period, especially of a textbook).

4.7 Copy Requests

The requesting library is responsible for complying with the provisions of Section 108(g)(2) Copyright Law[6] and the Guidelines for the Proviso of Subsection 108(g)(2) prepared by the National Commission on New Technological Uses of Copyrighted Works (the CONTU Guidelines).[7]

4.8 Responsibility of the Requester

The requesting library assumes an inherent risk when material is supplied through interlibrary loan. Although the number is small, some material is lost or damaged at some point along the route from the supplier and back again. The requesting library's responsibility for this loss is based on the concept that if the request had not been made, the material would not have left the supplier's shelf, and thus would not have been put at risk. This section clearly states that the requesting library is responsible for the material from the time it leaves the supplying library until its safe return to the supplying library.

If the requesting library asks for delivery at a location away from the library (such as to the user's home), the requesting library is likewise responsible for the material during this delivery and return process. In any case, a final decision regarding replacement, repair, or compensation rests with the supplying library.

Borrowed items should be returned in the condition in which they were received at the requesting library. In particular, adhesive labels or tape should not be affixed directly to any borrowed item.

It is the responsibility of the requesting library to pay invoices received or to notify the supplying library of any billing questions not later than six months from the billing date for the charges in question. The requesting library should also make every attempt to resolve billing questions within six months of notifying the supplying library of an apparent billing error.

Although the code stipulates that the requesting library is required to pay if billed for a lost or damaged item, the supplying library is not necessarily required to charge for a lost item. In the case of lost material, the requesting and supplying libraries may need to work together to resolve the matter. For instance, the library shipping the material may need to initiate a trace with the delivery firm.

4.9 Responsibility for Unmediated ILL Requests

Some requesting libraries permit users to initiate online ILL requests that are sent directly to potential supplying libraries. A requesting library that chooses to allow its users to order materials through interlibrary loan without mediation accepts responsibility for these requests as if they have been placed by library staff. The supplying library may assume that the user has been authenticated and authorized to place requests and that the requesting library assumes full responsibility for transaction charges, the safety and return of material, and the expense of replacement or repair.

4.10 Due Date and Use Restrictions

This code makes a departure from earlier codes that described due dates in terms of a "loan period," which was interpreted as the length of time a requesting library could retain the material before returning it. The primary object of this section is to provide a clear definition of due date as the date the material must be checked in at the supplying library. This definition brings ILL practice into alignment with automated circulation procedures and is intended to facilitate interoperability of ILL and circulation applications.

The requesting library should develop a method for monitoring due dates so that material can be returned to and checked in at the supplying library by the due date assigned by the supplying library.

The requesting library is responsible for ensuring compliance with any use restrictions specified by the supplying library such as "library use only" or "no photocopying."

4.11 Renewals

When the supplying library denies a renewal request the material should be returned by the original due date or as quickly as possible if the renewal is denied after the due date has passed.

4.12 Recalls

The response to a recall may be the immediate return of the material, or timely communication with the supplying library to negotiate a new due date.

When the material has been recalled, the requesting library is encouraged to return the material via an expedited delivery carrier such as UPS, FedEx, or USPS Priority Mail.

4.13 Shipping

It is the ultimate responsibility of the requesting library to return materials in the same condition in which they were received as noted in section 4.8 of the Interlibrary Loan Code for the United States.

It is the responsibility of the requesting library to follow the shipping and packaging requirements, including insurance and preferred shipping method, as stipulated by the supplying library. Packaging is defined as the outer material, which may be a box, padded envelope, etc. Wrapping is defined as an inner covering for the item such as paper or bubble wrap.

If no shipping or packaging methods are specified, the requesting library's regular form of shipment should be used.

If packaging material has been used previously, remove or mark out old addresses, postal marks, etc., to avoid misdirection. Do not reuse old, frayed, ripped, or decaying packaging and wrapping materials—discard it instead. Clearly address all packages with both the destination and return addresses properly attached to the packaging material.

In accordance with United States Postal Service guidelines, tape is the preferred sealing method on all types of packages. Remember that wrapping and packaging materials will most likely be reused. So, please use tape judiciously. If staples must be used, do not use industrial (e.g., copper) staples if at all possible. Copper staples make it very difficult to reuse wrapping and packaging materials and are not ergonomically sound.

Use wrapping and packaging material that is appropriate to the size and format of the material being shipped. Too small or too large packaging will not adequately protect materials during transportation. Remember to use appropriate wrapping to avoid shifting and damage to the contents.

For special formats, consult the appropriate ALA Guidelines:

- American Library Association. Association for Library Collections and Technical Services. Guidelines for Packaging and Shipping Magnetic Tape Recording and Optical Discs (CD-ROM and CD-R) Carrying Audio, Video, and/or Data, n.d.
- American Library Association. Association for Library Collections and Technical Services. Guidelines for Packaging and Shipping Microforms, 1989.
- American Library Association. Association for Library Collections and Technical Services. Guidelines for Preservation Photocopying of Replacement Pages, 1990.

- American Library Association. Video Round Table. Guidelines for the Interlibrary Loan of Audiovisual Formats, 1998.
- American Library Association. Association of College and Research Libraries. Ad Hoc Committee on the Interlibrary Loan of Rate and Unique Materials. Guidelines for the Interlibrary Loan of Rare and Unique Materials, 2004.

4.14 Suspension of Service

Repeated or egregious breaches of this code may result in the requesting library's inability to obtain material. Examples of actions that may result in suspension include lost or damaged books, allowing "library use only" books to leave the library, or failing to pay the supplier's charges. A supplying library should not suspend service to a requesting library without first attempting to resolve the problem(s).

5. Responsibilities of the Supplying Library

5.1 Lending Policy

The lending policy should be clear, detailed, and readily available to requesting libraries. The policy should include, among other things, schedule of fees and charges, overdue fines, noncirculating items/categories, current shipping instructions, calendar for service suspensions, penalties for late payments, etc. While a supplying library may charge additional fees for the rapid delivery of requested material, it is recommended that no additional fees be charged for the routine supply of documents via electronic means.

The supplying library is encouraged to make its lending policy available in print, on the library's website, and in resources such as the OCLC Policies Directory. The supplying library should be willing to fill requests for all types and classes of users, and all types of libraries, regardless of their size or geographic location.

5.2 Material Format

Supplying libraries are encouraged to lend as liberally as possible regardless of the format of the material requested, while retaining the right to determine what material will be supplied. It is the obligation of the supplying library to consider the loan of material on a case-by-case basis. Supplying libraries are encouraged to lend audiovisual material, newspapers, and other categories of material that have traditionally been noncirculating.

Supplying libraries are encouraged to follow ACRL's Guidelines for the Interlibrary Loan of Rare and Unique Materials[8] and the Guidelines for Interlibrary Loan of Audiovisual Formats.[9]

If permitted by copyright law, the supplying library should consider providing a copy in lieu of a loan rather than giving a negative response.

Supplying libraries should be aware of the provisions of license agreements for electronic resources that may either permit or prohibit use of an electronic resource to fill interlibrary copying requests.

5.3 Confidentiality

The supplying library has a responsibility to safeguard the confidentiality of the individual requesting the material. The sharing of the user's name between requesting and supplying library is not, of itself, a violation of confidentiality. However, the supplying library should not require the user's name if the requesting library chooses not to provide it. If the name is provided, the supplying library needs to take care not to divulge the identity of the person requesting the material.

5.4 Timely Processing

The supplying library has a responsibility to act promptly on all requests. If a supplying library cannot fill a request within a reasonable time, then it should respond promptly. The response should be sent via the same method the requesting library used to send the request, or by otherwise contacting the requesting library directly. Some ILL messaging systems such as OCLC and DOCLINE have built-in time periods after which requests will either expire or be sent to another institution. The supplying library should respond before this time expires rather than allow requests to time-out.

Providing a reason for an unfilled request helps the requesting library determine what additional steps, if any, may be taken to access the requested item. For example, "noncirculating" indicates the item is likely available for on-site use, while "in use" indicates that another request at a later date might be filled. Providing no reason or simply stating "policy problem" or "other" without providing additional information deprives the requesting library of important information and can lead to time-consuming follow-up for both libraries.

Timely processing of a loan or copy may involve other library departments, such as circulation, copy services, and the mailroom. The interlibrary loan department is responsible for ensuring that material is delivered expeditiously, irrespective of internal library organizational responsibilities.

The supplying library should, when charging for materials, make every effort to allow for a variety of payment options. Payment through electronic crediting and debiting services such as OCLC's ILL Fee Management (IFM) system or other noninvoicing payment forms such as IFLA vouchers should be encouraged. The supplying library that charges should make every effort to accept the use of vouchers, coupons, or credit cards.

It is the responsibility of the supplying library to send final bills for service not later than six months after the supply date, final overdue notices not later than six months after the final due date, and final bills for replacement of lost material not later than one year after the final due date. The supplying library should resolve billing questions within six months of receiving notice of an apparent billing error.

5.5 Identifying the Request

The supplying library should send sufficient identifying information with the material to allow the requesting library to identify the material and process the request quickly. Such information may include a copy of the request, the requestor's transaction number, or the user's ID or name. Failure to include identifying information with the material can unduly delay its processing and may risk the safety of the material.

Supplying libraries are encouraged to enclose an accurate and complete return mailing label.

5.6 Use Restrictions and Due Date

Although it is the responsibility of the requesting library to ensure the safe treatment and return of borrowed material, the supplying library should provide specific instructions when it is lending material that needs special handling. These instructions might include the requirement that material be used only in a monitored special collections area, no photocopying, library use only, specific return packaging/shipping instructions, etc. The supplying library should not send "library use only" material directly to a user.

The supplying library should clearly indicate the date on which it expects the loan to be discharged in its circulation system. As explained in section 4.10, this code has moved away from the concept of a loan period, to a definite date that accommodates the sending and return of material, as well as sufficient time for the use of the material. For example, a supplying library might establish a due date of six (6) weeks for the purpose of providing one (1) week for shipping, four (4) weeks for use, and one (1) week for the return trip and check-in.

5.7 Delivery and Packaging

The location specified by the requesting library may include the requesting library, a branch or departmental library, or the individual user.

It is the responsibility of the supplying library:

- to judge whether an item is suitable for shipment and circulation. If a damaged item is sent, the supplying library should note all prior damage (such as loose pages or loose spine) and not hold the requesting library responsible for subsequent damage.
- to take care that the material it sends out is properly packaged to protect the item from damage even though the requesting library will be held responsible for material damaged in shipment to specify the shipping method, as well as insurance, for returning materials and if any special wrapping or packaging is required. See section 4.13 for definitions and other important information regarding wrapping and packaging.
- to provide a complete street address if asking for return via UPS, FedEx, etc. (Many supplying libraries find it safer and more cost effective to ship all material via expedited carriers.)
- to work with the requesting library when tracing a lost or damaged item if the commercial delivery firm is responsible for reimbursement for losses in transit.

5.8 Renewals

The supplying library should respond affirmatively or negatively to all renewal requests. The supplying library is encouraged to grant the renewal request if the material is not needed by a local user.

5.9 Recalls

The supplying library may recall material at its discretion at any time. Increasingly, some libraries are finding it more effective to request the material on ILL for a local user rather than to recall material in use by another library.

5.10 Service Suspension

A supplying library should not suspend service without first attempting to address the problem(s) with the requesting library.[10, 11]

NOTES

1. Boucher, Virginia. *Interlibrary Loan Practices Handbook*. Chicago: American Library Association, 1997. Although written in light of an earlier code, the *Practices Handbook* contains many useful and practical details on interlibrary loan procedures.

2. International Federation of Library Associations and Institutions. International Lending: Principles and Guidelines for Procedure, 2001.

3. Transborder Interlibrary Loan: Shipping Interlibrary Loan Materials from the U.S. to Canada, 1999. (Note: Pricing information is out of date.)

4. American Library Association. Office for Intellectual Freedom. Policy on Confidentiality of Library Records, 1986. American Library Association. Office for Intellectual Freedom. Policy Concerning Confidentiality of Personally Identifiable Information about Library Users, 2004.

5. American Library Association. Committee on Professional Ethics. Code of Ethics. Chicago, American Library Association, 1995.

6. Copyright Law of the United States of America Chapter 1, Section 108: Limitations on the exclusive rights: Reproduction by libraries and archives.

7. National Commission on New Technological Uses of Copyrighted Works. Guidelines on Photocopying Under Interlibrary Loan Arrangements.

8. American Library Association. Association of College and Research Libraries. Ad Hoc Committee on the Interlibrary Loan of Rate and Unique Materials. Guidelines for the Loan of Rare and Unique Materials, 2004.

9. American Library Association. Video Round Table. Guidelines for Interlibrary Loan of Audiovisual Formats, 1998.

10. Hilyer, Lee. *Interlibrary Loan and Document Delivery: Best Practices for Operating and Managing Interlibrary Loan Services in All Libraries*. New York: Haworth Information Press, 2006. (Copublished simultaneously as *Journal of Interlibrary Loan, Document Delivery, and Electronic Reserve* 16, nos. 1/2, 2006.)

11. Hilyer, Lee. *Interlibrary Loan and Document Delivery in the Larger Academic Library: A Guide for University, Research, and Larger Public Libraries*. Binghamton, NY: Haworth Information Press, 2002. (Copublished simultaneously as *Journal of Interlibrary Loan, Document Delivery, and Information Supply* 13, nos. 1/2, 2002.)

Appendix D

ALA and ARL Response to the Section 108 Study Group Regarding Interlibrary Loan and Other Copies for Users

The mission of libraries is to preserve and provide access to information, regardless of format. Thus there is a legitimate societal interest in assuring that these trusted cultural institutions continue to have legal support for undertaking best practices for the preservation of and access to copyrighted content, without regard to the format by which the content is distributed.

Our ability to accomplish this mission is greatly enhanced by the exceptions currently offered in Sections 107 and 108. The American Library Association (ALA) and the Association of Research Libraries (ARL) believe that the combination of Sections 107 and 108 provides libraries and archives with the ability to take full advantage of digital technologies in support of user services. However, we believe that should Congress decide changes to 108 are required, under certain circumstances, there could be opportunities to clarify the intent of selected provisions in Section 108.

Maintaining flexibility in the statute is important in order for libraries to achieve their mission. Thus, any proposed changes to Section 108 should not be tied to the use of restrictive conditions or technologies such as those included in the TEACH Act. Such proposals would undermine the needs of libraries and archives in the digital environment.

ALA and ARL convened a second workshop on January 4–5, 2007, to receive and consider input from members of the library community regarding the continuing deliberations of the Section 108 Study Group. The January workshop focused on the recent Federal Register Notice issued by the Copyright Office concerning the Section 108 Study Group work on making and distributing copies for users.

To clarify our response to the Federal Register notice, we will briefly review the kinds of reproductions that are requested by library users. These can be categorized as

1. interlibrary loan copies, where the "lending" library makes a copy for a member of the "borrowing" library's user community upon receiving a request;
2. direct copies, where a library makes a copy from its own collection upon the request of a member of its user community; and
3. copies made by the library for noncommunity users. The third category—copies for noncommunity users—is a service that only a few libraries provide. For these copies, a royalty is paid to the rights-holder and libraries charge those users for these costs. Document delivery services, when a library provides copies to users on a fee basis, are also not included in this discussion.

An interlibrary loan copy under *category 1* is a "library to library" transaction allowing libraries to make limited copies from their own collections to supply to another library at the request of a library user. Only legitimate community users of the borrowing library are eligible for interlibrary loan service. The CONTU guidelines are widely practiced and control the kind of systematic copying that could interfere with market interests. Interlibrary loan is, by definition, a *mediated* activity in that library staff or systems screen requests from users before fulfilling them. Most libraries prefer to mediate these transactions (rather than allow the user of the borrowing library to contact the lending library directly) because frequently the user does not realize that the borrowing library already owns or licenses the material being requested. ARL libraries report that their studies indicate that the library already owns more commonly required materials, and it is very rare (1–1.5 percent) that the library ever fulfills the same request twice.

Category 2 copies—a library directly making a copy for a member of its user community—is also a mediated transaction and only involves works that the library already owns. In practice, such activity is minimal because most libraries make available to users reproducing equipment that allows the users to make their own copies pursuant to Section 108(f)(1).

TOPIC A: AMENDMENTS TO CURRENT SUBSECTIONS 108 (D), (E), AND (G)(2) REGARDING COPIES FOR USERS, INCLUDING INTERLIBRARY LOAN

General Issue: Should the provisions relating to libraries and archives making and distributing copies for users, including via interlibrary loan (which include the current subsections 108(d), (e), and (g), as well as the CONTU guidelines) be amended to reflect reasonable changes in the way copies are made and used by libraries and archives, taking into account the effect of these changes on rights-holders.

1. How can the copyright law better facilitate the ability of libraries and archives to make copies for users in the digital environment without unduly interfering with the interests of rights-holders?

Currently, libraries take full advantage of the provisions of the Copyright Act, Sections 107 and 108 in particular, to provide lawful access to information resources. The Copyright Act has built-in safeguards to balance the interests of authors, users, and owners of copyrighted information.

2. Should the single-copy restriction for copies made under subsections (d) and (e) be replaced with a flexible standard more appropriate to the nature of digital materials, such as "a limited number of copies as reasonably necessary for the library or archives to provide the requesting patron with a single copy of the requested work"? If so, should this amendment apply both to copies made for a library's or archives' own users and to interlibrary loan copies?

Yes, a flexible standard is more appropriate and should replace the single-copy restriction. This standard should apply to both library users and to interlibrary loan copies. We suggest the language "such copies as reasonably necessary" over "a limited numbers of copies as reasonably necessary."

However, the library community believes that digital reproduction and delivery is currently permitted under Section 108(d) and (e) and 107. Section 108(d) provides that "[t]he rights of reproduction and distribution under this section apply to a copy . . . of more than one article." We believe that a court would interpret this phrase to permit incidental copies—those copies that are temporary and have no monetary consequence—necessary to distribute a copy to a user. And if the court did not interpret Section 108(d) in this manner, we are confident that the court would treat these as fair-use copies that otherwise met the criteria of Section 108(d) (i.e., they became the property of the user; they were used for private study, scholarship, or research; and they met the requirements of section 108(g)).

3. How prevalent is library and archives use of subsection (d) for direct copies for their own users? For interlibrary loan copies? How would usage be affected if digital reproduction and/or delivery were explicitly permitted?

Interlibrary loan is a fairly common activity that libraries engage in to meet the information needs of our users. Only a member of the borrowing library's user community can request interlibrary loan service from the collections of other libraries. We anticipate that due to the use of remote storage and its functional equivalent—a library serving multiple campuses—making copies directly for library users will increase. We do not believe that digital reproduction and distribution will increase the use of interlibrary loan or other lawful copying. Most libraries currently provide copies in digital format, and the number of requests has not increased from when the copies were provided in analog format. We do not anticipate the number of requests increasing if digital reproduction and delivery were explicitly permitted.

4. How prevalent is library and archives use of subsection (e) for direct copies for their own users? For interlibrary loan copies? How would usage be affected if digital reproduction and/or delivery were explicitly permitted?

Rarely do libraries or archives use subsection (e) for direct copies or for interlibrary loan copies. Digital reproduction and distribution would not increase this already uncommon occurrence.

5. If the single-copy restriction is replaced with a flexible standard that allows digital copies for users, should restrictions be placed on the making and distribution of these copies? If so, what types of restrictions? For instance, should there be any conditions on digital distribution that would prevent users from further copying or distributing the materials for downstream use? Should user agreements or any technological measures, such as copy controls, be required? Should persistent identifiers on digital copies be required? How would libraries and archives implement such requirements? Should such requirements apply both to direct copies for users and to interlibrary loan copies?

In current practice, libraries already restrict further copying and distribution of digital copies by placing those works on a secure server that only the requesting user can access. Access to the copy is eliminated entirely after the "loan period" for the work has concluded. This method works best for libraries because it allows us to act in the spirit of the law, is secure, and is efficient for libraries. This approach also works well for our users. Sending an e-mail attachment of a work directly to a requesting user is not practical because of the size of files. Additionally, using attachments is more labor intensive and is not as secure, and many systems do not accept such files. We support the continuation of current practices rather than the use of technological protection measures that could be used to monitor and invade the privacy of our library users. Libraries routinely inform their users about copyright law implications, include the required notice on order forms (108(d)(2) and 108(e)(2)), include the original Copyright Notice on documents when available and the message, "No further reproduction or distribution of this copy is permitted by electronic transmission or any other means." This practice is so common that library supply vendors sell ink stamps and other materials for this very purpose.

6. Should digital copying for users be permitted only upon the request of a member of the library's or archives' traditional or defined user community in order to deter online shopping for user copies? If so, how should a user community be defined for these purposes?

Libraries currently provide copies to their defined user communities, or to that of a borrowing library under an interlibrary loan. This is long-standing practice and should not be codified. Interlibrary loan and direct copying is both time consuming and costly for libraries. Libraries have no incentive or desire to serve users beyond their existing client base. The number of libraries offering document delivery services to users outside of their user base (or the user base of a borrowing library) is quite small, and in these instances libraries pay royalties and seek cost recovery from the requester to offset costs.

7. Should subsections (d) and (e) be amended to clarify that interlibrary loan transactions of digital copies require the mediation of a library or archives on both ends, and to not permit direct electronic requests from, and/or delivery to, the user from another library or archives?

Typically, interlibrary loan transactions are, by definition, mediated so there is no need to change the law. It may appear that user-initiated requests via an electronic form are unmediated, but, in fact, these requests are routinely reviewed by interlibrary loan staff to ensure that the user is not requesting something that the library already owns.

8. In cases where no physical object is provided to the user, does it make sense to retain the requirement that "the copy or phonorecord becomes the property of the user" (17 U.S.C. 108(d)(1) and (e)(1))? In the digital context, would it be more appropriate to instead prohibit libraries and archives from using digital copies of works copied under subsections (d) and (e) to enlarge their collections or as source copies for fulfilling future requests?

In making copies for users who request materials for research, scholarship, and personal study, libraries follow the practice not to retain digital copies of works copied under subsections (d) and (e), not only because it is an infringement of copyright law, but also because it is not feasible technically or financially to retain the copies, and because the likelihood that the same work will be requested twice is slim.

9. Because there is a growing market for articles and other portions of copyrighted works, should a provision be added to subsection (d), similar to that in subsection (e), requiring libraries and archives to first determine on the basis of a reasonable investigation that a copy of a requested item cannot be readily obtained at a fair price before creating a copy of a portion of a work in response to a patron's request? Does the requirement, whether as applied to subsection (e) now or if applied to subsection (d), need to be revised to clarify whether a copy of the work available for license by the library or archives, but not for purchase, qualifies as one that can be "obtained"?

No. The proposed requirement that libraries first investigate whether a requested item under subsection (d) is readily obtained at a fair price before creating a copy in response to a user request would eliminate interlibrary loan altogether. Libraries pay institutional subscription fees for journals in order to account for the many people the library serves, and these uses are also included in the license agreements. No additional changes are required.

10. Should the Study Group be looking into recommendations for revising the CONTU guidelines on interlibrary loan? Should there be guidelines applicable to works older than five years? Should the record-keeping guideline apply to the borrowing, as well as the lending library, in order to help administer a broader exception? Should additional guidelines be developed to set limits on the number of copies of a work or copies of the same portion of a work that can be made directly for users, as the CONTU guidelines suggest for interlibrary loan copies? Are these records currently accessible by people outside of the library community? Should they be?

No. We do not recommend any revision to the CONTU guidelines. The CONTU guidelines, while not law, have served libraries well as a useful "best practice" document.

11. Should separate rules apply to international electronic interlibrary loan transactions? If so, how should they differ?

No.

TOPIC B: AMENDMENTS TO SUBSECTION 108 (I)

General Issue: Should subsection 108(i) be amended to expand the application of subsection (d) and (e) to any nontext-based works, or to any text-based works that incorporate musical or audiovisual works?

1. Should any or all of the subsection (i) exclusions of certain categories of works from the application of the subsection (d) and (e) exceptions be eliminated? What are the concerns presented by modifying the subsection (i) exclusions, and how should they be addressed?

The exclusion of certain categories of works from the application of subsection (d) and (e) is an antiquated way to deal with content, and therefore we recommend that subsection (i) be eliminated. Today, libraries purchase works that are multiformat—for example, books that include a CD. These titles are enhanced by the addition of multiformat content, and it should not matter in what form that content appears.

Subsection (e) would continue to prevent the copying of entire works that are readily available in the market place.

2. Would the ability of libraries and archives to make and/or distribute digital copies have additional or different effects on markets for nontext-based works than for text-based works? If so, should conditions be added to address these differences? For example: Should digital copies of visual works be limited to diminished resolution thumbnails, as opposed to a "small portion" of the work? Should persistent identifiers be required to identify the copy of a visual work and any progeny as one made by a library or archives under section 108, and stating that no further distribution is authorized? Should subsection (d) and (e), user copies of audiovisual works and sound recordings, if delivered electronically, be restricted to delivery by streaming in order to prevent downloading and further distribution? If so, how might scholarly practices requiring the retention of source materials be accommodated?

Libraries are willing to use technologies that would limit further reproduction or distribution of nontext-based works such as streaming. We believe, however, that libraries and archives should not be limited to one technological method, as new and innovative means of delivery will likely emerge. Thus, flexibility will be key in order for libraries to lawfully distribute digital copies.

With regard to thumbnails, these do not provide enough detail for scholarly research. Fidelity to the original work is important to research. Finally, persistent identifiers do not appear to be the right approach at this point in time. Libraries do not support any active monitoring of user behavior.

3. If the exclusions in subsection (i) were eliminated in whole or in part, should there be different restrictions on making direct copies for users of nontext-based works than on making interlibrary loan copies? Would applying the interlibrary loan framework to nontext-based works require any adjustments to the CONTU guidelines?

No. In addition, no changes are required to CONTU.

4. If the subsection (i) exclusions were not eliminated, should an additional exception be added to permit the application of subsections (d) and (e) to musical or audiovisual works embedded in textual works? Would doing so address the needs of scholars, researchers, and students for increased access to copies of such works?

If subsection (i) were not eliminated, then an additional exception for embedded works would be desirable. We anticipate that authors will create more works with embedded content in the future, and keeping the nature of the whole work as the author intended is essential for scholars, researchers, and students.

TOPIC C: LIMITATIONS ON ACCESS TO ELECTRONIC COPIES, INCLUDING VIA PERFORMANCE OR DISPLAY

General Issue: Should section 108 be amended to permit libraries and archives to make temporary and incidental copies of unlicensed digital works in order to provide user access to these works? Should any exceptions be added to the copyright law to permit limited public performance and display in certain circumstances in order to allow for user access to unlicensed digital works?

1. What types of unlicensed digital materials are libraries and archives acquiring now or are likely to acquire in the foreseeable future? How will these materials be acquired? Is the quantity of unlicensed digital material that libraries and archives are likely to acquire significant enough to warrant express exceptions for making temporary copies incidental to access?

We do not envision a future where all digital materials are licensed and reject the premise implicit in many of these questions that if materials are in digital form, access to them must be controlled in some way. In fact, libraries acquire digital materials that are not bound by license agreements. When a license is associated with a particular digital work, libraries comply with the terms of that license; therefore, when libraries receive donated materials, we comply with the terms of the donor agreement when acquiring the work. If there is no agreement, the library may deem it appropriate to make a copy for the user. Any temporary, incidental copies made as a result of making the user copy are not retained. As stated earlier in section A, any temporary incidental copies made as a result of meeting a user request are inevitable and of little consequence since they have no economic value. We maintain that the only copy that is of consequence is the copy provided to the user.

2. What uses should a library or archives be able to make of a lawfully acquired, unlicensed digital copy of a work? Is the EU model a good one, namely that access be limited to dedicated terminals on the premises of the library or archives to one user at a time for each copy lawfully acquired? Or could security be ensured through other measures, such as technological protections? Should simultaneous use by more than one user ever be permitted? Should remote access ever be permitted for unlicensed digital works? If so, under what conditions?

The EU model is too restrictive. It is not reasonable to insist that a user be tethered to a dedicated computer in the library in order to access the copy requested. In those cases where agreements with owners require some limitation on access, we prefer placing the copy on a secure server that only the requesting user may access.

3. Are there implied licenses to use and provide access to these types of works? If so, what are the parameters of such implied licenses for users? What about for library and archives staff?

Yes, there are implied licenses to use and provide access to these types of works. When libraries receive a user request for access to unlicensed digital material, they do everything legally within their power to meet the user's need.

4. Do libraries and archives currently rely on implied licenses to access unlicensed content, or do they rely instead on fair use? Is it current library and archives practice to attempt to provide access to unlicensed digital works in a way that mirrors the type of access provided to similar analog works?

It depends. If a donor agreement is linked to the work, then the donor agreement terms are followed. If there is no agreement, libraries provide access in the lawful ways available to them under Section 108. When Section 108 exceptions do not apply, the library turns to Section 107 and makes a fair-use assessment to determine if the user requests can be met. Additionally, certain uses may be permitted under an implied license. Yes, it is the goal to deliver information electronically and to take advantage of the benefits of the technology, and not restrain technologies to "mirror" the print environment.

5. Are the considerations different for digital works embedded in tangible media, such as DVDs or CDs, than for those acquired in purely electronic form? Under which circumstances should libraries and archives be permitted to make server copies in order to provide access? Should the law permit backup copies to be made?

Not really. The library again would turn to 108 and then 107 to meet the user request. Making backup copies is not necessary to provide access to a digital work.

6. Should conditions on providing access to unlicensed digital works be implemented differently based upon the category or media of work (text, audio, film, photographs, etc.)?

No. Copyright law is intended to be technology and format neutral.

7. Are public performance and/or display rights necessarily exercised in providing access to certain unlicensed digital materials? For what types of works? Does the copyright law need to be amended to address the need to make incidental copies in order to display an electronic work? Should an exception be added for libraries and archives to also perform unlicensed electronic works in certain circumstances, similar to the 109(c) exception for display? If so, under what conditions?

Yes, public performance or display rights might be exercised in order to provide access depending on the category of work. Obviously, audiovisual works cannot be accessed unless they are perceptible to the user, and this may implicate the public performance right. The Study Group seems to be attempting to suggest modifications in the law that we believe are too specific. Congress and the Supreme Court have long recognized the need to maintain flexibility in the law, especially during times of rapid technological change. We cannot anticipate what situations may arise in the future and so recommend that the Study Group not be bogged down by specifics that may unintentionally prevent the law from achieving its purpose.

In conclusion, we believe that if Congress determines that changes to Section 108 are necessary, we recommend that:

1. Subsection (i) should be eliminated.
2. Temporary and incidental copies should be allowed with language like "such copies as reasonably necessary."

If Congress does decide to consider changes to Section 108, we believe that it will be critically important that Section 108 retain its current flexibility that permits libraries and archives to effectively provide needed services to their users.

Used with permission from the American Library Association, www.ala.org.

Appendix E

Interlibrary Loans

ALA Library Fact Sheet Number 8

As defined by the Interlibrary Loan Code for the United States, "Interlibrary loan is the process by which a library requests material from, or supplies material to, another library. The purpose of interlibrary loan as defined by this code is to obtain, upon request of a library user, material not available in the user's local library."

This fact sheet has been designed for libraries in the United States and Canada. If you are outside of the United States and Canada, please see the section on international interlibrary loan and follow the guidelines set forth by IFLA.

INTERLIBRARY LOAN IN THE UNITED STATES

Libraries should follow the Interlibrary Loan Code for the United States, which was prepared by the Interlibrary Loan Committee of ALA's Reference and User Services Association (RUSA, a division of ALA) in 1994, and revised in 2001 (with the revision approved by the RUSA Board of Directors in January 2001). The full text of the Interlibrary Loan Code for the United States statement appears online and was published in the Summer 2001 issue of the official RUSA journal, the *Reference and User Services Quarterly* (v. 40, no. 4, pp. 318–19).

The Explanatory Supplement of the U.S. Interlibrary Loan Code also appears online and was published in the Summer 2001 *Reference and User Services Quarterly* (v. 40, no. 4, pp. 321–27).

Most state and regional library networks/consortia and state library agencies have interlibrary loan procedures, and libraries in their service areas should be familiar with these procedures.

INTERLIBRARY LOAN FORM

Libraries normally transmit requests either electronically (through OCLC or other networks) or using ALA-approved interlibrary loan forms. The interlibrary loan form, sometimes called "the ALA form," can be accessed as an Adobe Reader PDF document, as well as a Microsoft Word file (which can be edited). The form can also be purchased in bulk from library supply houses. A list of directories of library product suppliers is available on ALA Library Fact Sheet 9, Library Products and Services.

INTERLIBRARY LOAN IN CANADA

Loans to Canada are conducted on much the same basis as domestic loans, with slightly different mailing procedures (many Canadian libraries are part of OCLC or other networks). For more information on ILL in Canada contact:
Interlibrary Loan Division
Library and Archives Canada
395 Wellington Street
Ottawa, Ontario K1A 0N4 Canada
Telephone: (613) 996-7527
Fax: (613) 996-4424
E-mail: illservicespeb@lac-bac.gc.ca
Library and Archives Canada Interlibrary Loans (ILL) Web page: http://www.col lectionscanada.ca/ill/index-e.html

INTERLIBRARY LOAN INFORMATION RESOURCES

For more information on interlibrary loan, you may want to consult the following titles:

Boucher, Virginia. *Interlibrary Loan Practices Handbook*, 2nd ed. Chicago: American Library Association, 1997.
"Guidelines and Procedures for Telefacsimile and Electronic Delivery of Interlibrary Loan Requests and Materials." Chicago: ALA, Reference and Adult Services Division, 1994.
Higginbotham, Barbara Buckner, and Sally Bowdoin. *Access versus Assets: A Comprehensive Guide to Resource Sharing for Academic Librarians*. Chicago: American Library Association, 1993.
"Interlibrary Loan Packaging and Wrapping Guidelines." Chicago: ALA, Reference and User Services Association, 1997.
Morris, Leslie R., ed. *Interlibrary Loan Policies Directory*, 7th ed. New York: Neal-Schuman, 2002.

INTERNATIONAL INTERLIBRARY BORROWING

Any library may participate in international interlibrary loan activities. When seeking a loan from a library outside the United States and Canada, follow the guidelines set forth by IFLA in the following sources:

"International Lending: Principles and Guidelines for Procedure (1987)." *IFLA Journal* 14, no. 3 (1988): 258–264, or in *Interlending and Document Supply* 16 (January 1988): 28–32.

International Federation of Library Associations and Institutions. "The IFLA Fax Guidelines." *Journal of Interlibrary Loan, Document Delivery, and Supply* 6, no. 4 (1996): 5–10 (also at http://www.IFLA.org/VI/2/p3/g-fax.htm).

International Federation of Library Associations and Institutions. "IFLA Guidelines for Sending ILL Requests by E-mail." At http://www.IFLA.org/VI/2/p3/g-ill.htm.

Several procedures are particularly important when performing international interlibrary loan.

- Interview the patron to get a complete picture of what information or source is needed and how it is to be used.
- Verify the citation in a dependable source so that the record is complete and correct.
- Always check to be sure that the item cannot be found in the United States.
- If the item cannot be located in the United States, locate a foreign supplier. If a foreign library or document supply center is found, address this organization directly.
- If no location is known, find out if the country from which you wish to barrow has an international ILL center (use one of the sources listed in the "Selected Additional Sources" section).
- Be sure to inform the patron that the process could take up to six weeks (sometimes longer).
- (Summarized from chapter 6, "International Interlibrary Loan" in Boucher's *Interlibrary Loan Practices Handbook*, 2nd ed., 1997.)

Copyright regulations of the country from which the material is requested must be followed. OCLC PRISM Interlibrary Loan system serves a number of foreign libraries and is one of the best choices to use when transmitting a request. Fax and e-mail are the most common modes for transmitting a request. If the postal service is used, choose the fastest method available (preferably air mail). Charges should be expected and paid promptly as the lending library directs.

Always contact the foreign lending institution first because some institutions use their own ILL forms, but most accept the ILL forms designated by the IFLA Office for International Lending. These forms are available for overseas use at a price of $15.00 per 100 copies from:

British Library Document Supply Centre
Boston Spa, Wetherby
West Yorkshire, LS23 7BQ
United Kingdom
Telephone for information on the Document Supply Centre: +44 (0)1937 546060
Fax: +44 (0)1937 546333
E-mail: dsc-customer-services@bl.uk
Website for IFLA's ILL forms: http://www.ifla.org/VI/2/uap.htm
Document Supply Centre website: http://www.bl.uk/services/document/dsc.html

Note: some libraries will not lend internationally; however, one good source for materials, regardless of language, is the British Library Document Supply Centre. The Document Supply Centre focuses on remote document delivery covering every aspect of scientific, technical, medical, and human knowledge regardless of language. The Document Supply Centre does require that borrowing institutions register with them free of charge. There is a fee per completed request. Information about the Document Supply Centre's service, the particular forms required, and the costs involved can be obtained from the aforementioned information. Please note that the telephone number and website for the Document Supply Centre are different from the number and website for the IFLA ILL forms.

For more information on international interlibrary loan, you may want to consult the following titles:

Barwick, Margaret, and Pauline Connolly, eds. *A Guide to Centres of International Lending and Copying*, 5th ed. Boston Spa, UK: IFLA-UAP Publications, 1995. (ISBN 0 7123 21128)

Barwick, Margaret, and Pauline Connolly, eds. *Guide to Centres of International Document Delivery*, 5th ed. Boston Spa, UK: IFLA-UAP Publications, 1996. (ISBN 0 7123 21454)

Cornish, Graham P. *Model Handbook for Interlending and Copying*. Boston Spa, UK: IFLA-UAP Publications, 1991.

Gould, Sara, ed. *Charging for Document Delivery and Interlending*. Boston Spa, UK: IFLA-UA Publications, 1997. (ISBN 0 7123 2151 9)

For more information on this or other fact sheets, contact the ALA Library Reference Desk by telephone: 800-545-2433, extension 2153; fax: 312-280-3255; e-mail: library@ala.org; or regular mail: ALA Library, American Library Association, 50 East Huron Street, Chicago, IL 60611-2795. Used with permission from the American Library Association, www.ala.org.

Appendix F

Five Things Every New Resource-Sharing Librarian Should Know

1. Guidelines and Laws
2. Technology
3. Customer Service
4. Assessment
5. Education and Networking

1. GUIDELINES AND LAWS

Many library resource-sharing activities are guided, limited, and even made possible by federal laws—particularly those related to copyright and copyright exemptions. Core guidelines commonly adhered to in resource-sharing practices have grown out of these laws. Licenses and licensing agreements between libraries and library consortia and vendors supersede law and should be familiar to resource-sharing librarians. Knowledge of current laws and guidelines governing resource sharing can help librarians provide compliant, standardized services that enhance performance in their library's roles as both borrower and lender.

Best Practices

- As a borrower, follow the CONTU Rule of Five and do not request more than five articles from the last five years from a single journal title within a calendar year unless copyright fees are paid.
- As a borrower of copies and provider of local document scanning, comply with the U.S. copyright law (Title 17, U.S. Code) and its associated guidelines.

- Include a copyright notice of restrictions on copies provided to other libraries or your own patrons.
- Display a statement of copyright restrictions on material request forms.
- Work with the people in the library or consortium that negotiate electronic resource licenses to ensure there is nothing in them to prohibit lending the resources via interlibrary loan. Use a mechanism (e.g., a spreadsheet or a database) to track which subscriptions allow you to provide lending via ILL and those that do not.

Resources

Interlibrary Loan Code for the United States

Circular 21: Reproductions of Copyrighted Works by Educators and Librarians (U.S. Copyright Office)

STARS Legislation and Licensing Committee provides updates on legislative and regulatory developments affecting libraries and resources sharing. (You may have to log into ALA Connect to view.)

First Sale Doctrine—U.S. Code Title 17, Section 109. This is what allows libraries to lend materials they acquire under any condition they choose. In other words, this makes library resource sharing of physical materials possible.

CONTU (National Commission on New Technological Uses of Copyright Works) Rule of Five as presented by the Coalition for Networked Information

Library Copyright Alliance (LCA). This is a great resource for current topics related to libraries and copyright, including relevant cases wending their way through the U.S. judicial system. A document of current interest is the one on *Costco v. Omega.* The LAC is also a great resource for information on treaties and international copyright affecting libraries.

Copyright Clearance Center

2. TECHNOLOGY

Using technology to streamline your workflow and processes provides benefits to your organization and to your patrons. Using appropriate technologies saves staff time (and thus money), results in fewer errors, shortens patron wait times, and helps to integrate ILL processes with the rest of the library. This doesn't always mean you need to purchase the newest, most expensive product. Rather, aim for effective, efficient use of technology where it will have the most impact.

Best Practices

- Be familiar with technological offerings and tools
- Consider ILL management software either through your ILS or stand alone

- Use document transmission software
- Use all the features of your ILL system, such as custom holdings with OCLC
- Take advantage of tools developed by your colleagues
- Review your ILL automation annually
- Maximize technology whenever possible (e.g., be familiar with technological offerings and tools, use OCLC custom holdings, use DOCLINE routing tables, use ILLiad Odyssey trusted sender, take advantage of tools developed by colleagues, etc.)
- Implement an ILL management system (e.g., ILLiad, Clio, Relais) to manage ILL records for tracking and statistical purposes
- Provide adequate workstations for staff to access your ILS, OCLC, DOCLINE, Internet, and other electronic and bibliographic resources, as well as for scanning and electronic transmittal of copies
- Network individual workstations to share ILL data, forms, and other resources on a shared server/space
- Maintain up-to-date hardware and software
- Use state-of-the-art electronic methods to request items
- Use state-of-the-art technology to send copies electronically when possible
- Network with colleagues

Resources

IDS Project Workflow Toolkit
OCLC's WorldCat Resource Sharing Support
ShareILL's list of Systems, Software, and Standards

3. CUSTOMER SERVICE

Having a strong customer service philosophy will make ILL easier and more pleasant for your patrons.

- Keeps patrons coming back to use interlibrary loan
- Makes the process smoother and easier for you and your staff
- More efficient and saves money

Best Practices

- Use technology to save time and cost
- Have a fast turnaround time
- Reduce the amount of people through whom requests pass
- Promptly notify patrons when material arrives
- Make interlibrary loan policies and procedures easy to find and understand

- Be open to comments from patrons and listen to what works and what doesn't
- Focus on the preferences and needs of the end user
- Perform regular customer satisfaction evaluations

Resources

IFLA Guidelines for Best Practices for Interlibrary Loan and Document Delivery

Leon, Lars E., et al. "Enhanced Resource Sharing through Group Interlibrary Loan Best Practices: A Conceptual, Structural, and Procedural Approach." *Libraries and the Academy* 3, no. 3 (July 2003): 419–30.

ALA's Professional Tips Wiki entry on customer service

TED Talks, although not strictly library-focused, are a great resource for ideas and inspiration.

GiveMore Media is a for-profit company that develops and sells customer service training tools. They offer some great free videos to inspire.

Your patrons are your resources! Treat complaints as gifts!

4. ASSESSMENT

Whatever name you use—quality measurement, program evaluation, benchmarking—the purpose of assessment is to help you make decisions about your library's services. Some decisions may be what new services should be developed, what services need improvement—or, what should you stop doing completely? Assessment can be used to discover whether the quality, speed, price, or quantities of the services your library provides are similar to other libraries of your type and size.

Best Practices

Some of the most commonly measured or assessed ILL activities are as follows:

- Fill rate: How often does your department fill requests from borrowing libraries?
- Turnaround time: How long do your patrons wait for a book or journal to be delivered? How long does it take your ILL department to respond to borrowing library requests?
- Cost studies: How much does it cost your department to loan a returnable item? A photocopy?
- User studies: Who is using your ILL department? What academic group? Faculty? Graduate students versus undergraduate? Is usage on the rise? Are patrons happy with your services?
- What is being requested? What titles or types of materials are you being asked to borrow for your patrons? What titles or types of materials are you most frequently lending?
- Consortial borrowing statistics

Resources

Association of Research Libraries (ARL), www.arl.org
ARL's assesment blog
National Center for Education Statistics
Leon/Kress Resource-Sharing Cost Study Database
Journals
> *Journal of Interlibrary Loan, Document Delivery, and Electronic Reserve*
> *Interlending and Document Supply*
> *IFLA Journal*

Market research studies
> The Primary Research Group publishes market research studies focusing on higher education, including academic libraries. Their 2009 study, Higher Education Interlibrary Loan Benchmarks ($89.00 for downloadable pdf), features a wealth of ILL data from almost ninety academic libraries in the United States and Canada for you to measure your department against.

Checklists and "best practices" questionnaires
> Rethinking Resource Sharing "Checklist." This list of aggressive and forward-thinking questions will get you pondering how good your resource-sharing practices really are—or will be in the future.

> IFLA's "Guidelines for Best Practice in Interlibrary Loan and Document Delivery." This list is organized by lending library and borrowing library and will give you the opportunity to evaluate your practices against a list of key questions.

5. EDUCATION AND NETWORKING

Resource sharing is a rapidly changing field requiring ongoing familiarity with a wide range of topics, from scanners and software to copyright law. Continuing education is key to gaining new skills and keeping up with changing trends and technologies. Likewise, networking with other librarians in the field allows resource-sharing librarians to learn about changes, products, and trends. Networking also allows us to form personal relationships, key when you need a special request, a favor, or help finding that impossible to locate item.

Best Practices

- Attend national and regional conferences
- Join relevant discussion lists
- Take advantage of webinars and other free or low-cost trainings
- Volunteer for a STARS Committee (you will have to log into ALA Connect)
- Visit other ILL operations

Resources

ShareILL's list of ILL conferences
Douglas Hasty's *Library Conference Planner*
ShareILL's list of discussion lists and blogs
STARS-Atlas Systems Mentoring Award (provides funding for a new ILL librarian to attend ALA Annual)
Your resource-sharing colleagues. Resource-sharing librarians tend to be a friendly lot. Reach out to other resource-sharing practitioners in your area with questions or requests for advice.

Used with permission from the American Library Association, www.ala.org.

Appendix G

About IFLA

The International Federation of Library Associations and Institutions (IFLA) is the leading international body representing the interests of library and information services and their users. It is the global voice of the library and information profession.

Founded in Edinburgh, Scotland, on 30 September 1927, at an international conference, the organization celebrated their 75th birthday at the conference in Glasgow, Scotland, in 2002. The association now has 1,500 members in approximately 150 countries throughout the world. IFLA was registered in the Netherlands in 1971. The Royal Library, the national library of the Netherlands, in The Hague, generously provides the facilities for the group's headquarters.

INTERNATIONAL RESOURCE SHARING AND DOCUMENT DELIVERY: PRINCIPLES AND GUIDELINES FOR PROCEDURE

The shared use of individual library collections is a necessary element of international cooperation by libraries. Just as no library can be self-sufficient in meeting all the information needs of its users, no country can be self-sufficient. The supply of loans and copies between libraries in different countries is a valuable and necessary part of the interlibrary loan process.

Since every country must determine the ways in which it provides resource sharing and document supply, the principles and guidelines in appendix H have no mandatory force; however, individual countries and libraries are strongly encouraged to use these guidelines as a basis for the conduct of international lending. The principles protect the interests of all libraries and set out the recommended practice by individual nations for access to collections.

Used with the permission from the IFLA Document and Delivery Section, www .IFLA.org.

Appendix H

IFLA Guidelines for Best Practice in Interlibrary Loan and Document Delivery

These guidelines stem from discussions held among members of the Document Delivery and Resource Sharing Section of IFLA (International Federation of Library Associations and Institutions). They are based on best practices formulated from the following studies:

Vattulainen, Pentti. *Performance of Interlending in Nordic Academic Libraries: Report for NORDINFO Board*, 2003.
Jakcson, Mary E. *Measuring the Performance of Interlibrary Loan Operations in North American Research and College Libraries*. Washington, DC: Association of Research Libraries, 1998.
National Resource Sharing Working Group. *Interlibrary Loan and Document Delivery Benchmarking Study*. Canberra: National Library of Australia, 2001.

These are brief guidelines for use within your own interlibrary loan department and are standards to strive for. We are aware that not all libraries will be able to implement all the recommendations, but we would nevertheless encourage libraries to use these guidelines as a basis for their current service and to influence future development.

GENERAL RECOMMENDATIONS

- Streamline the process within your own library.
  - Define performance indicators for service levels and turnaround time and monitor your performance against them.

- Evaluate your own routines and change them accordingly.
- Reduce the number of hands through which the requests are passing.
- All requests should be handled in one electronic system, preferably with the ability to interoperate with other ILL/DD systems.
- Keep statistics to suit national monitoring schemes and local needs.
- Make holdings available on Union Catalogs and keep them up-to-date, with an indication of availability for resource sharing.
- Explore reciprocal arrangements.

STAFF

- Use the expertise of skilled staff members.
- Staff members should continuously be able to develop competencies and be trained in using new tools and resources.
- Encourage the exchange of experience at the local or international levels.

TECHNOLOGY

- Update hardware and software.
- Encourage users to submit requests electronically.
- Give the end users the ability to check the status of requests online.
- Handle all communication about requests electronically.

USERS

- Focus on the needs and preferences of the end user.
- Perform user surveys on a regular basis.

RECOMMENDATIONS FOR THE REQUESTING LIBRARY

- ILL should be an integrated part of the library's service to users.
- Introduce new technology in all processes.
- Do not limit unreasonably the number of requests from users.
- Involve the end user as much as possible in requesting.
  - Give end users access to union catalogs with requesting facilities.
- Process requests from end users quickly.
- Use your experience to select supplying libraries according to speed of service and cost.
- Adhere to conditions of suppliers and treat material with care.

- Offer IFLA vouchers as payment.
- Deliver the material as fast as possible to the end user.
  - Send copies electronically if at all possible.
  - Check speed of supply on a regular basis.

RECOMMENDATIONS FOR THE SUPPLYING LIBRARY

- Use experienced staff to collect requested material from your collections in order to minimize mistakes.
- Use the fastest delivery methods.
- Try to satisfy requests in the best possible way.
- Be sure that your license agreements for your e-resources will allow ILL/DD.
- Create online order forms and/or interoperate with other ILL/DD systems.
- Make your library's lending policies available on your website and in policy directories.
- Accept IFLA vouchers.

Used with the permission from the IFLA Document and Delivery Section, www .IFLA.org.

Appendix I

Libraries Very Interested in Sharing (LVIS) Fact Sheet, Illinois State Library

Libraries Very Interested in Sharing (LVIS) represents the first global OCLC no-charge Resource Sharing Group agreement. LVIS, which was established in 1993, began out of a shared goal of the Illinois State Library and the Missouri Library Network Corporation (MLNC) to encourage and provide greater opportunities for no-charge resource sharing throughout the Midwest region. During the first year, LVIS members included more than two hundred multi-type libraries in Illinois and Missouri. There are now more than 2,700 members worldwide.

LVIS MEMBER LISTING

Alphabetical by state/country and OCLE symbol
Alphabetical by OCLC symbol

The LVIS member listing is provided for the convenience of LVIS group members. If there is a question regarding membership in the LVIS group, please consult OCLC's Policies Directory and look under "Group Affiliations."

If you have questions regarding the LVIS member list, please call 217-785-1537 or e-mail sburkholder@ilsos.net.

PARTICIPATION IN LVIS

To participate in LVIS, a library must agree to comply with the following resource-sharing arrangement:

1. Set holdings in WorldCat.
2. Maintain supplier status in WorldCat Resource Sharing.
3. Commit to resource sharing with all LVIS members.
4. Provide loans of all circulating (returnable) items to LVIS members at no charge.
5. Provide electronic copies, if possible.
6. Provide photocopies for a maximum of thirty pages per bibliographic citation to LVIS members at no charge. (A cost recovery charge for photocopies exceeding the thirty pages limit is permissible and may be determined by the library.)

BENEFITS OF LVIS MEMBERSHIP

- Greater work flow efficiency. Libraries can quickly and easily identify no-charge libraries in OCLC and therefore streamline ILL transactions.
- Greater load leveling. LVIS encourages the strengthening of local ILL networks, which ultimately lessens the lending burden of major research libraries.
- Greater resource-sharing alternatives. LVIS supplements the ILLINET ILL Code by providing a resource-sharing option for those libraries that desire an overall no-charge policy for ILL transactions.
- Broader ILL scope. LVIS expands the geographic ILL scope by encouraging interstate and international resource sharing.

ACCESS TO LVIS DATA

LVIS participants access the groups' holdings via OCLC WorldCat.

JOINING LVIS

There is no charge to join LVIS. You may complete the LVIS Participation Agreement Form and return it via e-mail as a PDF attachment to sburkholder@ilsos.net or lvisshare@gmail.com. You may also fax the completed form to 217-782-6062. For more information about LVIS, please call 217-785-1537 or e-mail sburkholder@ilsos.net or lvisshare@gmail.com.

Used with permission from the Illinois State Library, http://www.cyberdriveillinois.com/departments/library/libraries/OCLC/lvis.html.

Index

AACR. *See* Anglo-American Cataloging Rules

AASL, 20

AbeBooks, 104

Abel, Richard, 34

Access for All, 51

Access Services, 89–90

ACRL, 43, 153, 169

AddAll.com, 104

African Studies Association, Archives Libraries Committee, 136

Against the Grain: Linking Publishers, Vendors, and Librarians, 8

ALA. *See* American Library Association

ALBRS. *See* Alibris

Albany Public Library, 74; Interlibrary Loan Guidelines, 75–76;

Albany University, 88

Albert Einstein College of Medicine, Center for Public Health Services, 74

Alder, Nancy Lichten, 100

Alford, Larry, 37

ALIAS, 112, 119

Alibris (ALBRS), 93, 103, 104

Alliant International University, 132

Amazon, 61, 65, 93, 98–99, 103–5

American Association of School Librarians (AASL), 20

American Experience (television series), 48

American Express, 87

American Library Association (ALA), x, 4, 20, 26, 41, 87, 91, 97, 102, 126, 133, 166; Code of Ethics, 157–58, 165; College Reference Section, 42; Cooperation Committee, 42; Core Competences of Librarianship, 94; Interlibrary Loan Code for the United States, 43, 51, 74, 80, 119, 126–27, 137–38, 140, 159–61, 163–72, 183; Interlibrary Loan Form, 140–42, *144*, 184; Library Fact Sheets, 80–81, 183–86; Library-Related Acronyms, 11, 52; meetings of, 38, 39, 89, 101; name changes of journals of, 20–21; Office for Intellectual Freedom, 165; Reference Services Division, 88; Resources and Technical Services Committee, 43; response to Section 108 study group, 173–82. *See also* References and User Services Association (RUSA)

American Medical Association journals, 20

Ameritech, 35

AMIGOS, 31

AmLib library management system, 36

Anderson, Rick, 64, 97–98

Anglo-American Cataloging Rules (AACR), 16–18, 23; RDA and, 24, 25
Archive Grid, 34
Archives of Internal Medicine, 20
Ariel, 92, 112
ARL. *See* Association of Research Libraries
Article exchange, 112
Article License Information Availability Service (ALIAS), 112, 119
ASERL, 61, 112
Ash, Lee, 151
Association of College and Research Libraries (ACRL), 43, 153, 169
Association of Research Libraries (ARL), 32, 57, 101, 105, 121, 174; *ARL Statistics 2012-2013*, 91; Collections and Access Programs, 91; Research Libraries Information Network (RLIN), 139; *Special Collections in ARL Libraries*, 154; Transborder Interlibrary Loan, 164
Association of Southeastern Regional Libraries (ASERL), 61, 112; Kudzu ILL project, 112
Arthur D. Little Associates, 36
Atlas Systems, 36, 45, 51, 119
Australia, 36
Avatar, 35
Avram, Henriette, 16

Ballard, Thomas H., 142
BALLOTS, 139
Baltimore, University of, School of Law, 39
Baltimore County Public Library, 101
Barnhart, Anne C., 101
Baseball (television series), 48
Battelle, 36
Bavarian State Library, 128, 150
BCR, 31
Beth Israel Hospital (Boston), 47
Bethune-Cookman University, 50
Better World Books (QUICK), 93, 103
BIBFRAME (bibliographic framework), 23, 26–27
Bible, 24
Bibliographic Center for Research (BCR), 31

Bibliographic Retrieval Services (BRS), 46–47
Biomedical Communications Network, 46
Blackwell North America, 36
BLDSS, 128, 186
BNMEX, 132
Bond GmbH & Co.KG, 36
Books on Demand, 98-100, 103, 104
Boone County Public Library, 49
Borrow Direct, 61
Boston Public Library, 42
Boucher, Virginia, 6
Bourg, Chris, 154
Bowker, Richard R., 126
Brigham Young University, 100, 102
British Columbia, University of, 5
British Library, 22, 43
British Library Association, 85, 86
British Library Document Supply Service (BLDSS), 128, 186
Brodman, Estelle, 47–48
Brooklyn Museum, Digital Collections and Services, 85
Brothers Grimm, 153
Brown, Rowland C. W., 33
Brown University, 105
BRS Search Software, 46–47
Bruno, Tom, 59
Bucknell University, Bertrand Library, 98
Budapest Open Access Initiative, 120
Burgess, L. A., 142
Burns, Ken, 48
Butler, Margaret, 111

Cain, Alexander, 46
California, University of, 42, 43; Santa Barbara, 100
Calvert, Kristin, 93, 110
Campbell, Sharon A., 101
Canada, 37, 43, 81, 130, 151, 164, 183–85, 191; Institute for Scientific and Technical Information (CISTI), 50; MARC in (CANMARC), 17; National Library of, 61; OCLC Customer Support in, 9
CAPCON, 31
Capital District Library Council, 74

Carroll, Lewis, 109

Carter, Jimmy, 151

cataloging, 42–43, 26–27, 88; chronology of, 22–23; machine readable, *see* MARC

Cataloging Rules and Principles (Lubetsky), 23

CCC, 64

CCLC, 31

CD Plus Technologies, 46

CEA, 150

CEA Critic, 150

Center for Research Libraries, 50, 51

Central Florida, University of, Library, 50

Chambers, Mary Beth, 110

Chandler, Alice, 148

Cheung, Ophelia, 104

Chicago, University of, 4

Chronogram, 148

CIC, 51, 61

CIRCPLUS listserv, 90

CISTI, 50

Citadel, College of Charleston, 8

citations, 114–16, 128, 152, 200; complete bibliographic, 165; verification of, 115–16, 185

The Civil War (television series), 48

Claremont Total Library System, 35

Clark-Bridges, Robyn, 141

Classified Catalogue Code (Ranganathan), 23

Clio, 9, 10, 112, 131

CLR, 33

COBOL, 113

Coe College, 141

COKAMO, 51

Coleman, Ross, 154

College English Association (CEA), 150

Colorado State University, Morgan Library, 49–50

Columbia University, 4, 34, 105, 115, 105, 151

Committee on Institutional Cooperation (CIC), 51, 61

A Community Resource Manual, 151–52

Condill, Kit, 116

Confidentiality, 170

Congress, U.S., 81, 115, 182; Commission on New Technological Uses of

Copyrighted Works, 83, 166; Post Office Committee, 87

Consortium of Universities of the Washington Metropolitan Area (CAPCON), 31

Constitution, U.S., Copyright Clause, 81

CONTENTdm, 33, 36

CONTU Guidelines, 83, 118, 166, 174, 178, 179; Rule of Five, 187

Cooperation theory, 11-12

Cooperative College Library Center (CCLC), 31

Copyright Clearance Center (CCC), 64

Copyright Law, 81–83, 92, 166, 187; photocopying rights and guidelines for libraries (Section 108), 82–83, 173–82

Copyright Office, Federal Register notice issued by 173–74

Cornel College, 141

Cornell University, 74, 105

Council for Library Resources (CLR), 33

C&RL News, 154

Croft, Janet Brennan, 119

Cutter, Charles Ammi, 23

Daly, James, 47

Dana, John Cotton, 97, 102

Dartmouth College, 105

DataCite, 50

Data Phase, 35

Dataware Technologies, 46

Davis, Phil, 20

Declaration of Independence, 149

Denver, University of, 100

Depression, 87

Deutsche Nationalbibliothek, 33

Deutscher Gesamtkatalog, 43

Dewey, Melville, 4, 126

Dewey Decimal System (DDC), 16, 34

Digital Media Management (DiMeMa), 36

Digital Millennium Copyright Act (1998), 118

Digital Public Library of America (DPLA), 60

digital rights management (DRM), 63

digitization, 154

DiMeMa, 36

Directory of Open Access Journals, 120
discovery portals, 92
discovery to delivery (D2D), x, 51
DOCLINE, 9, 47, 48, 114, 165, 166, 170, 189
Donham, Jean, 20
DPLA, 60
Drake, Paul B., 142
DRM, 63
D2D, x, 51

E-book Library, 103
ebrary, 103
EBSCO, 36, 114
Effective Data, 112
Einstein, Albert, 73
eJournal Availability Server, 49
Electronic Fund Transfer System, 165
Elting Memorial Library (New Paltz, NY), 74, 126
Emmy Awards, 48
Empire State College, 136
EndNote, 115
ephemera, 151
Erway, Ricky, 154
eSerials Holdings, 112
Excel, 113
Exhaustion of Rights, 81
EXProxy, 36

Fabri de Peiresc, Nicolas Claude, 125 [this is correct]
Facebook, 7, 112
Fair Use, 81
Fashion Institute of Technology, 34
FAUL, 31
Federal Library Committee (FEDLINK), 31
FedEx, 168, 171
FEDLINK, 31
Feltsman, Vladimir, 148
FFA, 47
First Sale Doctrine, 81
FirstSearch platform, 38
Fischetti, Judy, 141
Five Associated University Libraries (FAUL), 31
Five Laws of Library Science, 153

Fleming, Rachel, 93, 110
Florida, University of, 100, 102, 104, 110
Ford, Kevin, 44–45
Ford, Kevin L., 26
Forest Press, 34
France, 21; Bibliothéque nationale de, 33, 43
FRBR, 23
FreeForAll (FFA), 47
FreeShare, 47
Fretwell-Downing Informatics Group, 36
Frontline (television series), 48
Functional Requirements for Blbliographic Records (FRBR), 23

Gabel, Linda, 18
Gale databases, 36
Gardner, Andy, 12
Gasaway, Laura, 83
Gates Foundation, 33
GEBAY, 128, 150
"Geek the Library" website, 33
Germany, 36, 43; GEBAY, 128, 150
Get It Now, 112
Getting It System Toolkit (GIST) software, 105, 106, 120
Gilmer, Lois, 12
GIST software, 105, 106, 120
Glover, M. Jason, 44, 45
Goodman, Paul, 4
Google, 59, 61, 65, 86, 91; Books, 60; Docs, 12; Scholar, 120; Translate, 128, 129
Gopher, 47
Gore Technologies, 36
Gorey, Edward, 3
The Graduate (movie), 148
Green, Samuel S., 41–43
Gregory, Jennifer, 49
Greyhound busline, 51
grey literature, 150–54
Guam, University of, 142

Half-Price Books, 104
Handbook on Human Rights and Citizenship, 151
Hand Press Books and Art Sales Catalogs, 34

Hardin, G., 11–12
HathiTrust, 60
Harvard University, 34, 98, 139
Hawaii, University of, 5
Hawley, Lorin M., 7
Heims, Steve, 52
HHS, 126
hidden collections, 153
Hill, Katherine, 93, 110
historical manuscripts, 125
Historic Huguenot Street (HHS), 126
Holmes, Oliver Wendell, Sr., 147
Hopkins, Judith, 30
Hopper, Grace Murray, 112
Housewright, Ross, 147

IBM Storage and Information Retrieval
  Systems (STAIRS), 46
IDS. *See* Information Delivery Services
  Project
IFLA. *See* International Federation of
  Library Associations and Institutions
IFLA Journal, 8
IFM, 65, 103, 128, 130, 165, 170
ILDS, 8, 58
ILLiad. *See* Interlibrary Loan Internet
  Accessible Database
ILLNET, 31, 200
ILS, 35, 188
INCOLSA, 31
Interlibrary Loan Internet Accessible
  Database (ILLiad), 36, 44–45, 49, 51,
  112, 116, 131, 142, 189; Atlas Systems,
  9, 45, 119; listserv, 10; management
  software, 106; Trusted Sender, x
Illinois, University of, 87, 119;
Illinois Research and Reference Center
  (ILLNET), 31, 200
Illinois State Library, 10, 199–200
Illinois Heartland, 61
ILL-L listserv, 10, 119
Imhotep: Journal of Afrocentric Thought, 148
Indiana Cooperative Library Services
  Authority (INCOLSA), 31
Indian Head, 46
Indian Library Association, 153
Indicommons blog, 85

Information Delivery Services (IDS) Project,
  48–49, 61, 112, 113, 119; User Groups,
  52
Information Dimensions, 36
Information Handling Services, 33
Information Technology and Libraries
  (journal), 33
Informix RDMS (relational database
  management system), 105
Inforonics Ltd., 16
Ingram Content Group, 39
Innovative Interfaces, 35
integrated library system (ILS), 35, 188
integrated workflow, 127–28
Interlending and Document Supply
  Conference, 51
International Federation of Library
  Associations and Institutions (IFLA),
  x, 8, 23, 91, 128, 129, 185, 193–94;
  e-mail or fax request details for, *132–33*;
  established policy documents for, 126–
  27; integrated workflow for, 127–28;
  payment methods for, 130–31, *131*;
  record keeping on, 131–32; searches
  for lenders for, 126, 128; shipping and
  customs for, 130; translator tools and,
  129; using IFLA form for nonsystem
  requests, 129, *130*; Interlending and
  Document Supply (ILDS) section, 8,
  58; International Lending Principles
  and Guidelines for Procedure, 80, 160,
  164, 183, 185; Office for International
  Lending, 186; Resource Sharing and
  Document Delivery Section, 127, 193–
  97; vouchers, 131, *131*, 170, 187. *See
  also* Rethinking and Resource Sharing
  Initiative
international interlibrary loans, 125–34
Internet, 26, 45–47, 85, 128, 154
ISBD (International Standard Bibliographic
  Description), 23
ISBN (International Standard Book
  Number), 17
ISO ILL, 91, 92
ISSN, (International Standard Serial
  Number), 150
ITHAKA, 91, 147, 154

Ivy League, 61, 105. *See also specific universities*

Jackson, Mary, 57, 91–92, 102
JAMA Internal Medicine, 20
Jaques, Elliot, 19
Jast, Louis Stanley, 85
Jazz (television series), 48
Johnson, Kay G., 19
Jordan, Jay, 33, 39
Journal of Interlibrary Loan, Document Delivery, and Electronic Reserve, 8, 20, 29
journals, 19–20; cancellation of subscriptions to, 109–10; name changes of, 20–21; open-access, 120. *See also titles of journals*
Journalseek.net, 116
Journal Storage (JSTOR), 91, 147
JSTOR, 91, 147

Karlsruher Virtueiler Katalog (KVC), 128
Karr, Jean-Baptiste Alphonse, 55
Katz, William, 88
Kelly, Michael, 4
Kentucky Libraries Unbound, 49
Keplar, John, 115
Kilgour, Frederick G., 30, 32–33
King, Donald, 120
Kirkwood Community College, 141
Kress, Nancy, 121
Kriz, Harry, 44, 45, 116–17
Kudzu ILL project, 112
Kuhn, Maggie, 29
Kuhns, Judy, 7
KVC, 128

LC. *See* Library of Congress
Learning to Be Human (Stern), 148
Leman, Hope, 13, 51
Leon, Lars, 121
LexisNexis, 39
Libraries Very Interested in Sharing (LVIS), 10, 199–200
Library of Congress (LC), 13, 16, 23, 33, 34, 44, 148, 150; bibliographic framework (BIBFRAME) under development by, 26–27; catalog card

numbers of, 30, 32; Catalog of Printed Books, 87; monumental collection of, 98; Network Development and MARC Standards Office (NDMSO), 26; union catalog project of, 87, 115
Library Hotel (New York City), 34
Library Journal, 4, 5, 41–42, 87, 88, 102, 120, 147
LIBREF-L listserv, 90
licensing agreements, 118–19
Lincoln, Abraham, 73, 155
Linda Hall Library, 50
LIS-Ill, 10
listservs, 10
Locating Books for Interlibrary Loan (Winchell), 115
The Lonely Africanist, 136
LS/2000 library automation system, 35
Lubetsky, Seymour, 23
LVIS, 10, 199–200

Mabee, Carleton, 149
Machine-Readable Bibliographic Implementation Committee (MARBI), 23
MAchine-Readable Cataloging (MARC), 15–27, 30, 44, 52, 150; levels of serials holdings data in, *114*
Mak, Collette, 137
Manchester Public Library, 85, 86
manuscripts, historical, 125
MARBI, 23
MARC. *See* MAchine-Readable Cataloging
Martin, J. Paul, 151
Massachusetts Institute of Technology (MIT), 61; Press, 52
Massachusetts Library Association, 61
Massive Open Online Courses (MOOCs), 38, 59
Matthews, Brian, 154
Maxwell, Robert, 46
McHone-Chase, Sarah, 66
McNamee, Roger, 86
MEDLINE, 46
Melvin, Tony, 29, 38
Mendeley, 115
Menlo College, 100

Metadata, 50, 114
Mexico, 130, 164; Biblioteca Nacional de (BNMEX), 132
Michigan, University of, 36
Michigan Library Consortium (MLC), 31
Michigan State University, 35
microfilm, 140, 154
Microsoft SQL Server, 44
Mid-American Library Alliance (MALA), 51
Mid-Hudson Library System, 138
Midwestern Regional Library Network (MRLN), 31
Miller, Jonathan, 86
Minnesota, University of, Law Library, 103
Minnesota Interlibrary Teletype Exchange (MINTEX), 31
MINTEX, 31
mission statements, 73–74
Mississippi, University of, 100
Missouri, University of, 30
Missouri Library Network Corporation (MLNC), 10, 31, 199
MIT, 61; Press, 52
Mitchell, Sydney, 57
MLNC, 10, 31, 199
Mobipocket Reader platform, 18
Montgomery, Susan, 86
monumental collections, 98
MOOCs, 38, 59
Morris, Leslie R., 29
Mosaic, 47
Mount Mercy University, 141
MRLN, 31
Mueller, Kurt, 46–47
Museum of Seminole County History, 50

name changes of journals, 19-21
National Information Standards Organization (NISO); Circulation Interchange Protocol, 92; Computer to Computer Protocol, 47, 51
National Library of Medicine (NLM), 9, 46, 47; Lister Hill Center, Integrated Library System, 35
National Medical Library, 42
National Television System Committee (NTSC), 21

National Union Catalog of Pre-1956 Imprints (Mansell), ix, 43, 52, 87
Navy, U.S., 113
NDMSO, 26
NEBASE, 31
Nebraska, University of, 100
Nebraska Library Commission (NEBASE), 31
NELINET, 30, 31
Netherlands Royal Library, 36, 193
netLibrary, 36, 103
New England Library Information Network (NELINET), 30, 31
new normal, 86
New Paltz public schools, 126
New York, City College of New York, 4
New York, State University of (SUNY), 136–37, 148; Geneseo, 48–49, 52, 106; New Paltz, 74, 126, 149, 151; NYLINK, 31; Oswego, 76–79, 112; Press, 148; Upstate Medical Center, 46
New York African Studies Association Newsletter, 150
New York City School Board, 4
New York Public Library, 34, 52, 139
New York State Education Department, 151
New York State Library, 52
NISO Circulation Interchange Protocol (Z39.83), 92
NLM. *See* National Library of Medicine
North Carolina, University of, at Chapel Hill, School of Information and Library Science, 31–32
North Carolina State Library of, NC LIVE Media Collection, 48
Notre Dame University, x
NYLINK, 31

OAIster, 36
Oberlander, Cyril, 62, 66, 89–90, 120
OCLC. *See* Ohio College Library Center
OCLC, *See also* Online Computer Library Center
OCLC PICA, 36
OCTONET, 47
ODLIS: Online Dictionary for Library and Information Science, 11

Odyssey, 112

Ohio College Association, 30, 32

Ohio College Library Center, 30

OhioLink, 112

OHIONET, 31

Ohio State University, 100

Olive Software, 36

Online Computer Library Center (OCLC), 6, 8, 11, 21, 24, 29–39, 44, 45, 49, 51, 68, 88, 91, 119, 127–29, 133, 149; accession numbers of, 32; acquisitions of, 35–36; Americas Regional Council (ARC), 38; annual processing of requests by, 58; Batch Processing, 112; Board of Trustees, 37–38; Customer Support, 38, *39*; custom holdings with, 189; Direct Request, x, 89; electronically submitted requests through, 166, 184; global programs of, 10, 37, 60–61, 92; information on individual libraries from, 126; Interlibrary Loan Subsystem, ix; international payment vouchers available from, 131; Interlibrary Loan Fee Management (IFM) system, 65, 103, 128, 130, 165, 170; levels of serials holdings data in, *114*; listservs of, 10; *NextSpace* newsletter, 121; Policies Directory, 128, 165, 169, 199; Programs and Research Division, 34; Public purpose, 35; Regional Councils, 37; Research Libraries Group merger with, 139; Research website, 139, 140; response to Section 108 study group, 173–82; Review Board, 34–35; training from, 113; trusted sender, x, 18; Turnaround Time, 52; User's Council, 31, 36; virtual monumental collection of, 98; Western Service Center (PACNET, OCLC Pacific), 31; Worldshare ILL, 9, 67. *ee also* WorldCat

online public access catalogs (OPACs), 35

on-the-spot ILL, 135–45

OPACs, 35

Open Access (OA), 60, 61, 63, 120, 133

Open Archives Initiative Protocol for Metadata Harvesting, 92

OpenURL, 49, 57, 92

Orange County Library System, 50

Orange County Regional History Center, 50

Orbis Cascade Alliance, 61, 103–5

Oregon State University, 104

Orlando Memory Project, 50

out-of-print (OP) materials, 98

Oxford University, Bodleian Library, John Johnson Collection, 151

PACNET, 31

PAIS, 36

PAL, 21

PALINET, 31

PBS, 48

PDA, 100–106

Panizzi, Anthony, 15, 22

Paris Principles, 23

Parker, Ralph, 30

Parker, Sara, 98

Parry, Michelle, 112

patron-driven acquisition (PDA), 100–106

Pennsylvania, University of, 105

Pennsylvania Network Area (PALINET), 31

Periodical Holdings in the Library of the School of Medicine (PHILSOM), 47–48

Phase Alternating Line (PAL), 21

PHILSOM, 47–48

PICA, 36

Pittsburgh Regional Library Center (PRLC), 31

Pizer, Irwin, 46

policies, 148-49, 164, 169

POD, 93, 103–5

PORTICO, 91

Portland State University, 152

Posner, Beth, 48,

Pratt Institute, 4

Pride and Prejudice (Austen), 16, 17, 19

primary sources, 149

Princeton University, 42, 105, 140

Pritchard, David "Skip," 38, 39

Pritchard, Sara, 153

ProQuest, 36, 39

Public Affairs Information Service (PAIS), 36

Public Broadcasting System (PBS), 48

Publisher's Weekly, 102
purchase-on-demand (POD), 93, 103–5
Purdue University Books on Demand
    program, 98–100, 103, 104
Putnam, Herbert, 43

QuickDoc, 47

Ranganathan, S. R., 23, 86, 153
RapidILL, 49–50, 112
Rawlinson, Nora, 102
RDA, 23–27
RDMS, 105
ReadCube, 61, 64
Reagan, Ronald, 148
RECAP, 61
Reciprocal Faculty Borrowing Program
    Cards, 139
Reference and User Services Association
    (RUSA), 101, 159, 161, 183;
    Professional Tools website, 8; Sharing
    and Transforming Access to Resources
    Section (STARS), x, 7, 8, 58, 80, 109
Reference and User Services Quarterly, 183
RefWorks, 115
regional medical libraries (RMLs), 47
Reitz, Joan M., 11
Relais, 112; Discovery-to-Delivery (D2D),
    x, 51
Research Libraries Group (RLG), 34, 36
Research Libraries Information Network
    (RLIN), 34
ResearchRaven, 13, 51
Resource, Description, and Access (RDA),
    23–27; Toolkit, 25–26
Rethinking Resource Sharing Initiative
    (RRSI), 58; Innovation Awards, 39,
    48–52; manifesto of, 58–59, 153
Reynolds, Leslie J., 106
Richardson, Ernest C., 42–43
Ridgway Library (Philadelphia), 42
RLG, 34, 36
RLIN, 139
RMLs, 47
The Rocky and Bullwinkle Show, 154
Rollins College, Olin Library, 50
Rothstein, Samuel, 5

Rowman & Littlefield, 24
Royal Library (Paris), 125
RRSI. *See* Rethinking Resource Sharing
    Initiative
Rudasill, Lynne, 116
RUSA. *See* References and User Services
    Association
Russia, 21

Samaritan Health Services, 13; "Access for
    All" Projects, 51
Samuel, Bunford, 42, 43
Samuel Dorsky Museum of Art, 126
ScanGrants, 51
Schonfeld, Roger C., 147
School Library Media Research, 20
School Library Quarterly Online, 20
School Library Research (SLR), 20
SCIPIO database, 34
Searcher magazine, 46
SECAM, 21–22
Seneca, Lucius Annaeus, 125
Sequential Color with Memory (SECAM),
    21–22
SERHOLD, 47
serials changes, 19-21
Shakespeare, William, 135
ShareILL, 8–9, 128
SHAREit, 112
SHARES, 34, 139–40
Shelley, Percy Bysshe, 41
Simpson, Evan, 58
Sisis Information Systems, 36
SkyRiver, 35
Smith, K. Wayne, 33
Smithsonian Institution, 43
So, Soo Young, 110
SOLINET, 31
Sonny Bono Copyright Term Extension Act
    (1998), 92
Southeastern Library Network (SOLINET),
    31
Southeastern New York Library Resources
    Council Referral Card, *143*
Southern Illinois University, 100
special collections, 153–54
STAIRS, 46

Stanford University, 139
STARS, x, 7, 8, 58, 80, 109
Stern, Jason, 148
Stetson University, DuPont-Ball Library, 50
Straw, Joseph E., 87
Striker, Bridget, 49
Sturr, Natalie, 112
Subject Collection (Ash), 151
Sullivan, Mark, 49, 52
Summon discovery service, 36
SUNY. *See* New York, State University of
SUNY/OCLC, 31
Supreme Court, U.S., 182
SWAN, 61
System Wide Automatic Network (SWAN),
61

teachable moments, 89–90
TEACH Act (2002), 173
Telex messaging system, ix
Temple University, 148
Tenopir, Carol, 120
Texas, University of, 100
Texas A&M University, 106
Thomas Canada LTD., 36
Thyssen-Bornemisza, 46
Toronto, University of, Library Automated
System (UTLAS), 36
Towson University, 39
TPAM, 49
tragedy of the commons, 11–12
Transaction Performance Analysis Module
(TPAM), 49
translator tools, 129–30
TROEL, 132
True Serials, 112
Truth, Sojourner, 3, 149, 155
Twenty-First Century Access Services, x
TWX, ix
Tyler, David, 93

U.S. Postal Service (USPS), 43, 86, 130,
131, 168
UBorrow, 51
Ulster County School Library System, 126
Union Catalogs, 196
Union List of Serials, 87

United Kingdom, 8, 154; MARC in
(UKMARC), 17
United Nations, 128, 151
United Parcel Service (UPS), 105, 168, 171
Upper Hudson Library System, 75
UPS, 105, 168, 171
Useful Utilities, 36
USPS. *See* U.S. Postal Service
Utah, University of, Willard Marriot
Library, 97
UTLAS, 36

van Dyk, Gerrit, 102
Vassar College, 113
Vatican Library, 125
Vermont, University of, 100
VIAF, 33
Virginia Tech, 36, 44–45
Virtual International Authority File (VIAF),
33

W.I.L.L. program, 138
Wake Forest University, 141
"Walk-in Interlibrary Loan" (W.I.L.L.)
program, 138
Walters, William H., 100
WANGO, 128
Washington, University of, 33
Washington Library Network (WLN), 36
Washington State University, 104
Washington University School of Medicine
(WUSM), 47
Washoe County Library System, 101
Wayback Machine, 154
Webopedia, 114
Wells Fargo, 87
Wertheimer, Andrew, 5
Western Carolina University, 110
Western Connecticut State University, 11
West Virginia Tech, 116
Wiener, Norbert, 52
Wikipedia, 26
Williams, Joseph, 111
WiLS, 31
Winchell, Constance, 76, 115–16
Windows NT, 44
Wisconsin Library Consortium (WiLS), 31

Wisner, William H., 120
Woolwine, David E., 111
Worchester Public Library, 41
Word, 112
workflow, integrated, 127–28
Workflow Toolkit, IDS, 52
World Book Encyclopedia, 33
WorldCat, ix, 5, 12, 32–36, 91, 98, 105, 116, 117, 120, 135, 148, 150, 200; Connexion Browser, 113; entries for journal name changes in, 20; finding foreign lenders through, 128; Open Access materials located through, 120; Quality Management Unit, 18; RDA records in, 24, 25; Registry, 126, 131; Resource Sharing, 29, 38

WorldShare, 30, 38, 112, 131
World Wide Web, 97, 98, 152; digital archive of, 154. *See also* Internet; *specific websites*
WUSM, 47
Wythe, Deborah, 85

Xerox, 88

Yale University, 30, 34, 105, 113, 139
Yankee Book Publishers, 103
York (England), University of, 100

Zotero, 115
Z39.50, 47, 51
Z39.83, 92

About the Author

Corinne Nyquist is a librarian at the Sojourner Truth Library at the State University of New York at New Paltz, and has been a librarian for more than forty years in public and academic libraries in the United States—New York, Illinois, Minnesota, Montana—and Africa—Sudan and South Africa. She has been in charge of interlibrary loan for more than twenty-five years and has been active in the ALA RUSA STARS (Sharing and Transforming Access to Resources Section), as well as in the Rethinking Resource Sharing group. She was a member of the ALA Committee that revised the Interlibrary Loan Code for the United States in 2008. She is currently a member of the ALA Library School Accreditation External Review Panel.

CPSIA information can be obtained at www.ICGtesting.com
Printed in the USA
BVOW05s1155180714

359469BV00002B/2/P